Little Known Adventures Under Sail
499 -1999

by Jeff Markell

Little Known Adventures Under Sail
499 - 1999

by Jeff Markell

a Lighthouse Press Publication

division of **ProStar** Publications, Inc.

ISBN: 1-57785-294-X
Printed in the United States

Published by:

Lighthouse Press

division of **ProStar** *Publications*, **Inc.**

3 Church Circle

Suite 109

Annapolis, MD 21401

(800) 481-6277

Email: www.editor@prostarpublications.com

Other Titles by Jeff Markell

Sailor's Weather Guide

Coastal Navigation for the Small Boat Sailor

Coastal Weather Guide for Southern California & Western Mexico

A Practical Guide to Coastal Navigation

Cover and Book Design and Production by

Carole Ann Thomas

ACKNOWLEDGEMENTS

I would like to thank the following people for their invaluable assistance in preparing both the accompanying text and illustrations:

Mr. Teoman Arsay

Messers Daniel & David Hayes

Dr. Charles F. Herberger

Mr. Hassan Kacmaz

Mrs. Grace Lary

Mr. Myron Markell

Mr. Colin Mudie

Mr. Norman C. Otman, Jr

Mrs. Florence Piver

Ms. Nancy Piver

CONTENTS

INTRODUCTION

Weather, sea state, or other conditions can be either so beautiful, or so ghastly, as to make any trip under sail become an adventure, whether it be just an afternoon jaunt across the bay or a trans-oceanic passage. However, some voyages are by their very nature obviously destined to be adventurous long before they actually get under way. That is true of the voyages described here. Each one is unusual in a different way from all the others. It was my purpose in this book to focus attention on some mariners and voyages that are not well known, but just as memorable as those of such well known sailors as Joshua Slocum, Sir Francis Chichester, Tristram Jones and various others. These outstanding sailors have unfortunately remained obscure.

Those who have gone to sea and sailed fairly long distances have unavoidably run into wretched conditions sooner or later. Therefore, tales of sailing vessels making lengthy passages in which they encounter ferocious weather and sea conditions while experiencing hull, rigging, or other equipment failures are no longer uncommon. What follows are not stories of such misadventures at sea.

What makes the initial story of the trans-Pacific voyage of Hoei Shin in 499 AD unusual is the very fact that a written record of this voyage from so long ago still exists. While it appears possible, even likely, that trans-Pacific passages may have been made earlier, no actual written records proving that such voyages did in fact occur, have yet been found. So up to now, a little known Buddhist monk leads them all.

On the Atlantic side some artifacts have been found indicating that Phoenecians and perhaps Romans may have made very early crossings. However, the tale of St. Brendan told in the Latin text of the "Navagatio" is the first story we have of a specific Atlantic crossing. The Vikings were early, but not that early. As far as we know, the Irish, who were later to be repeatedly plundered by the Vikings, were well ahead of them in this case.

The immense fleet built in China to explore the Indian Ocean returned with specimens that amazed the Chinese.

While Captain Joshua Slocum's single-handed crossing of the Atlantic in the 34′ Spray is well known, the single-handed crossing shortly afterward by Captain Howard Blackburn should perhaps be better known than that of Slocum. You'll soon see why.

Then we come to the tale of two grown men squeezing into a 20′ sloop to make an Atlantic crossing from Great Britain to Barbados simply to show that such a small vessel could get them safely across. They must have been far more uncomfortable along the way than they ever admitted.

Then another two men sailed from the eastern U.S. in a 25′ sloop all the way around South America, including Cape Horn and back up to the U.S. a total of 17,000 miles. Both of these two-man voyages certainly deserve to be better remembered than they are.

In the Mediterranean, Captain Bradford attempts to put to rest the idea that the Odyssey is merely a myth. He is able to trace, by boat, most of the route Odysseus followed around that Sea, as described by Homer. A couple places seem to be off the track, but it is remarkable how much of it works out when actually retraced by boat. See if you think he has made his point.

Much of the interest in multi-hulled sailboats, the catamaran and the tri-maran, which currently exists is owed to Arthur Piver, the pioneer sailor and designer who is now nearly forgotten. Piver was a bit opinionated and some-what testy at times, but those who disagreed with him found out, to their dis-may, that more often than not he was right. While he had no formal training as a naval architect it became difficult to prove that his design and construc-tion ideas were unsound and unsafe after he had built the boats he designed and then successfully made both Atlantic and Pacific ocean crossings in them.

How and why Captain Clark made sailing all the way through the inland waterway system of European Russian from north to south a lifetime ambi-tion is unclear, but he finally succeeded in doing just that. Actually, unless one has had occasion to go to Russia and make an extensive study of their inland waterway system, and even sail part of it as I did, there would be no way to know that such a trip is even remotely possible. Certainly, none of the information we normally get about that country gives any indication of the extent of that immense inland system of interconnected rivers, lakes, and canals.

The cruise described in the last story is primarily notable, not only for the fact that it passes straight through the most volatile part of the turbulent Middle East, but also for the fact that it has been repeated every year since 1989. While so many of the people of that area have ancient and implacable hatreds toward each other, mysteriously they have uniformly extended the most cordial of welcomes year after year to these peaceable visiting sailors.

Hopefully, the stories that follow will help to make you aware of some sailors you previously knew little or nothing about. Their accomplishments deserve considerably better recognition than they have been given.

CHAPTER 1

A Buddhist Priest Crosses the Pacific in 499 A.D.

Excerpt from "The Great Summons" of Chu Yuan translated by Arthur Waley

Oh soul come back again and do not go east or west or north or south!
For to the east a mighty water drowneth the Earth's other shore
Tossed on its waves and heaving with its tides
The hornless Dragon of the Ocean ridest
Clouds gather low and fogs enfold the sea
And gleaming ice drifts past
Oh soul go not to the east,
To the silent Valley of Sunrise!

Our histories traditionally tell us that the continents of the Western Hemisphere were first discovered and then settled by Western Europeans in the late 1400s and early 1500s. They do then admit that a few Vikings are believed to have gotten here earlier, but made no permanent settlements. This view is now being seriously challenged .

Only fairly recently have surprising relics been found pointing to the possibility that Phoenecians may have gotten to what is now New Hampshire, as far back as 480 B.C. Another curious find is a clay sculptured head found near Toluca, Mexico that has been identified as Roman, circa 200 A.D., by the distinguished classical archaeologist Robert Heine-Gildern. In addition, in New Mexico at a site about 30 miles south of Albuquerque, is a large rock inscribed in Old Phonecian/Hebrew script that has been deciphered as an abridged version of the Ten Commandments. These, and other discoveries indicate that contacts between the "old world" and the "new world" go back far earlier than has long been believed.

Historians and archeologists have traditionally been agreed that the remote ancestors of the aborigines of the Western Hemisphere arrived in North America by crossing a land bridge from Siberia to Alaska which appears to have existed during the last Ice Age. Further, it is postulated that they, in turn, were descended from peoples who had migrated from the west into northeastern Asia many thousands of years earlier than that. The crossing to the American Continents was made at least as long ago as 40,000 years. These numerous tribes of people were mistakenly described initially as "Indians" by early European explorers, and that name has persisted long after it became clear that the Caribbean Islands are not the East Indies, and the continent northwest of them is not connected to the subcontinent of India.

Curiously, although these wanderers developed many extremely elaborate and sophisticated civilizations in diverse parts of the Americas such as Mexico, Guatamala, Chaco Canyon, and Peru thousands of years before the Europeans arrived, they simply cannot be considered to have "discovered" these continents. When it comes to gaining credit for discovery, among western historians, simple migration apparently does not count. Discoveries, it appears, have only been made when Europeans have arrived!

When the Ice Age ended, the sea level rose, the land bridge disappeared, and presumably that ended the migration of the peoples from Asia into North America. Intercontinental contacts with Asia are assumed to have stopped as well, except for a few Eskimo groups who have maintained a tenuous contact, even to this day, between Siberia and Alaska. These contacts have been maintained down through the Aleutian and Komandorski Island chains, and thence across the Bering Straits.

This entire scenario dealing with the "discovery" of the Western Hemisphere by European explorers has come under serious question as the result of findings such as those mentioned above, as well as many others. On one hand, the Siberia to Alaska land bridge theory easily accounts for populating part of the Western Hemisphere, but since the start of the European Age of Exploration in the 1400s humans have been found living from the high Arctic to Tierra del Fuego, on the plains, in the forests, on mountain tops in the Andes, and in the jungles of Central America and the Amazon. Are they *all* descendants of migrants from Siberia?? And are the various physical differences among them explained as simple evolutionary adaptations? Perhaps, but evidence is surfacing of other possible explanations.

Until fairly recently, the idea that North America might have been "rediscovered" by people from the Far East long before the start of the European Age of Discovery in the 15th and 16th centuries had not been seriously considered. However, much evidence does exist indicating that this is indeed what happened. How many Asians may have crossed by water to the Americas in ancient

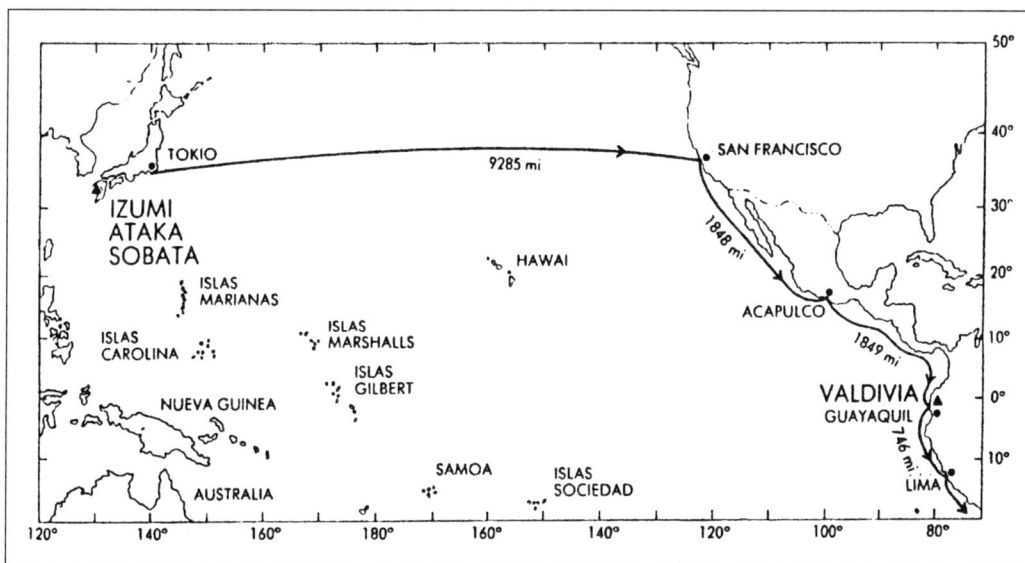

*Fig. HS-1 Route of the Yasei-Go III and distances in Nautical Miles
from "Across Before Columbus"– NEARA Publications 1998*

times is impossible to guess, but interesting indications of very ancient crossings have been found, such as pottery in Valdivia, Equador, dating from 4 to 5 thousand years ago containing many remarkably close resemblances to Jomon pottery made in Japan as early as 8000 years ago. Authorities such as Betty J. Meggers of the Smithsonian Institution believe there are too many resemblances between them to be the result of pure chance. To counter the objection that the Japanese could not have crossed the Pacific at that time, a double canoe, the Yasei-go III, a vessel of a type used by the Japanese as long as 3000 years ago, was built in Japan in 1980. She was equipped, as the boats of that period were, with the traditional sails, rudder and centerboard. She was then sailed from Shimoda, near Tokyo, on May 8, crossing the Pacific non-stop in 51 days, to arrive in San Francisco June 28. (Fig. HS-1). She was then sailed down the west coast to Equador, and from there, further south as far as Chile, proving that Japanese-type pottery design could well have found its way across the Pacific to South America as early as 3000 years ago.

In addition, written records exist of one specific Chinese trans-Pacific crossing that also occurred long before Europeans arrived on the Caribbean Islands and the east coasts of the Americas. These Chinese records were studied by Karl Freidrich Neumann, a German Sinologist, and his commentaries were later translated into English and published by an American historian named Charles G. Leland. This record shows that a Chinese monk named Hoei Shin led a party of Buddhists to the west coast of North America in 499 AD. He came on a missionary journey to bring the true faith of the Buddha to its unenlightened inhabitants.

Looking at western Europe during the 5th century AD, there is evidence the so called *Dark Ages* had begun. Rome had fallen under the repeated assaults of barbarian hordes bringing tumult, disorder, destruction, and devastation in their wake. The Huns, the Visigoths, the Ostrogoths, the Vandals, the Franks, and other barbarians had thoroughly trampled over and destroyed the western Roman Empire. The arts, literature, philosophy, and learning of all kinds had come to a halt in Western Europe. Although in the Middle East the Byzantine Empire lasted for another several hundred years, much of what we like to think of as "civilization" was at a very low ebb in Western Europe. Throughout Western Europe, the Roman Catholic version of Christianity was gaining ascendancy, while at the same time the majority of the common people lived in constant terror of the power struggles between the mighty Christian princes who had risen to positions of immense power. These princes found that, in addition to a guaranteed place in Heaven in the hereafter, great earthly power in the here and now was also very convenient to have. In addition, the fact that they had such power clearly proved that God *wanted* them to have it.

CHINA IN THE FIFTH CENTURY AD

Meanwhile in China, conditions in that period were very different indeed. In the Far East during the fifth century AD, the Celestial Kingdom was in the midst of a brilliant renaissance. Great cultural changes were breaking down the traditional smug haughtiness of the Chinese with regard to other nations, and other peoples of every kind.

Previously, the traditional Chinese attitude was that they, and they alone, had already achieved the *highest* degree of civilization. The Celestial Kingdom had long been, in its own opinion, the unquestioned center of the universe, and all other societies and peoples were regarded as barbarians and totally beneath their exalted consideration.

This traditional feeling of aloof superiority was now being replaced by an interest in, and curiosity about, outsiders. One major contributing reason for this was that Buddhism, a foreign religious faith, had spread into China from India. It had now become extremely important and influential, and the basic tenets of Buddhism were at considerable variance from the conventional smug superiority of the Chinese. This had produced a group of devout and energetic missionaries who were intent on spreading the sacred word of the Buddha everywhere in the world that they possibly could.

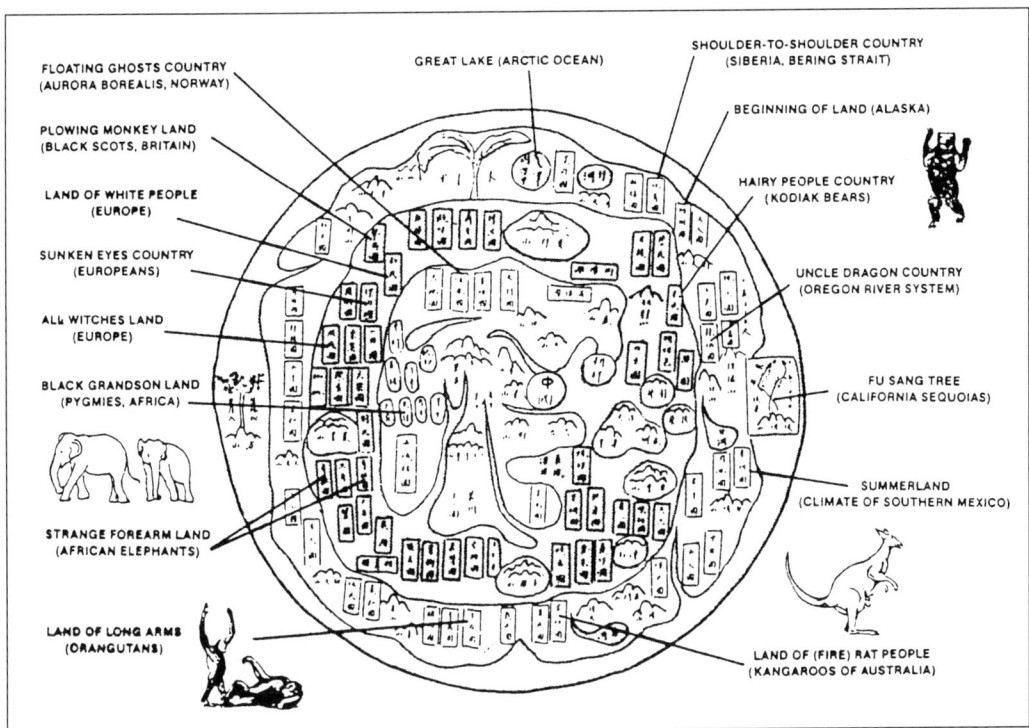

Fig. HS-2 Ancient Chinese World Map with the Harris Translations

By the late 5th Century AD, Buddhism was already well established throughout India, China, Tibet, and southeastern Asia. It was then the zealous and pious monk Hoei Shin looked eastward over the restless waters of the China Sea hoping to find additional people in need of enlightenment. He had heard stories of a land existing far across that sea toward the rising sun called *Tahan*. Those tales told of strange inhabitants dwelling there who were called the *Painted People*, because they painted their bodies. Instantly it was clear to the good monk that these were people in desperate need of the truth. Any people as misguided as were these poor unfortunate souls, clearly showed a serious need to become acquainted with the holy message of the Buddha.

How Hoei Shin learned of the existence of these lands across the sea to the east, it is unclear. However, a scholar named Hendon Harris found and translated the Chinese labeling on a map (Fig. HS-2) similar to a number of other existing early Chinese maps. It, and they, are copies of copies of truly ancient maps which Harris guessed could date back as far as 2200 BC. Judging by the labels Harris deciphered, the Chinese appear to have known a great deal about lands extremely far away from China, at a very early time. There are references that appear to refer to the elephants of Africa, the white men of Europe, the Arctic Ocean, the huge Kodiak bears of Alaska, the giant sequoia trees of California, and even the kangaroos of Australia.

From an early age, the Chinese had seagoing ships far larger than those the Europeans had been able to build, it is therefore very likely they made extensive voyages and numerous discoveries as well.

Unfortunately, details of the vessel, or vessels, which Hoei Shin used to make his crossing of the Pacific Ocean are not to be found in the works of Karl Freidrich Neumann as translated by Charles G. Leland. Coincidentally, at the time Leland came across Neumann's work, he was doing research on early American Indians, and since they were then believed to be of oriental origin, Neumann's story of Hoei Shin's crossing the Pacific was of particular interest to him.

Leland's version of the story of Hoei Shin was published in New York City in 1875 under the title *Fusang*; Fusang being the name the Chinese then used for North America. It was also the Chinese name for a tree which has since been identified by some as the aloe, and by others, including Harris, as the giant Sequoia. Since the Chinese believed the tree to be abundant there they identified the place with the tree. If the Fusang tree was in fact the aloe, rather than the sequoia, and Hoei Shin indeed went where the aloe was abundant, he must then have traveled at least as far south as Mexico, and possibly further.

You are quite possibly wondering, just as I did, how such a revolutionary discovery as the tale of a Pacific crossing by the Chinese in 499 AD failed to become a sensational story when it was originally published, and why it is still virtually unknown today. This is quite probably due to the fact that when Leland's translation was published in New York in 1875 it appeared only in a relatively obscure academic journal. Such publications, even today, usually reach only a limited number of scholars, and consequently seldom come to the the attention of the general public. Had the Internet and todays news-hungry media existed then, it would doubtless have been widely publicized, but it failed to get much notoriety at the time. As a result, it has remained in obscurity ever since.

In 1875 another American historian, Edward P. Vining produced a large book also dealing with the story of Hoei-Shin called *An Inglorious Columbus*. His version also agrees that the Chinese expedition must have reached Mexico, but he has no additional new information to add to Leland's account.

THE SHIP, OR SHIPS OF HOEI SHIN

Unfortunately, the account of Hoei Shin's trip to *Tahan* and *Fusang* gives no description of the vessel or vessels on which he and his companions crossed the

Pacific Ocean. However, clearly at that time, the Chinese had long been building ships fully capable of making the journey. There exists an additional account of the travels of another Chinese Buddhist, one Fa-Hsein, in which slightly more descriptive information is given regarding a large Chinese ship on which he made an ocean passage a few years prior to the voyage of Hoei Shin. His tale begins to give us an idea as to how far advanced the Chinese art of shipbuilding had become by then.

Fa-Hsein tells of traveling overland from China across the Gobi Desert, over the Hindu Kush, and down into India. His story then goes on to say that, in what would be the year 414 AD, he sailed from Ceylon aboard "a large merchant vessel on which there were over 200 souls". En route they were struck by a gale lasting 13 days. During this gale he notes that the ship sprang a leak, but after considerable difficulty finally arrived at Java. Fa-Hsein gives no detailed description of this ship, but to have carried 200 people it certainly was a very large ship compared to anything the Europeans were building at that time. It was likely to have been designed along the lines of a junk, very similar to those still in use today, except considerably bigger. From Java, Fa-Hsein embarked again for Canton on another ship of the same size, carrying another 200 souls. They ran into gales again, but finally arrived safely at Canton after a passage at sea of 82 days! A ship that could carry 200 people on a voyage requiring 82 days had to be large enough to carry a great deal in the way of stores, in addition to its many passengers. Even if the 82 days at sea is a monumental exaggeration, and the count of 200 people aboard was reached by counting some of them

Fig. HS-3 South China Junk
from "The Story of Sail"– Laszlo & Woodman

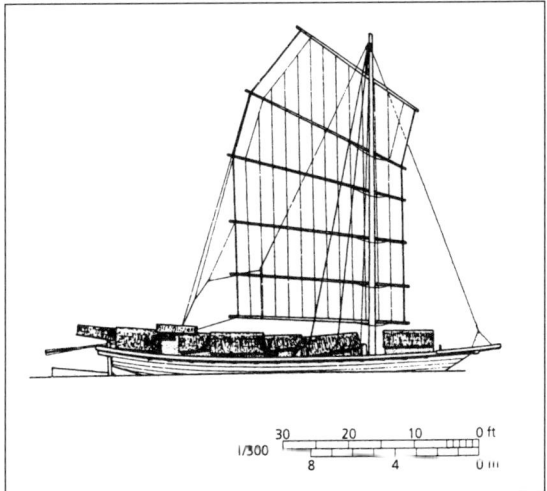

Fig. HS-4 South China Junk
from "The Story of Sail"– Laszlo & Woodman

Fig. HS-5 Petchili Junk
from "The Story of Sail"– Laszlo & Woodman

twice - the Chinese still had some very big ships at that early time.

The origin of the traditional large sea-going Chinese junk design (Fig. HS-3) is lost in far distant antiquity. In a colorful old explanation an ancient Chinese scribe wrote that it was the Emperor Fu Hsi, reputedly the offspring of a nymph and a rainbow, who taught the Chinese to build boats. The early ones were most likely quite simple, small, flat-bottom river craft modeled after a log raft. These were gradually developed into the lug rigged sampan. (Fig. HS-4) If the sampan's lines are enlarged, a cabin added over the stern, and a rudder and battened lug sails added as well, the vessel becomes a typical junk The masts were, and still are, a single heavy pole firmly secured so as to require no wire shrouds or stays to hold it in place. Each mast supports a single large lug-rigged sail with a series of stiffeners, or battens, running completely through it. Since there are no supporting lines around each mast the lug sails can be swung freely around the masts giving the junk rig great maneuverability.

A great many sailing sampans and junks are still in use in the Far East today. A good many are now motorized but the hulls continue follow the ancient and well proven traditional lines.

While we use the word "junk" to refer essentially to trash, the origin of the word we use is an old Middle English word "jonke" which referred to the type of rushes used to weave rope. The history is obscure as to how the the word "junk" came to describe this type of vessel. One explanation is that it comes from the word "junce", a name for this type of vessel used by the Portugese who were the first Europeans to reach China by sea. Another possible origin is the Javanese word for ship: "djong". A third possibility is the Malay word for boat: "adjong". Take your own choice of these various explanations - or with imagination, come up with one of your own.

Incidentally, the ships on which Fa-Hsein sailed were considerably larger than the junks commonly in use today. However, until recently some large junks, descendants of the truly huge ones of the past, were still in service (Fig. HS-5). This Petchili junk was about 170' long and subdivided into 20 watertight compartments, making it nearly unsinkable. Note that when the Chinese built bigger vessels needing larger sail areas, instead of making the available masts higher, as those in the west did, they simply added more masts each with its own sail. The Petchili junk thus carried 5 masts.

In 1330, one Ibn-Batuta described a voyage he made on a large junk out of Calcutta. He was traveling in company with his wives and his slave girls. He was incensed that he could not get a 1st Class cabin and he very unhappily wrote that he

Fig. HS-6

Junk from the fleet of Admiral Zheng in 1431 AD was 440' long and 180' wide

At approximately 90' long in 1492 the Santa Maria of Columbus was very small by comparison

had to travel without a private lavatory and bathroom, amenities which he obviously expected on that ship and which he felt were due a person of his great importance.

It seems doubtful that a missionary monk would have available to him a ship anywhere near the size of the ones on which Fa-Hsein is reported to have booked passage, but we also know that both Europeans and Polynesians have repeatedly crossed thousands of miles of open ocean in considerably smaller vessels. Based on other earlier recorded Chinese voyages, it is not difficult, therefore, to believe that Hoei Shin found a seaworthy ship in which he was able safely to cross the Pacific, as early as 499 AD.

THE TRANS-PACIFIC VOYAGE

The land of *Tahan*, known in China at the time of Hoei Shin in a rather sketchy way, was the land of Painted People or alternately, the land of Marked Bodies. Knowledge as to its location and extent appears to have been vague, at best. The Painted People could have been a reference to the peoples of the Aleutian Islands and Alaska, who were often elaborately tattooed. In order to reach them the Chinese would have had the help of two very important natural forces. East of Japan (Fig. HS-7), the strong, warm Kuroshio Current flows northeast toward the Aleutians, and as it moves northward, it moves ever deeper into

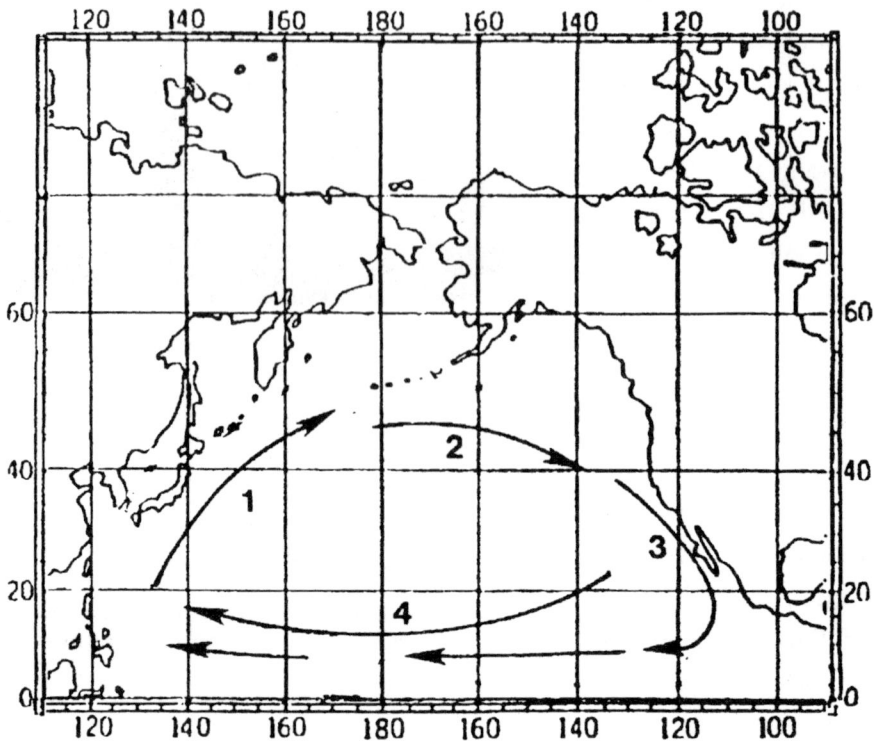

**PACIFIC OCEAN CURRENTS THAT HELPED HOEI SHIN
ON HIS WAY TO AND FROM NORTH AMERICA**

TO:
   1. Kuroshio Current
   2. North Pacific Current
   3. California Current

FROM:
   4. North Equatorial Current

Fig. HS-7

the belt of the Prevailing Westerly Winds which help a sailing vessel on its way toward the east and the North American continent. The Kuroshio Current north of Japan gradually broadens, slows, and turns toward the east becoming the North Pacific Current, further helping a sailing ship heading toward the land, or lands, of *Tahan*.

   As to the actual route Hoei Shin took from China, there is no surviving information. He could well have gone first to Japan, then sailed northward up the Sea of Japan. North of Japan he could easily have hopped across to the Kurile Islands, and next coasted up the east side of Kamchatka, and on out to the Komandorski Islands. From there it is not a long voyage to Attu, the first of the Aleutians, and then on through the Aleutian chain to Alaska.

Hoei's story, as translated, makes no comments regarding *Tahan* so we have no way of knowing for certain whether he ever even found it. His record concentrates instead on what he encountered in *Fusang*. Fusang, as mentioned earlier, is a Chinese name for either the sequoia or the aloe. In order to reach the land where the aloe grows he had to have worked his way southeast along the North American coast with the help of the persistent west winds and the southward flowing California Current, to a point at least as far as somewhere in Mexico.

The lack of any comments regarding *Tahan* encourages consideration of a possible alternate scenario. We know from the tale of Fa-Hsein that the Chinese at that time did have big ships capable of long passages. Perhaps Hoei did succeed in acquiring a large ship for his trip and sailed directly out into the Pacific and used favorable winds and currents to make a direct crossing, ending on what is now the west coast of either the U.S. or Mexico. In any event, by whatever route he took he finally arrived in Fusang and later returned to China with descriptions of many things he saw. For his return to China from southern Mexico, he again would have had the help of favorable winds and current. The North Equatorial Current (Fig. HS-7) and the easterly Trade Winds of the lower latitudes would speed him homeward from Mexico toward China.

FUSANG

The story of Hoei Shin found in ancient manuscripts by Neumann and translated by Leland begins:

"During the reign of the dynasty of Tsi, in the first year of the year-naming "Everlasting Origin" (AD 499) came a Buddhist priest from this kingdom who bore the name Hoei Shin, Universal Compassion, to the present district of Hukuang, who narrated that Fusang is about 20,000 (Chinese) miles in an easterly direction from Tahan and east of the Middle Kingdom.

"Many Fusang trees grow there - - the sprouts resemble those of the bamboo tree and are eaten by the inhabitants of the land. The fruit is like a pear in form, but is red. From the bark they prepare a sort of linen which they use for clothing - - The houses are built of wooden beams. Fortified and walled places are there unknown.

They have written characters in this land, and prepare paper from the bark of the Fusang. The people have no weapons, and make no wars - -"

Hoei goes on to describe the criminal justice system as well as marriage and funeral customs. He mentions that the king is called *"Ichi"*, and also notes that gold, silver, and copper are not prized among these people. However, by noting that they are not prized by these people he is also noting that these metals are known to them.

Several of the following details he mentions indicate he may be describing the Maya of Central America:

1. From the description given, the Fusang tree appears to be the aloe also known as the century plant, commonly found in Mexico and was plentiful in the Maya territory

2. Neither the Maya nor any of the other Indians in the area are known to have prized gold or silver.

3. The Maya had a written language. As far as we know no other tribes to the north or south of them had writing at that time.

4. The Maya were not a warring people until long after this time.

5. The title of the king given as *"Ichi"* could perhaps have been confused with the word *"Itza"* which was the Maya name for one of their major tribes.

Some of the observations attributed to Hoei Shin regarding what he found in Fusang, fit very well with the Mayans of Mexico. while many others simply cannot be either be confirmed or denied since so much of our present information regarding the Maya is sketchy. For example, his comments on criminal justice, marriage, and funeral customs simply cannot be corroborated, nor have we enough information to discard them as nonsense, either.

The chronicle of Hoei Shin is also said to mention his seeing horses, oxen, and stags being harnessed to wagons This most certainly is absolute nonsense. Neither the Maya nor any other people in the Americas had the wheel or used wagons at that time. However, the story of Hoei Shin is a very old one. Could it be that this is a fantasy inserted by someone transcribing the tale? The Odyssey and the chronicle of St Brendan both also contain fantastic nonsense very likely to have been added by later scribes Such a fabrication is entirely possible, but then an imaginary addition of this kind raises the question of whether the entire chronicle might be an elaborate fabrication.

WERE THERE OTHER EARLY TRANSPACIFIC CONTACTS

The first thought that comes to mind in connection with that question is, naturally, how did Hoei Shin or anyone else in China, know about either the Painted People of *Tahan* or of the existence of *Fusang*. For these things to be known there had to have been earlier voyages. Either trips of exploration were made deliberately, or some luckless ships were blown far off course, but were subsequently able to return to China.

The Chinese are believed to have had a form of the compass by about 2000 BC. This is extremely important as this makes it entirely possible for them to have undertaken long voyages into unknown waters in very ancient times feeling confident they could safely find their way back. At the very end of the chronicle of Hoei Shin, he mentions that in the year of the "Great Light of Song" which translates to be 458 AD five beggar monks had gone to Fusang and taught there, the religion of Buddha. That was 41 years before Hoei says he got there.

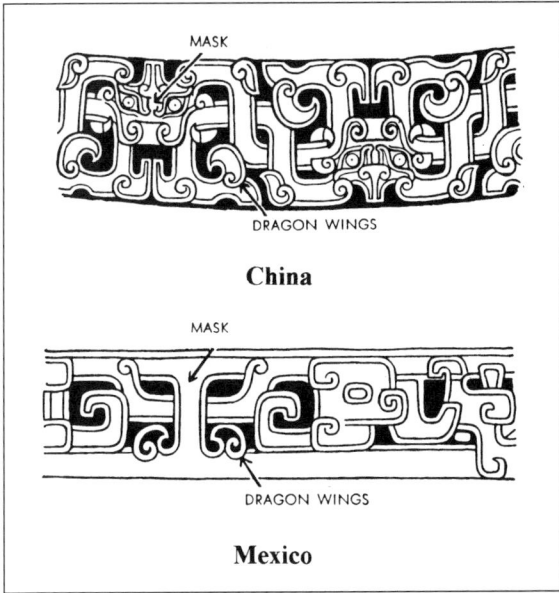

Fig. HS-8 Decorative Design Examples from from "They All Discovered America"

There is also an ancient Chinese story, the *Shan Hai Ching*, telling of travels to foreign places. Sixteen of the original 32 book are lost, but one of the lands described in one of the remaining books is *Fu Sang*. It is described as a strange and fabulous land where, among other wonders, there is a bird that flies backwards. Could this be the hummingbird, a bird that appears to do this, and which is found in the Western Hemisphere but not in China?

There is no way for us to be certain today as to how much trans-Pacific traffic

Fig. HS-9 Wheeled Toy Found in Central America from "They All Discovered America"– Boland

there may have been in ancient times. Perhaps if the Spanish Catholic priesthood had been somewhat less zealous about destroying the books of the Aztecs and the Maya there might still be records on this side of the Pacific telling of strangers arriving from the west. However, in the absence of written records, some curious physical evidence of outside influences have been found. In Fig. HS-8 a piece of ancient Mexican decorative design appears curiously similar to an ancient Chinese decorative design. The Mexican version is greatly simplified, but uses very similar shapes and patterns. Also, although wheeled carts or other vehicles were unknown in early Central America, wheeled toys (Fig. HS-9) have been found that are curiously similar to Asian wheeled toys. The discovery of a definitely oriental-looking sculptured head (Fig. HS-10) found near Vera Cruz is certainly another indication of the possibility of meaningful ancient contacts between China and Mexico.

As we have seen in the chronicle of Hoei Shin, he came in contact with people who were similar to the Maya in many ways. We still have much to learn about the Maya, and we actually have no idea where they came from, or when. Hopefully, one day archaeologists will unearth more concrete information as to their origins and whether there actually were early trans-Pacific contacts between the Maya and the Chinese.

While we may never be able to fully corroborate the story of Hoei Shin and his early exploration of the West Coast, we certainly cannot disprove it either. In light of the known shipbuilding capability of the Chinese at that period,

Fig. HS-10 This happy Chinese looking person was found in the Vera Cruz area of Mexico. It was carved centuries before the arrival of the Spanish. Could it be a portrait of one of Hoei Shin's people? from "They All Discovered America"– Boland

and knowing what we now do regarding ocean currents and prevailing winds, it seems highly probable that Chinese ships crossed the Pacific very long ago. A crossing as early as the Fifth Century AD is well within the realm, not only of possibility, but also of probability.

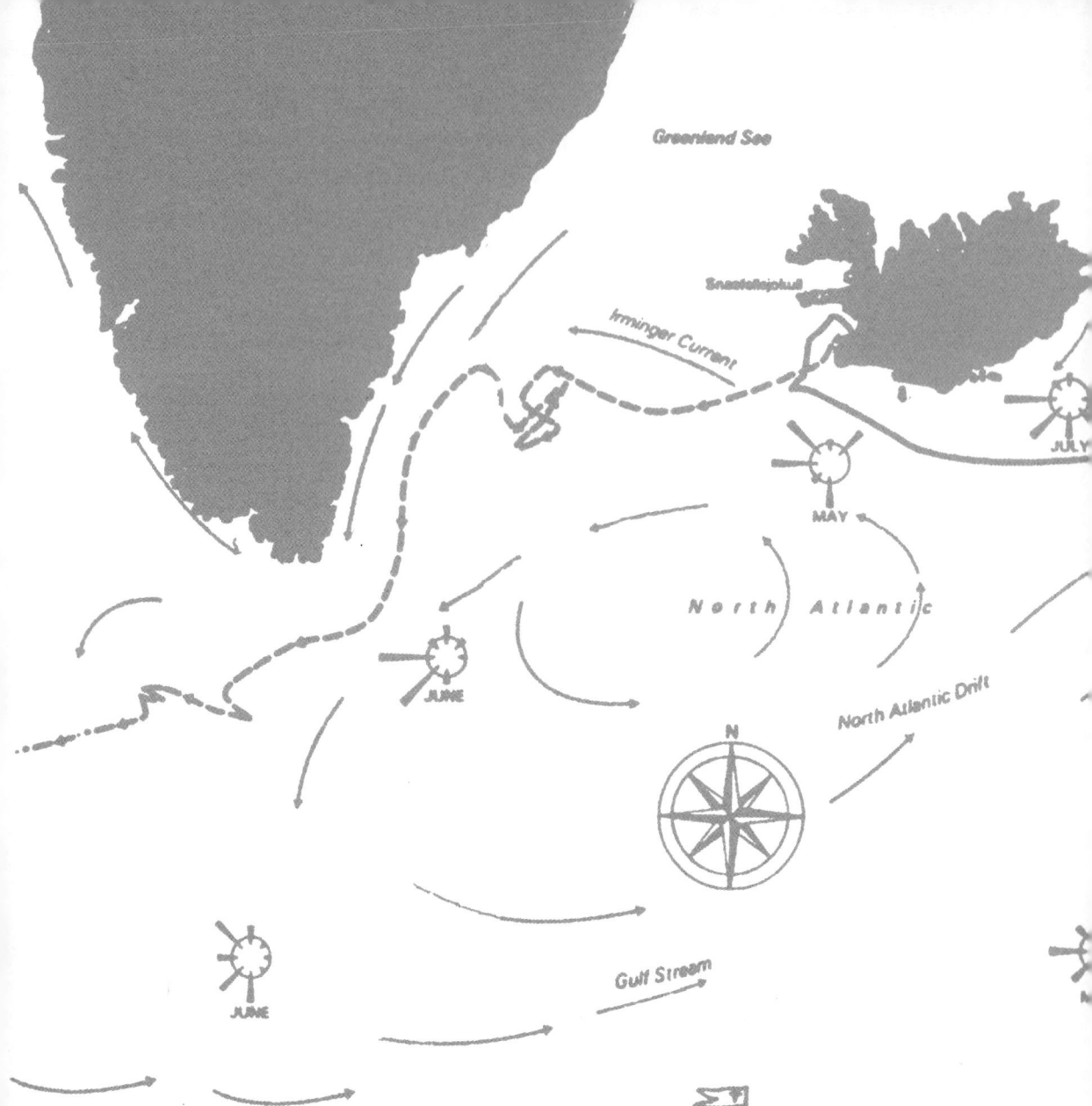

Greenland See

Snæfellsjökull

Irminger Current

North Atlantic

North Atlantic Drift

MAY

JULY

JUNE

N

Gulf Stream

JUNE

North Atlantic

AZORES

CHAPTER 2

Across the Atlantic in a Leather Boat 545-52 A.D.

A song from the Hebrides islands, one of Brendan's stops on his trans-Atlantic voyage

MINGULAY BOAT SONG

What care we how white the Minch is
What care we for the wind or weather
Bring her 'round boys for every inch is
Wearing home toward Mingulay

Chorus
Hilya ho boys. Let her go boys
Bring her head 'round into the weather
Ilya ho boys, Let her go boys
Sailin' homeward to Mingulay

Far behind us the hills of Quilon
Soon before us the hills of heather
And you know boys, the candles glow boys
In the windows of Mingulay

Wives are waitin' in the bank
Lookin' seaward from the heather
Bring her 'round boys, and then we'll anchor
E'er the sun sets on Mingulay

Ireland and its people are famous for many things from keen and witty conversation, to lively song and dance, to strife with England, to strife with each other. However, we do not normally think of the Irish as a major seafaring people in the same way as we do such groups as the Scandinavians, the British, the Spanish, the Portuguese, or the Dutch. This fact makes the tale of St. Brendan, also known in Ireland as Brendan the Bold, and Brendan the Navigator, all the more unusual.

He was born in County Kerry about 489 AD. County Kerry being a part of Ireland called the "sea country" through which the scenic River Shannon flows down to the restless and turbulent Atlantic. In the Fifth Century AD, many of the men of County Kerry had found scratching a living from their rocky land, by farming, extremely difficult. Therefor, some turned to building the uniquely Irish, small open boats called "curraghs", in which they put to sea and swapped the dangers and uncertainties of farming for the equally, if not more dangerous and uncertain occupation of fishing for a living. The earliest curraghs were very small boats used for coastal fishing.

This was also an era when many newly converted and extremely devout Christian monks felt an overpowering need to serve God by "mortifying" their flesh in a wide variety of imaginative ways. Some were able to satisfy this perceived need by living humbly in complete solitude, in remote and lonely parts of Ireland. Others gathered in groups to set up isolated monasteries where they fasted, prayed, and together, eeked out a meager living from the earth and the sea around them.

While many of these pious monks remained in Ireland, others found traveling to the remote windswept Atlantic islands of the Hebrides, the Faroes, the Orkneys, or Iceland, and apparently in some cases even further, to be more satisfactory places to serve God in appropriate discomfort. By Brendan's time, a small quantity of monks were widely scattered throughout these Atlantic islands.

Brendan was educated in a convent school, and as a young man felt called to the mission of spreading the Christian faith to the unenlightened. He was ordained a priest when he was 26, and soon founded a monastic group that settled on a mountain in Ireland, west of the Bay of Tralee.

The reason for the movement of many of these god-inspired monks out to the islands north and west of Ireland was prompted by a combination of Christian evangelism mingled with the ancient pagan Celtic belief in a glorious land that lay beyond the sunset. Legend had it that this land was peopled by the souls of departed heroes such as Oisin, the great mythical Irish leader, as well as by various strange and wondrous creatures. The story of this distant land appeared in the poetry of the early Irish bards who described the journeys of famous heroes to this fabulous place and their wondrous exploits while there. Frequently, the bards described this Other World as being mysterious, but also attainable, which meant that particularly fortunate and worthy mortals, under special conditions, could reach it.

When Christianity was introduced into Ireland, the myth of the Land of the Heroes was necessarily passed on into the Christian belief system, because the

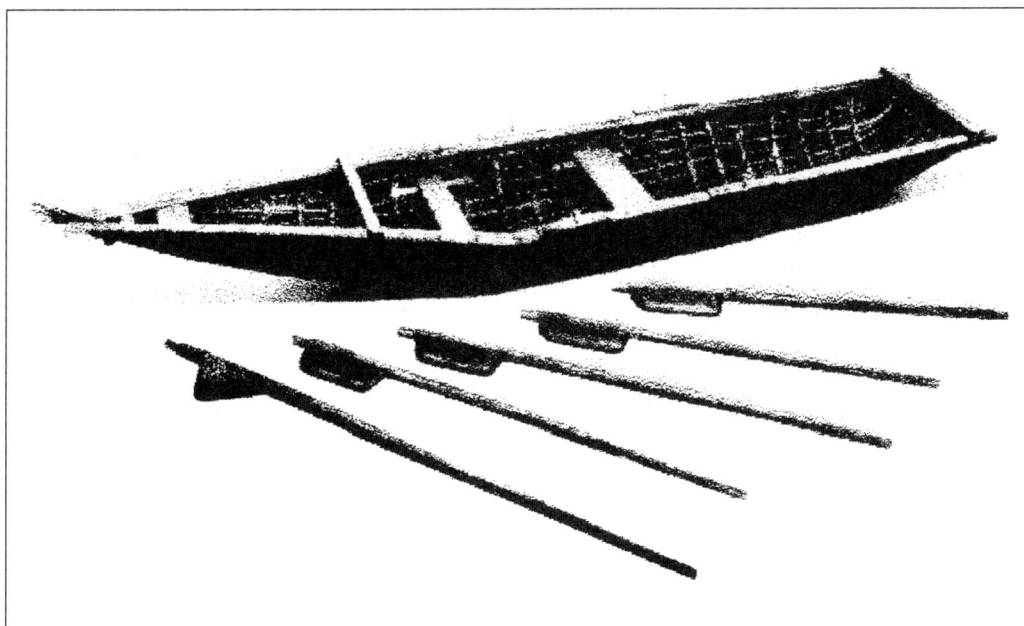

Fig. B-1 A small curragh of the traditional type from Mulroy Bay County Donegal from "Archaeology of Boats and Ships"– Greenhill & Morrison

Christian priests had no choice but to work and live alongside the traditional old Celtic seers and sages, if they wanted their message to be heard at all. The result was the ancient myth of an "Other World" was gradually given a Christian twist. It was still attainable by mortals, but it developed into a land promised by God to men of great virtue, and became peopled with a constellation of Christian saints and holy men. It became a most worthy objective for pious men to attempt to reach this land, and the journey itself became a commendable act of devotion and faith.

Irish monks were also able, at least in part, to fit this story into the framework of known geography, since they had studied many of the Greek and Roman authors. Consequently, from the proof of Eratosthanes they knew perfectly well that the earth was round. They understood Ptolemy's concept of world geography, and they knew, in addition, that the Romans had sailed around Scotland and found islands to the north of it. Consequently, a scattering of monks now went to these islands to cleanse themselves and prepare their souls for a better world to come. Thus, when Brendan decided he wished to attempt a journey to the wondrous lands to the west, his desire to do so was completely understandable to the monks around him. What made it unique and quite phenomenal from our point of view, but quite normal in his time, was the way he went about doing it. He decided to sail there in a traditional Irish leather curragh, which was the same type of boat used by those who had already reached the various Atlantic islands.

THE CURRAGH

Small boats called *curraghs* are still being built in Ireland to this day, and they are still remarkably similar to those made at the time of Brendan, in the late Fifth and early Sixth Centuries (Fig. B-1). The curragh of today consists of an elaborate latticelike frame of thin ashwood strips lashed to each other and connected to a stout oak gunwale. This frame, today, is covered with a tight skin of canvas that is then tarred inside and out to make it waterproof. This modern curragh is the descendant of one of the oldest types of boats known, the skin boat, which appears to date back to the Stone Age. The primary difference between today's curraghs and those of St. Brendan's time is the outer covering. The boats of Brendan's day were covered with well tanned oxhides. Thus, in his day, they routinely made lengthy sea voyages in leather boats!

As further evidence of the antiquity of the skin boat, not only had the Irish sailed north and westward to the Atlantic islands in such boats long before the 6th Century, but Vincent Cassidy of Louisiana State University reports that American Indians are thought to have reached Ireland and Germany up to 2000 years ago, also in skin boats. It was then, and still is, far easier to sail across the North Atlantic going eastward with the prevailing wind, rather than west, against it.

A scholar and researcher in the area of ancient Irish lore named Tim Severin found in the course of his studies, the chronicle of Brendan's voyage across the Atlantic starting in the year 545 A D., and was fascinated by this tale. Skepticism gradually grew into an intense interest to prove that an ocean crossing in a leather boat is indeed feasible, and that the chronicle of this voyage, therefor, is quite possibly true. If so, the legends of Irish monks having been scattered across the North Atlantic islands as far as Greenland, are doubtless true, as well.

To do this, Severn first had to search out a design as close as possible to the boat used by Brendan, and then he had to build such a boat using materials of the same types as those used in Brendan's day.

With the help of Colin Mudie, a prominent British naval architect, and supplemented by the advice of contemporary curragh builders along the Irish coast, a vessel was designed, which he named the "Brendan". (Fig. B-2) To resemble the curraghs that traveled to the Atlantic Islands it also had to be much larger than the earliest fishing dories.

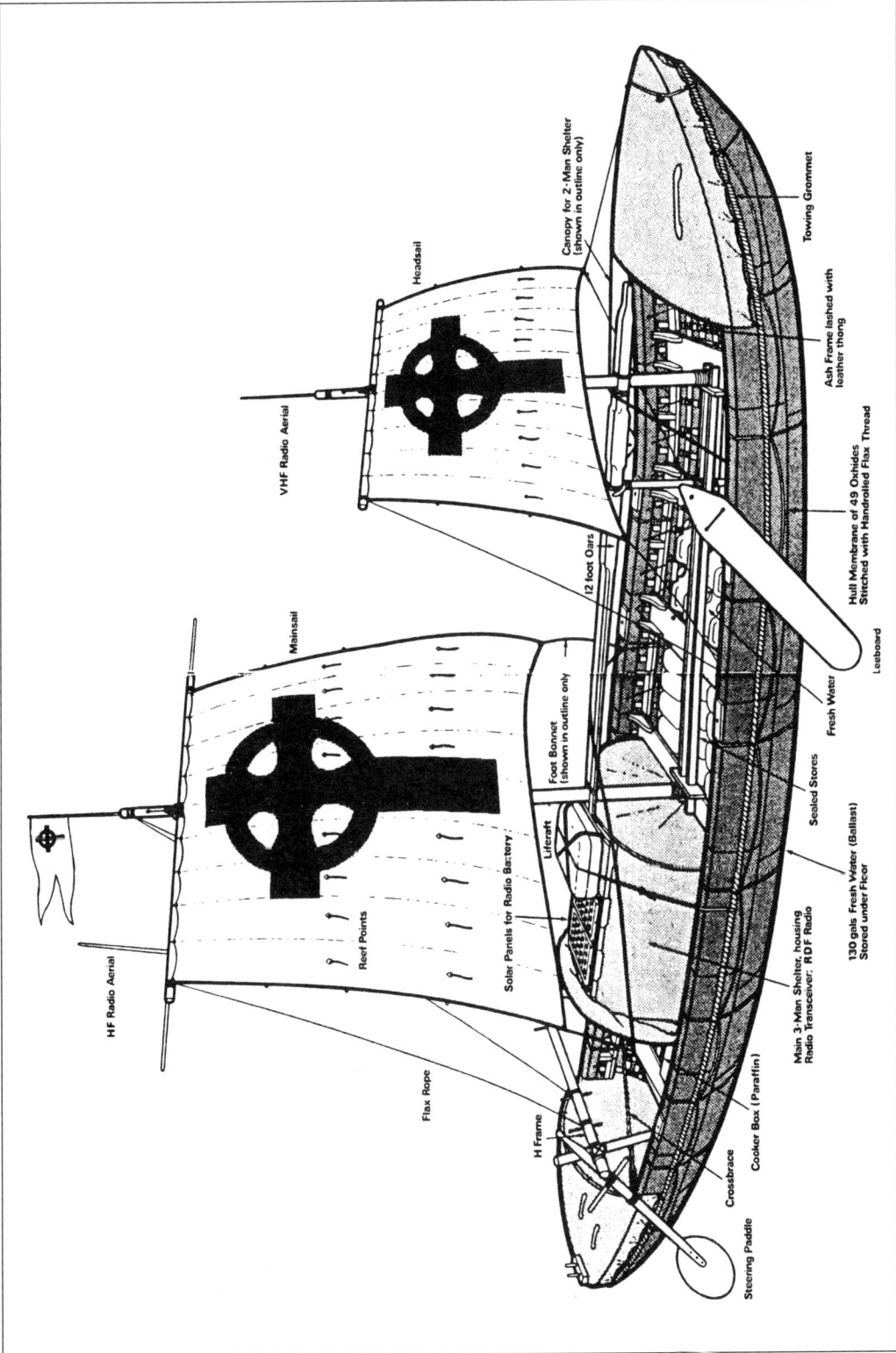

Fig. B-2 Drawing of the "Brendan" from "The Brendan Voyage"– Severin

If Severin was to prove his point, the construction of the ash and oak framework had to be done using the tools and methods available in Brendan's time. It was a laborious job but the final result was a frame very similar to those still being made by builders of curraghs today.

It was the leather outer skin that turned out to be the major problem, as it quickly became apparent that the modern methods employed for tanning leather, as presently used by cobblers, saddlemakers, and harness makers is definitely not suitable for prolonged immersion in salt water. They tried immersing some modern leather in ocean water, and it quickly disintegrated. At first, Severin was dejected, but after further research, was fortunate to find some ancient records indicating that a nearly obsolete method of tanning leather using an extract from oak bark was the normal tanning method in use during Brendan's time, and thus was undoubtedly the method used for the leather on his boat.

After considerable searching, a tannery was finally found that was familiar with this procedure. It is a very slow and laborious method, which perhaps explains why it is now obsolete, but this tannery agreed that they could, and would, tan some oxhides by the old oak bark method when the desired use for the hides had been explained to them. Leather tanned in this manner, and then dressed with the grease from sheep wool, which also was what St. Brendan had done, was then tested in salt water. The leather tanned and dressed using this ancient traditional method held up perfectly. It was now possible to complete the boat using a covering of oak bark tanned oxhides prepared in the same historical manner as indicated for use by St. Brendan and his companions.

THE "NAVIGATIO SANCTI BRENDANI ABBATIS"

The "Navigatio" is the ancient Latin chronicle of the Voyage of the Abbot St. Brendan. Several different Latin manuscript versions of the Navagatio exist describing this voyage. Naturally, there were many variations and discrepancies between these versions of the story. These various versions were finally reconciled and then compiled by a Notre Dame University professor, Carl Selmer, into a single comprehensive Latin edition in 1959. This edition was subsequently translated into English, and it now appeared that the Atlantic crossing was not St. Brendan's first sea voyage. He apparently went on three major voyages with which his Trans-Atlantic passage appearing to have been the second.

In some ways, the account of the long sea voyage of the Navigatio of St. Brendan resembles Homer's Odyssey, in containing many sections with very accurate descriptions of places which can, with reasonable certainty, be located today, mixed with many episodes of strange, wondrous, and imaginative fantasy. Partly, this results from the fact that, like the Odyssey, it was finally written down long after the fact, which accounts for much of the elaborate and exaggerated embroidery added to both stories by the imaginations of the many bards who told them over and over again, from memory, for the entertainment of their listeners long before they were finally written down. Since these bards were basically entertainers it is understandable that they would make additions to the tale to make it more thrilling and wondrous to their audiences.

The Navigatio starts with Brendan living as Abbot at the head of a community of 3,000 monks. For that period in Ireland this number sounds immediately like a tremendous exaggeration. In any event, the story goes on to say he was visited there by a traveling monk who told him the tale of a wondrous voyage to the west that this monk himself had taken to the Promised Land of the Saints in the company of another monk, Saint Mernoc. After the traveling monk had told his story and departed, Brendan decided he wanted also make this journey. He picked fourteen men from his own community and told them he greatly wanted to visit this promised land himself, and they agreed at once to accompany him.

They now built a traditional Irish curragh consisting of a wood frame which was then covered with oak bark tanned oxhides. The method of tanning used on these hides is specifically mentioned in the Latin texts. The joints between the hides were sewed with flax thread and smeared with sheep fat to seal them. The boat was then rigged with mast and sails, and a steering oar was installed. The hinged rudder we now use had not been invented at that time. Brendan and his companions then put aboard spare hides and fat, and supplies for forty days.

The sail they rigged would have to have been a square sail of the type used in earlier times by the Greeks and Romans. The triangular type sail, such as the lateen used in the middle east, or the bermudian fore and aft sail used on Colonial coastwise cargo schooners and what we use on yachts today, did not appear until many centuries after Brendan's time. The importance of this difference is that square sail could not go upwind as the triangular fore and aft rigged sail can. They could only sail with the wind or across it. This caused a major problem because they wanted to go *to* the west, and in the middle latitudes the prevailing wind blows *from* the west. Thus, they had no choice but to sail many miles off their course and do a lot of rowing as well, to make progress toward the west.

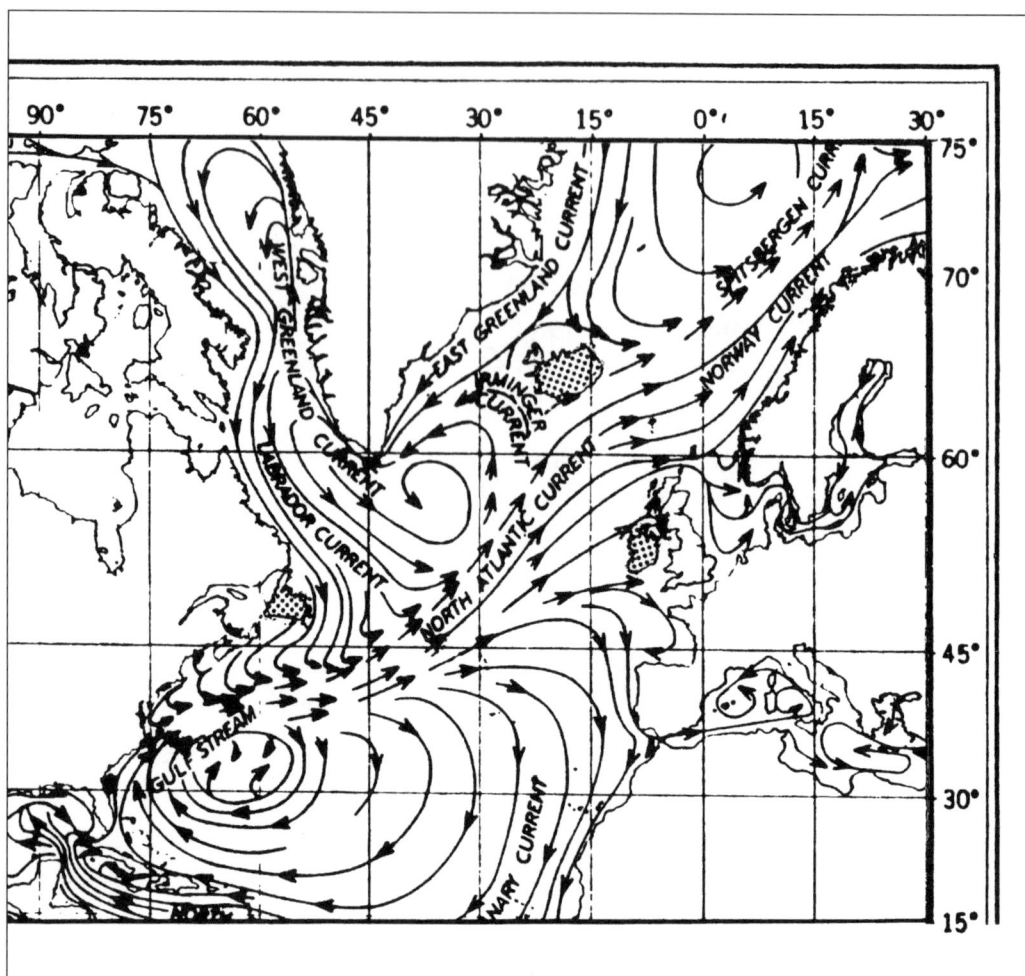

Fig. B-3 North American Currents
from "The American Practical Navigator"– Bowditch

In addition, in heading west from Ireland they soon ran into the North Atlantic Current, also moving against them from the southwest. Only after they have worked their way so far to the northwestward that they are south of Iceland, will they finally reach the westward flowing Irmiger Current which then flows into the East Greenland Current, which in turn flows toward the southwest. When they finally reach them these two currents will help take them southwestward toward their objective (Fig. B-3). None of these currents are strong ones, but when a lot of your progress is made by sailing across a generally adverse wind, and by rowing against the same adverse wind, any current, whether with you or against you, quickly becomes significant.

When St, Brendan and his people put to sea they initially sailed for two weeks, lost their bearings in a calm, and were then blown to a tall, rocky island where they stayed for several days. It is quite likely from the description that this island was one of the Hebrides. When leaving there, one of the less admirable of Brendan's monks tried to steal a silver bridle. Brendan rebuked him whereupon, the Navigatio states, a small devil jumped out of the man's chest and he promptly died.

Their next landfall was named in the Navigatio as the Island of Sheep. From the description of this island, and two others they landed on close by, they seem to resemble the Faroes, which are well to the north of the Hebrides. On the third island of this group, which was named the Paradise of the Birds, they spent Easter. According to the Navigatio, they then voyaged from there for three months before again sighting land. Thoroughly exhausted, they now had to row against the wind to reach a small landing area which, conveniently enough, was only 200 yards from a monastery. The abbot of the monastery pointed out to Brendan that here loaves of bread miraculously appear in the larder, and the lamps in the chapel never burn out.

Brendan and his people obviously lingered at this monastery for some time because the Navigatio says they spent Christmas with these hospitable monks and at some time after that, put to sea again. After stopping at a couple more islands they were blown back eastward to the Island of the Sheep. The Navigatio then says they repeated the same cycle for seven years - Island of Sheep, Paradise of the Birds for Easter, then back to the remote island monastery which they again leave after Christmas. The North Atlantic being no place for a small boat in mid-winter it would seem likely that they actually went back eastward to the Island of the Sheep quite a long while after Christmas. Very likely they were unable to sail westward, but were repeatedly blown back eastward by the prevailing westerly winds of those latitudes.

The Navigatio now describes a series of passages to various islands where all manner of miraculous and holy events occur. An eminent historian, archeologist and member of the Maritime Institute of Ireland, a Dr. Little, has carefully analyzed the Navigatio and other available material, and worked out a track indicating that Brendan and his group probably arrived at Iceland, and subsequently at Newfoundland. As they were sailing the coast of Newfoundland, one of their number died. He was a court jester named Crosan, and there is no explanation as to why he left the court to make this voyage. In any event, they stopped and buried him with appropriate ceremonies, before moving on. Some time later after they had again put to sea, another crewman died, and this time it was their smith. After appropriate services his body was consigned to the deep; but very soon they will regret his absence.

They then continued at sea for many days without incident. Now there is some disagreement between Dr. Little and other authorities as to whether the next island landfall was in the Bahamas or Bermuda. Dr. Little opts for the Bahamas, but he says their next run was eight days to reach Florida. That seems a very long sailing time for so short a distance. Other scholars believe they landed next at Bermuda. Eight days to sail from there to Florida would make more sense, but the chances of their finding Bermuda by accident so far out in the Atlantic also seems very strange.

Wherever it was, they no sooner anchored than they saw an old monk alone on the island. He said he had been there for many years and had come with twelve others, who were now all dead. Brendan and his people stayed seven days before moving on. When they were ready to leave they found their anchor was fouled and could not be raised, but after they cut themselves loose they found they needed another anchor. With the smith dead, one of the other monks made another anchor and they sailed on for eight days over "summer seas with spiced breezes".

One scholar believes they landed near Miami, another picks St. Augustine. Wherever it was, it appeared to them as a flowery, fragrant, abundant land. This had to be the fabled Fortunate Isle. Again, as seemed to happen everywhere they went, they were met by another old monk! This fellow was named Festivus. He had been there for thirty years and had come there with a number of other monks from Ireland.

For forty days the party explored what appears to have been inland Florida before deciding to return to Ireland. This they did by reversing their course. The return trip had to have been a great deal easier than the outbound trip, since both the prevailing wind and ocean currents were then favorable.

THE VOYAGE OF THE BRENDAN - 1976

After building the "Brendan" Tim Severin gathered a crew and set out to prove the seaworthiness of the leather curragh, and thus the feasibility of the voyage of St. Brendan, as described in the Navigatio by making the same trip themselves. They carried aboard many items that St. Brendan obviously lacked but what was thought to be be helpful, such as radio, compass, sextant, navigation tables, and charts, as well as more modern clothing and dehydrated food supplies. Let's remember they were not out to prove they were as tough as 6th Century monks, but only that a leather boat of the type used in that time could have made the voyage. Also, they didn't intend to spend seven years doing it either! Interestingly enough, it turned out later that

Fig. B-4 Track of the "Brendan" May and June 1976 from "The Brendan Voyage"– Severin

modern synthetic clothing didn't stand up as well on their cruise as traditional homespun wool. Also, modern dehydrated and freeze dried food didn't keep as well as the more "primitive" foods of the sort St. Brendan would have taken, such as smoked sausage, smoked beef, salt pork, hazelnuts, oat cereal and cheese.

Finally, on May 17, 1976, Severin and a crew consisting of an Irishman, a Cockney, a Norwegian, and an Englishman put to sea aboard their leather boat from Brandon Creek, on the west coast of Ireland. In a very few days they were caught in a gale. For 24 hours they ran before the storm blowing them nearly 100 miles offshore to the northwest. (Fig. B-4). The Brendan weathered the blow far better than her crew. After the storm, the wind came up from the west taking them back toward land where one of the crew, injured during the gale, had to be taken off.

A replacement was quickly found. They again set out working their way northward through the Hebrides Islands, passing and/or stopping at various places where monasteries existed in St. Brendan's time. They stopped at various other ports as well, where they were cordially welcomed by the local island people who were aware and supportive of their mission.

From Stornoway, the northernmost of the Hebrides, northward to the first of the Faroe Islands, *Brendan* made her first long run of about 200 miles over open ocean. The Faroes lie nearly half way from Scotland to Iceland. These islands are believed to be the ones referred to as the *Sheep Islands,* in the Navigatio, and one of them is thought to have been the island named *Paradise of the Birds.* Today's historians feel that the original settlers of these remote islands were in fact Irish monks. On the last day of the run to the Faroes, a gale struck again. Their arrival and final landing at the Faroes became a wild and memorable one. The boat handily weathered the storm again, although they did need to make some repairs to the rigging before starting on the next leg of the trip.

They were again most cordially greeted this time by the Faroese, with one of them signing on to join the crew for the upcoming long passage to Iceland. When under way again, this Faroese sailor turned out to be an extremely valuable and expert boatman, showing his fellow crewmen how the Faroese fish for cod which turned out to be a very useful supplement to the vessel's food supply. Certainly, in the time of St. Brendan his crewmen were familiar with many of the sailing and fishing skills known to this modern Faroese sailor.

When departing the Faroes, they had unusually favorable winds, at times reaching gale force for over a week. This again strained the rigging but it also placed them in an excellent position to reach Iceland Along the way they encountered a great many whales of several different species. Encountering a group of killer whales gave them some particularly nervous moments, but after the whales inspected them they decided the *Brendan* was not at all appetizing, and moved on.

In the *Navigatio* an incident is described where St. Brendan's people saw a very low island and decided to land and cook a meal ashore. They lit a fire, only to discover that what they had mistaken for an island turned out to be a very large whale. The animal was not amused and dove under, leaving them in the water. St. Brendan, who had stayed in the boat, came to their rescue and they proceeded on their way.

At about the time Severin began to fear the gale winds would drive them on past Iceland, it slacked and shifted. They were now only a short distance south of Iceland, but it took another 6 days in very light southerly winds to finally reach Reykjavik.

The Navigatio records a similar time when St. Brendan and his crew were blown by a southerly wind toward a stony island "very rough, rocky and full of slag, without trees or grass and full of smith's forges". Soon, according to this chronicle, a shaggy savage threw a great burning lump of slag at them passing out beyond them and falling into the sea causing it to boil and smoke. All the other shaggy inhabitants of the island threw more burning lumps at them, until it looked as if the whole island was on fire and there was a great clamor and a terrible stench.

Edit out the fanciful shaggy inhabitants and you have a good description of a volcanic eruption. The only place along the route where volcanic activity occurs is the south coast of Iceland. Here, there is ample evidence of volcanic activity, and St. Brendan approached the island from the south just as the modern crew did in retracing his voyage. The *Navigatio* identifies this place as the *Island of the Smiths*.

When the Norsemen first arrived on Iceland old chronicles indicate that they found a group they called "papars". These were Christians, and the Norse word "papar" means father. This would indicate they may well have been Christian monks, and the Icelanders believe they were Irish refugees who had come here from islands further to the east which they had abandoned after being plundered by Norse sea raiders. In any event, the Brendan had already proven that in earlier times Irish monks could certainly have reached as far as Iceland in leather boats.

By this time, the *Brendan* had been at sea for eight weeks on its way from Ireland. A small boatyard in Reykjavik now offered to haul the *Brendan* for inspection an offer Severin quickly accepted. He had repeatedly been told that they had already been at sea longer than a skin boat could be expected stay afloat, without regreasing the leather. When hauled, the grease coating was found to be in excellent condition, except for a few small areas where flotsam had scraped off the grease. The remaining grease was then all scraped off to check the condition of the leather underneath, which happily, was found to still be in perfect condition, and a new coating of grease was applied.

The boat was then completely emptied so the inside and everything aboard could be inspected. During this process the Icelandic Coast Guard was most helpful. They gave the *Brendan* a berth at the Coast Guard base during the unloading, and when this was under way supplied a spare anchor, extra line, a spare radio battery, and an oil bag for use in case of storm conditions. *Brendan* was now ready to sail, but the weather now turned against the expedition.

For three weeks Severin and his crew waited while a strong wind, intermittently at gale force, blew continuously out of the west to southwest. Now it was fall and too late in the season to start the long passage to Newfoundland, particularly since were absolutely no harbors of refuge along the way. The North Atlantic in fall and winter is a very stormy and uncomfortable ocean for large ships going west let alone this small boat. Also, the *Navigatio* clearly stated that St. Brendan advanced on his way "as the seasons allowed" so that it took him a total of seven years to complete his voyage. Therefor, Severin decided he could still prove his point if he left the boat in Iceland for the winter and continued the voyage when the spring "season allowed". The boat was then unloaded and taken ashore, spending the winter in a hangar at the Coast Guard base in Reykjavik.

VOYAGE OF THE BRENDAN IS COMPLETED – 1977

The following spring, two of the original crew were unable to return to complete the voyage, so the boat left Iceland with a crew of only four aboard. On the trip from Ireland to Iceland, they were able to repeatedly stop at various islands along the way to make repairs, rest, and pick up stores and water. The voyage from Iceland to Newfoundland provided no such convenient stopping places - none at all! This had to be a single, very long passage, so when they began they had to carry enough supplies for the entire trip. That being the case, reducing the crew to four had its advantages - more space to store supplies and fewer people to need and use them.

With everything ready they left Reykjavik May 7 of 1977 for, by far, the

Fig. B-5 "Brendon" under way at sea

longest, most difficult, and most dangerous part of the trip. (Fig. B-5) For the first few days the winds were very light as they headed westward toward Greenland. The weather remained favorable and for the rest of the week progress was slow, but they moved steadily westward.

Then the wind shifted to the southwest and the weather quickly deteriorated, turning to cold and rain. The next week brought extremely foul weather. Strong adverse winds, heavy seas, rain, and cold. The boat was so low in the water due to her heavy load of supplies that seas kept coming aboard requiring constant pumping to keep her afloat. When they turned to run with the seas they were repeatedly overtaken by waves breaking over the stern and pouring into the boat. Eventually, Severin thought of using some spare ox-hides to make a cover over the stern to block the incoming water. This worked very well and cut down considerably on the amount of pumping needed.

During this gale there was no thought of trying to keep to a course since every possible effort was needed just to keep the boat afloat. She very nearly foundered several times By the time the storm had passed *Brendan* had lost some distance, but the seemingly fragile leather boat had again proved her seaworthiness by surviving another North Atlantic gale.

This storm was by far the worst they had encountered thus far, and when it subsided, Severin and his crew believed that after this, they and their vessel could get through just about anything. That confidence would be tested repeatedly during the remaining passage of nearly 1500 miles to Newfoundland, as they would still encounter further storms, adverse winds, and fogs.

Off Labrador, they got into an ice field that could well have tragically ended their voyage; however, with phenomenal good luck, a Faorese fishing vessel happened by and saw their signal. The fishermen offered to tow them clear, and did. Shortly afterward they happened to meet a U.S. Navy supply ship returning from Greenland. The officers on the Navy ship had a hard time believing that this little skin boat (Fig. B-6) had sailed there from Iceland. The Navy gave them some supplies, a satellite check on their position, wished them well, and left wondering about how foolhardy some people can be.

By the 17th of June they were working their way south off Labrador when they ran into what is called, in Arctic terminology, "Very Open Pack" ice. This is a jumble of broken sea ice of all sizes and shapes, large and small, floating with channels of clear water opening and closing between them. On the 18th after zigging and zagging and twisting and turning to slip through between ice floes in the night, *Brendan's* luck ran out. A piece of sea ice cut a 4″ rip in the skin of their leather boat. In the dark they could do nothing but pump and wait for daylight so they could see to find the leak and attempt a repair. By another stroke of great, good fortune, the break was just on the waterline Although it was difficult to reach, they were able to successfully repair it by sewing a piece of a spare ox-hide over the cut. After heavily coating the patch with grease it became completely water tight, and they were able to continue on their way.

For days after clearing the pack ice they still saw and passed many lone ice bergs floating south along with them in the Labrador Current, but they also began to see signs they were nearing land; such as floating logs, patches of weed, and increasing numbers of birds. They now had many days of light winds and fog until finally, after 50 days at sea, they made landfall on a small island off Newfoundland. Their necessarily erratic track from Iceland to Newfoundland is clearly shown in Fig. B-6.

They had passed Greenland but did not attempt to land because of the dangerous pack ice along its shores, However, it is believed that in medieval times the climate there was considerably warmer than now, making it more likely that St. Brendan could have landed there on his way to North America.

Severin and his crew did not feel it necessary to fully complete St. Brendan's voyage to Florida and back to Ireland, since they had proved what they had

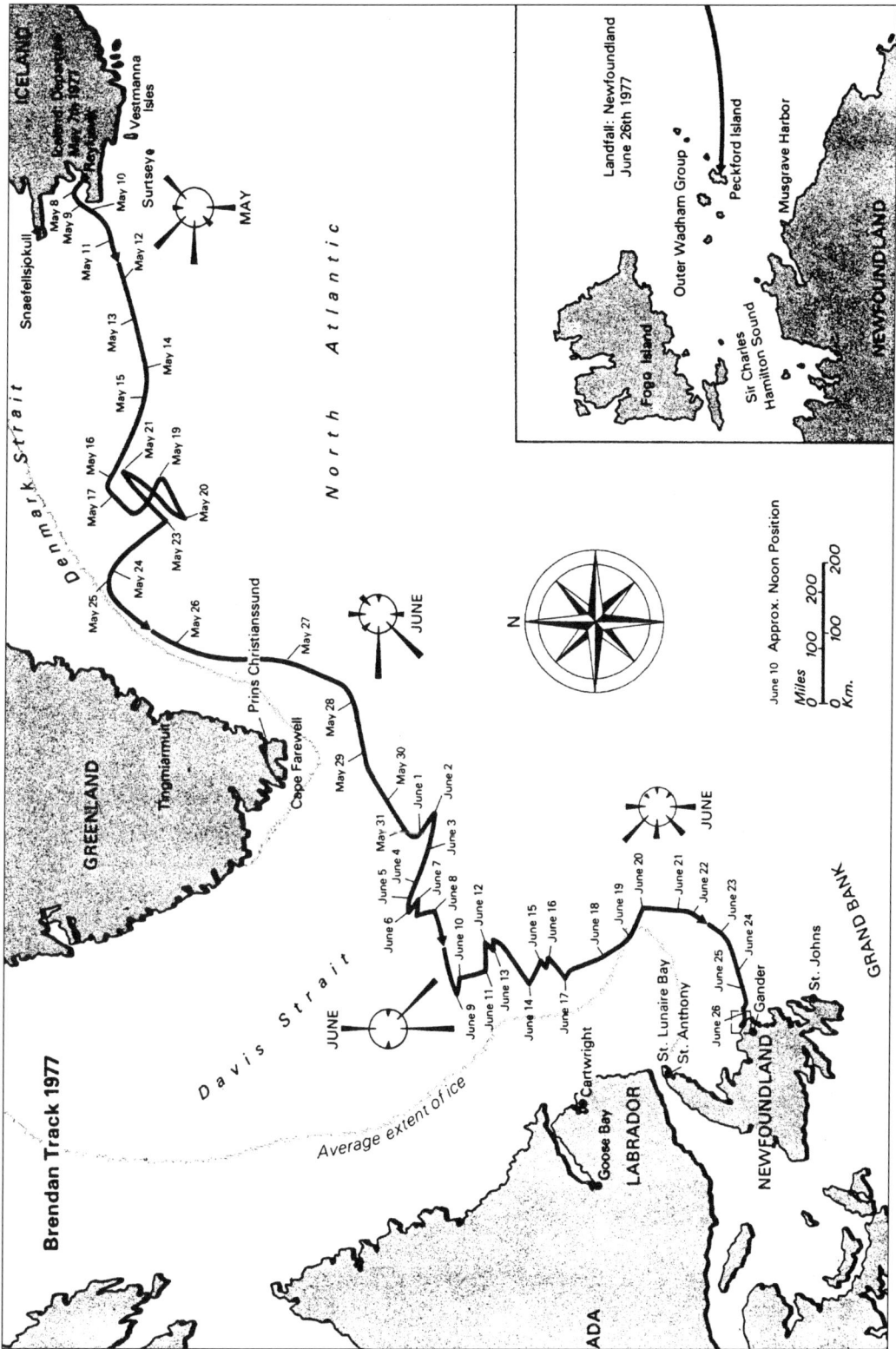

Fig. B-6 Track of "Brendan"–May & June1977 from "The Brendan Voyage"– Severin

intended to prove. The Navigatio, stripped of the mythology, allegory, exaggeration, and imaginative fabrication it contains, could well be a true account of a very real voyage across the Atlantic in a leather boat, by St. Brendan and his companions, around 550 AD.

In addition, it seems highly *un*likely that Brendan's group was the only one to cross the Atlantic in a leather boat at that early time in history. According to the distinguished archeological scholar, Dr. C.F. Herberger, ancient Irish-type stoneworks exist in New Hampshire and Connecticut, along with petroglyphs that can be dated. These are accompanied by the early Christian Chi Rho symbol. There is nothing in the record of St. Brendan's voyage to indicate he landed in New England, but clearly other Irish clerics did land there very long ago!!

A POSSIBLE ALTERNATE ROUTE

The *Navigatio*, as mentioned earlier, contains many strange and fanciful events and descriptions added by the bards who told and retold the story from memory through the many years before it was finally written down. Paul H. Chapman, also a student of the same *Navigatio*, has arrived at a very different route for St. Brendan's Atlantic crossing. than the one followed by Tim Severin.

Using Chapman's interpretation of the story, Brendan originally started out, just as Severin did, by going north past the Hebrides to the Faroes and then trying to head west. Chapman sees St. Brendan twice blown back to the Faroes. Then on the third try, he sees St. Brendan arriving at Flores Island in the Azores as identified by hot and cold water springs found together on the shore. From there, Brendan sailed into the Sargasso Sea and after being becalmed, was blown back to San Miguel in the Azores. He identifies San Miguel by thier lakes of mineral waters. On leaving San Miguel, Brendan is blown south to the Trade Wind belt, and now with the wind behind him, easily crosses to the Bahamas.

Chapman is also convinced that Columbus had read the *Navigatio* and sailed south to the Canary Islands before turning west, because he believed that Brendan had found steady winds to carry him west at that latitude. Chapman agrees that the Norsemen sailed across the Atlantic via the northern route, but this was before Greenland and its surrounding waters were frozen.

The Chapman theory raises the possibility that Severin sailed a shorter, but much more difficult route that St. Brendan. However, in that case there are parts of the *Navigatio*, such as the Island of the Smiths, that are difficult to fit into the

Chapman scenario.

In either case, it is clear that the Atlantic was crossed from east to west far earlier than we have been led to believe, and St Brendan and others as well, could certainly have crossed the water in leather boats.

CHAPTER 3

Single Handed Voyages of The Fingerless Captain Howard Blackburn

An American version of a popular British capstan chanty. Gloucester, Massachusetts was Captain Blackburn's homeport

GLOUCESTER GIRLS

Gloucester girls don't have no combs
Haul away! Haul away!
They comb their hair with codfish bones, An' we're
away for Australia

Refrain:
So heave her up my bully bully boys now,
Haul away! Haul away!
Heave her up an' don't you make noise An'we're
Bound away for Australia

Gloucester boys don't have no sleds
Haul awa!, Haul away!
They slide down hills on Codfish heads. An' we're
Bound away for Australia

Gloucester cats don't have no tails
Haul away! Haul away!
They got blown off in a Nor'east gale. An'we're
Bound away for Australia

Gloucester dogs don't have no bite
Haul away! Haul away!
They lost it barkin' at Gloucester Light. An' we're
Bound away for Australia

Gloucester ladies don't have no frills
Haul away! Haul away!
They're plain and skinny as a Codfish gill. An' we're
Bound away for Australia

On April 24, 1895, Captain Joshua Slocum started out from Gloucester to make a single-handed crossing of the North Atlantic Ocean in the 37' long rebuilt sloop

Fig. BL-1 Captain Howard Blackburn

Spray at the start of his famous single-handed, round-the-world-voyage. Twenty two months later, Captain Howard Blackburn (Fig. BL-1) also started from Gloucester in the much smaller 30' long sailboat, *Great Western,* to make his considerably less well known single-handed crossing of the Atlantic. He was headed for Gloucester, England and arrived there, successfully.

Although Captain Blackburn made his first of *two* singlehanded crossings shortly after the far better known Captain Slocum, what makes his achievement considerably more impressive, even more than that of Slocum, is the fact that he accomplished both crossings with no fingers on either hand! In addition, he was missing half of his toes as well!

Captain Blackburn's single-handed voyages across the Atlantic were only two of many unusual events in the life of this extraordinary mariner. To begin to understand how and why he made these voyages, disabled as he was, we must look back at his personality and life leading up to them.

Howard Blackburn was born to a seagoing family on February 17, 1859 in the small coastal town of Port Medway, Nova Scotia. He was the sixth of eight children, five boys and three girls.

Port Medway was then a major seaport for the export of lumber and fish. Millions of board feet of timber were floated down the Medway River from the huge inland forests. In spring, the river teemed with salmon, and in summer, the fishermen sailed out to to the many nearby off-shore banks to fish for cod and mackerel from the huge schools that massed there. The seagoing tradition of the family went back to Howard's grandfather, who was captain of a coastwise cargo schooner. His father, Bill Blackburn, was a sailor as well, so during his childhood, the boy was constantly in contact with ships and the sea, both at home and in the town.

Because school failed to interest the boy, he quit at the age of 10, and at 13, shipped out on a square-rigger bound for the Madeiras. After seven years as a hand at sea, on various ships, he landed in Gloucester at the age of 20. He was now a tough, handsome, hard-drinking, fun loving, giant of a man and a fully seasoned sailor. He now quickly proved himself valuable on the famous Gloucester banks-

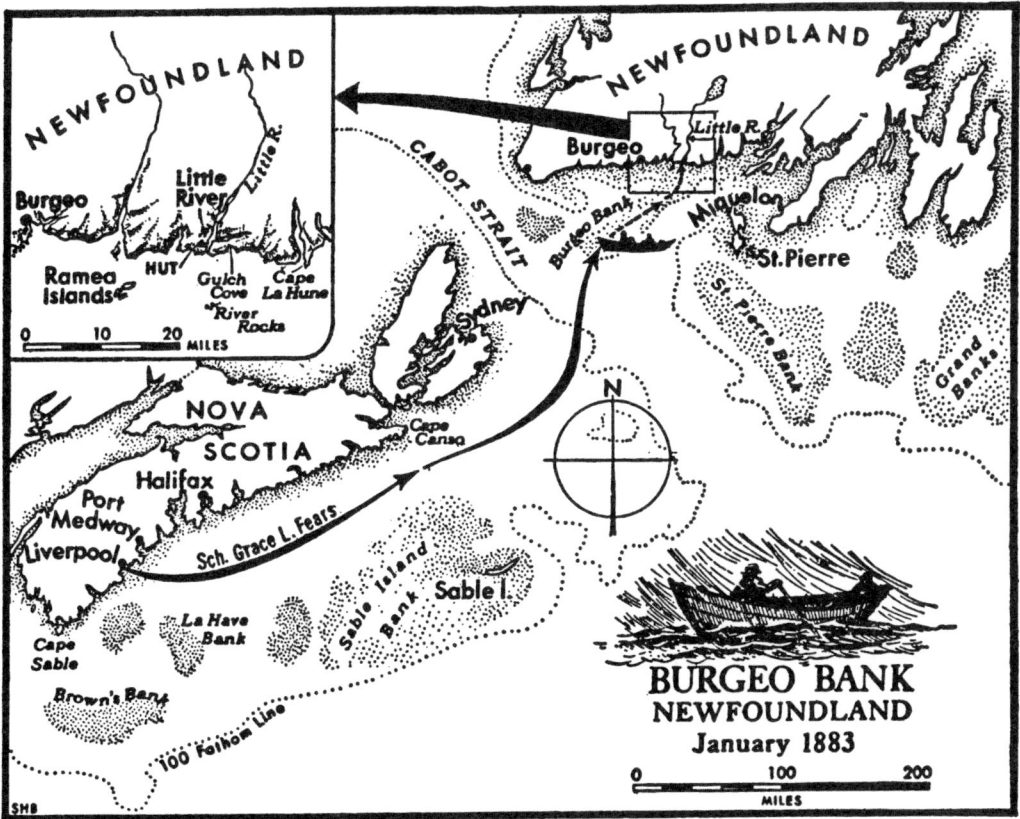

Fig. BL-2 Route of the "Grace L. Fears" to Burgeo Bank & Blackburn's row to Little River
from "Lone Voyager"– Garland

fishing schooners, on which he sailed for the next 3 1/2 years, all year , in all kinds
of weather.

THE DISASTROUS VOYAGE

In January 1883, at Liverpool, Nova Scotia, the *Grace L. Fears*, a banks fishing schooner (Frontispiece), arrived in port, short one crewman. Howard happened to be spending the holidays at his home in nearby Port Medway, and
while there, he chanced to meet up with Alec Griffin, acting as skipper of this
vessel while the locally well known and highly regarded regular skipper,
Captain Nat Greenleaf took off for some holiday time ashore. Blackburn and
Griffin had previously met and become friends in Gloucester. Griffin asked
Howard if he would take the empty berth and he agreed to sign on for the voyage to the Burgeo Bank off Newfoundland. Howard was to find this voyage
would completely change his life.

Burgeo Bank (Fig. BL-2) lies sixty miles south of the fijords of Newfoundland,
and well west of the much larger, and better known Grand Banks. The ship

cleared Liverpool on January 21 to go after halibut. This popular fish is a bottom dwelling flatfish similar to flounder, but vastly larger. A single fish may weigh as much as 350 pounds.

The ship reached the southern slope of the bank on the night of the 24th. Captain Griffin felt his way over the bank casting the lead line again and again to find the kind of bottom these fish like. At daybreak he found it and dropped his anchor.

The port and starboard dories, kept nested on deck, were now heaved up, swung out, and launched. These were the usual rowing dories normally used at that time – 18 feet long with flared sides, a flat bottom, and a small triangular transom at the stern. This design was much safer in the rough seas over the banks than the more common rowboat which has a wider, flat stern. This *"banks dory"* (Fig. BL-3) was, and still is, a remarkably tough, seaworthy boat. These fine rowing boats are still being built in Gloucester by a very small number of surviving craftsmen, precisely following that old, traditional design.

Six dories were launched to set out the trawl which, when fully extended, was nearly a mile and a half long with 480 fish hooks attached. Obviously, "long-lining" is by no means a new idea. After setting the trawl, the dorymen returned to the ship to rest and to allow time for the fish to hook on to the trawl.

In only two hours, an unusually short time, Captain Alex ordered the dorymen over the side to pick up the trawl. As an experienced banks fisherman he saw a look to the sky and a feel in the air that did not bode well. Foul weather was coming, and soon. The catch would be thin, but he did not want to wait and risk the chance of either loosing his trawl or having his dories caught away from the ship in boisterous wind and sea conditions.

Blackburn had been teamed with a burly Newfoundlander named Tom Welch and they worked well together. They went back all the way to the far end of the trawl and started hauling it in. As Welch heaved up the line Blackburn stood in the waist of the dory with the killing club in hand. As a thrashing halibut came to the surface he pulled in the line, got the flapping fish to the gunwale so he could club it on the head, drag it over the side into the bottom of the boat, and pull the hook from its mouth. When they had half a mile of trawl back aboard they noticed that the breeze from the southeast was picking up. At the moment this was fine since it would help them back toward the ship.

It had already begun to snow but they could still see the nearest of the other dories through the snow so continued on with their job. When Blackburn and Welch had their last section of the trawl aboard, the other dories were already heading back to the schooner, and they started back as well. At first the wind dropped to an ominous calm, then a squall hit, but from the northwest, exactly the wrong direction! They were now to leeward rather than to windward of the schooner, and it was out of sight in the flying snow. The sudden squall caused them to lose their bearings. The snow thickened, the wind increased, and the sea built into a

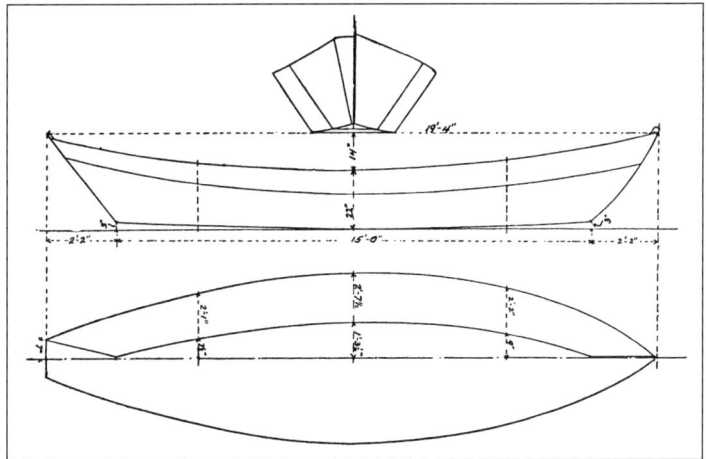

Fig. BL-3 Gloucester "banks dory",
The boat Blackburn rowed from Burgeo Bank to Newfoundland from "American Sailing Ships"– Charles G. Davis – Dover, New York

nasty chop, throwing spindrift on them from breaking wave crests.

They rowed steadily on, but could see nothing. After an hour of hard rowing they agreed they must be beyond, and to windward, of the schooner. In these prevailing conditions, they knew they could easily have passed within yards of the ship and not seen her in the wind and snow, so they decided to anchor and wait until the snow stopped when they could see the ship and row back to her. However, when the snow stopped after dark they found they were as far downwind as ever. They knew this because they now saw a lantern raised in the rigging of the ship. For all their rowing until now, they had made no headway at all.

Since they could now see the ship they pulled up the anchor and tried to get over to her. However, the wind and the sea were still too strong for them to make any headway so they again dropped the anchor. This time, as the dory backed down, the rising swells made the anchor line pull tight on the bow. This caused it to plow into every oncoming wave, each time pouring water into the boat. By constantly bailing all night with a bailing scoop and a buoy keg from the trawl they managed to just keep up with the incoming water. Meanwhile, spray was freezing, and covered the little boat with a glaze of ice. Their boat grew sluggish under the heavy load. To relieve her weight, they threw the trawl line overboard, along with all the fish they had caught, except for one cod which they kept to eat, raw if necessary.

Every so often during the night, a particularly high wave raised them up enough to briefly see the light in the rigging of the schooner, but by morning there was nothing to see or hear but the churning waves and the howling wind. The schooner and its crew had given them up and left for port, assuming they had drowned. Newfoundland, the nearest land, lay about 60 miles away to the north.

They again pulled up anchor and tried to row, but it was useless so they gave up. With the regular anchor down, they had constantly taken on water so they decided to try using a sea anchor instead. While Welch kept the boat head to the wind with the oars, Blackburn improvised a sea anchor. In order to do this he had to pull off his thick mittens which he dropped in the bilge so as not to lose them. As soon as the sea anchor was streamed overboard, the boat swung head to the wind and a large sea came aboard again, filling the boat with water. Welch shipped his oars and grabbed the bailer. As the first of the water went over the side, Blackburn's mittens were unseen in the bailer and went over as well. Neither of them noticed the loss until they stopped to rest and Blackburn looked for them in the bilge, and they were gone. Since there was nothing to be done about it, they went back to bailing.

For another hour or so of bailing Blackburn didn't really miss the mittens. Then Welch noticed that his hands looked strange – grey and colorless. Now that his mate had pointed it out Blackburn knew his hands were freezing. He felt no pain, only numbness, but he knew his hands would soon stiffen and become useless making it impossible for him to row. He bent down, picked up his oars, and slowly, slowly forced his fingers to curl around the handles. Very soon they became frozen to the curve of the oar handles..

All day they alternately bailed and broke ice off the boat to keep from sinking. The storm continued, and by that night, the second night, Welch was exhausted, lay down in the bow, and gave up. Blackburn had no intention of giving up and continued to bail and break ice to keep the boat afloat. During that night, Welch died of exhaustion and exposure.

By the dawn of the third day the storm finally let up, leaving a nearly calm sea. During the storm one pair of oars had been lost, but the other pair remained. Although his hands were frozen to the curve of the oar handles Blackburn was able to get the sea anchor aboard and start rowing for Newfoundland. He rowed all of that third day and part of the night; then stopped and again dropped the sea anchor over the side. It was a long night; there had been no food nor water since leaving the schooner, and the wind picked up again during the third night, with Blackburn's dead companion, Tom Welch, providing no help or company.

By dawn of the fourth day the wind again died down, and the sea was calm. Howard saw what appeared to be an island a fair distance away, but saw no signs of life so he continued to row on in the direction where he expected to find

*Fig. BL-4 Hands frozen to the oars, Blackburn arrives at Little River on the fifth night of his ordeal
from: "A Fearless Fisherman"*

Newfoundland. Late in the afternoon he saw the coast in the distance. He continued to row, and by dusk was at the mouth of a small river. Inside the river
mouth he found a broken-down wharf with a decrepit shed on it. He finally got
to the wharf, secured the dory, and dragged himself ashore to spend a miserable
night in the shed. As he crawled from the dory to the shed, the numbness in his
feet told him they were frozen also.

There was no settlement visible anywhere nearby. He knew his only choice
was to use the dory to row eastward along the coast, until he could find one. By
the morning of the fifth day he found the dory had been pounded on the rocks
during the night and was now badly damaged. With great difficulty he managed
at last to get the body of Tom Welch out of the boat. Then, by sitting off center to
keep a damaged plank out of the water, he started rowing along the coast, stopping frequently to bail as the damaged boat leaked badly. Finally, late in the fifth
night he reached a settlement called Little River (Fig. BL-4). Here, three men on
shore saw him, pulled in the dory, and took him to the nearby house of a family
named Lishman. There was no medical service available in Little River, or anywhere nearby, but in the past the Lishmans, having lived long on this bleak coast,

had seen many cases of frostbite, recognized it at once, knew exactly what must be done, and did it.

For weeks, Mrs. Lishman nursed poor Howard day and night. For several weeks it was doubtful whether he would survive. The results of the frostbite left him completely helpless. One by one he lost all the fingers on both hands and half of both thumbs. In addition he lost 3 toes on the left foot, as well as 2 toes and the heel on the right foot. At the end of April, partially recovered, he was well enough to be taken to the town of Burgeo where there was a doctor. The doctor could do no more for Blackburn than the Lishmans had already done. He could only complete the treatment they had started.

A NEW LIFE IN GLOUCESTER

Eventually, with the help of the U.S. Consular Service he obtained passage back to Massachusetts, arriving in Gloucester on the 4th of June. His recuperation had taken a bit over 4 months. He immediately became a great celebrity in Gloucester, but what was he to do now? Obviously he was done as a fisherman. His back pay from the schooner added to a popular subscription that was taken up to assist him, enabled him to start a small business in cigars, tobacco, and the various sundries fishermen needed. It was quickly a successful, although a limited business.

Liquor offered far more profitable possibilities. Having spent considerable time, along with other sailors, on the consuming side of the bar, Howard knew that a harbor saloon would be an excellent business. Therefor, he applied for a liquor license, and a food license as well, so he could serve light snacks to ease the hunger and increase the thirst of his seagoing customers. The problem with a saloon business, at that time, was that the control of local politics was passing back and forth between the local contingent of "wets" and their constant opposition the "drys". Unfortunately, the drys took control in Gloucester just before his application was processed. The food license was approved, but the liquor license was held up. For Howard, a food license without the liquor license was useless, but he managed to sell his booze clandestinely, anyway.

With his saloon successfully in operation, Blackburn made a very public donation of $500 to the widows and orphans of Gloucester's fishermen in repayment of the money raised for him in his time of need. This move again made him a local hero, so that when he was raided for selling liquor, the raids did not arouse much disapproval. Thereafter in spite of repeated raids by the "drys" he continued to run his covert saloon.

Finally, in 1890 the "wets" again regained control of local government and Blackburn was more than ready. Among seagoing people, his bar and restaurant became known as one of the best and busiest on the East Coast. He was normally behind his bar from opening to closing and he prospered greatly. Also, he had learned to use those injured hands in an astonishing variety of ways. He could pick up pen or pencil with the stubs of his thumbs and handle many other objects as well.

He personally indulged in both roast beef and drink with great relish. He was a giant of a man with an appetite and a thirst to match, with the result that he developed an imposing paunch. This he covered with a truly impressive waist-coat with silver buttons, a gold watch chain with a string of charms, and an array of change pockets which he could delve into with amazing skill, using his thumb stubs. His saloon was a workingman's bar where he allowed no rowdiness. He was an imposing figure so that on the rare occasions when he had to raise his voice to maintain peace, plates and glasses rattled, and silence fell at once in deference to his thundering order.

Having known want himself, Howard's largesse to others in need around Gloucester was legendary, now that he was successful. He also was particularly generous to the Lishmans, who had taken such very good care of him when he was totally helpless, and at death's door. Every year, when the Gloucester herring fleet sailed for Newfoundland, he sent a special shipment of food and clothing to the Lishmans, and he also rounded up supplies from all around town to send to the many helpful, poor people he had known along that bleak Newfoundland coast.

AROUND THE HORN TO THE KLONDIKE

Financially, Blackburn was doing well, but he was a sailor at heart and just not happy hanging about ashore while those around him continued to go to sea. Then in 1897 the news of the great gold find in the Alaskan Klondike reached Gloucester. Here was something really challenging. Of the various possible ways to get to the gold fields he felt the available transportation via the overland route presented many disadvantages that would put the traveler at the mercy of too many unscrupulous knaves living along the way, as well as all the greedy gold seekers who had preceded him. Sailing a schooner around the Horn and up to Alaska appeared to him to be the better route by far. He thus set about to organize the Gloucester Mining Company. His idea was to collect a group of fellow enthusiasts, buy a schooner, load her with coal and various other items that could be sold at a profit on the west coast, and sail out in the fall, hoping to pass the Horn of South America during the southern hemisphere summer. When arriving in San Francisco they would sell their cargo, buy mining equipment and sail on north to Alaska.

*Fig. BL-5 The schooner "Hattie I. Phillips" leaving Gloucester bound around Cape Horn
with fingerless Captain Howard Blackburn in command.*

Blackburn was the sparkplug and leader of the group. They bought a schooner, the *Hattie I. Phillips* (Fig. BL-5), fitted her out and sailed south in October with Blackburn as captain. As luck would have it when only three days out they ran into an Atlantic hurricane which thoroughly buffeted both them and their vessel, but they escaped without being seriously damaged, and from there on, the trip to the Horn was quite smooth. They were becalmed for a while in the Horse Latitudes, but then bowled along through the southern Trade Wind belt making good time down along eastern South America. They reached the Horn in late December and stopped at Punta Arenas for six days to make repairs to the schooner, and pick up supplies before sailing on.

They finally reached San Francisco on the 23d of February after a voyage taking 129 days (Fig.BL-6). Of two New England clipper ships that sailed the same route at about the same time, one reached San Francisco in 138 days, the other in 140, and neither of them made that six day stop at Punta Arenas on the way!

The fingerless Captain Blackburn was now a happy man and decided he had not had this good a time in fifteen years. Unfortunately, there was soon a falling out among the members of the Gloucester Mining Co. as to how to proceed from there on. After considerable bickering, the final result was that Blackburn left them at San

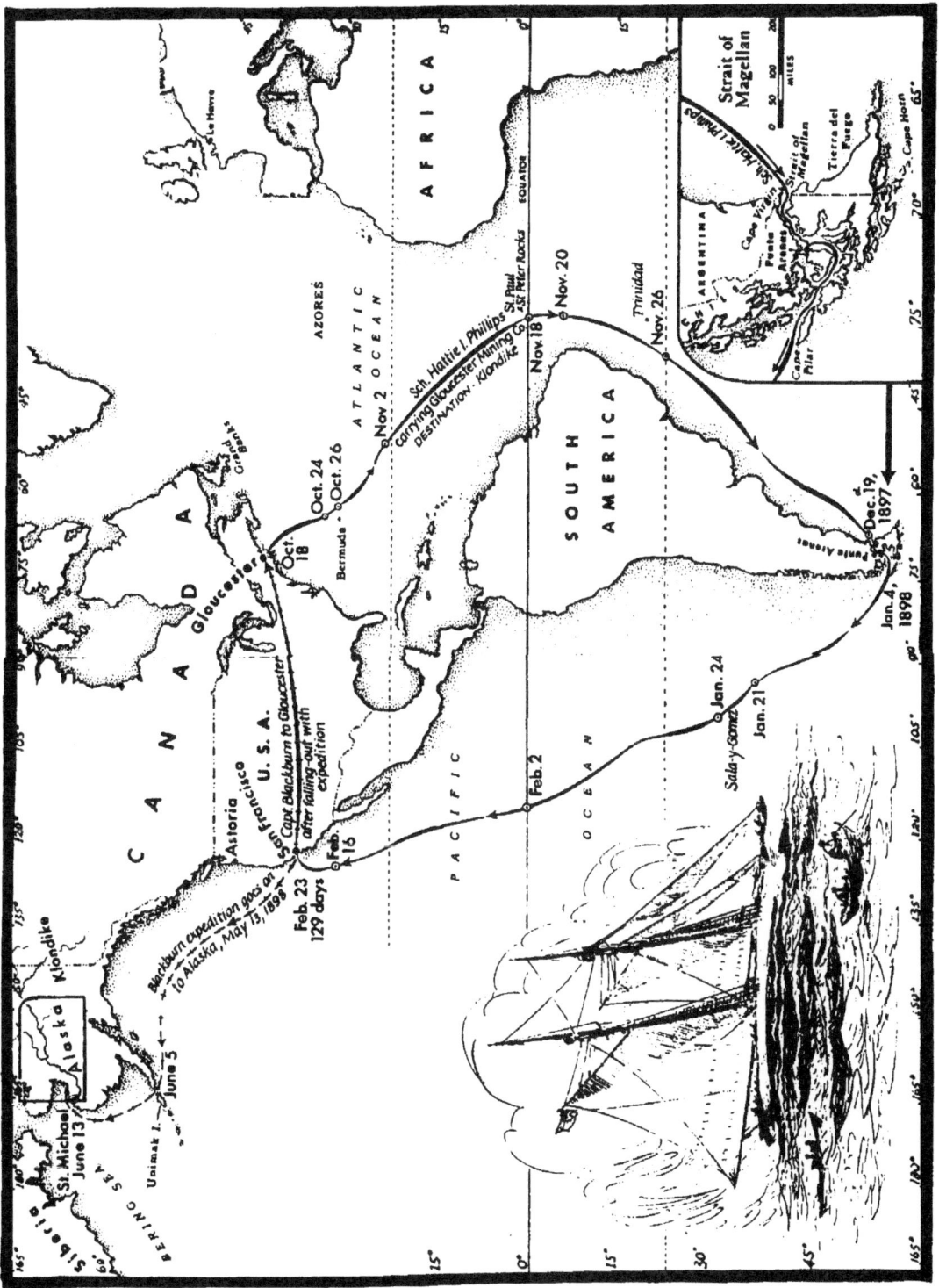

Fig. BL-6 Voyage of Captain Howard Blackburn and the Gloucester Mining Co. from Gloucester, Mass. to San Francisco Ca. The Gloucester Mining Co. continued on to Alaska without Blackburn. from "Lone Voyage"– Garland

Francisco in disgust, and returned across country to Gloucester. When the others did finally reach the Klondike, they received very little gold for their trouble.

SINGLE-HANDED ACROSS THE ATLANTIC IN GREAT WESTERN

Howard had failed to reach the gold fields, but he had happily learned that he could still pull his weight at sea, in spite of his handicap, and this was worth more to him than any amount of gold he could possibly have found. He became obsessed with the idea that he had to return to the sea, not in company with others on a large ship, but rather alone as he had been during those awful days in the dory, off the Burgeo Bank. In 1899, he had a thirty foot sloop built which he named *"Great Western"* as a bit of satire on the recent disastrous problems of the huge British steamship that had been named the *"Great Eastern".* That steamer had been the largest ship ever built, but she was too big and was a notorious commercial failure.

The GREAT WESTERN
Capt. HOWARD BLACKBURN.
DIMENSIONS: Length over all 30 feet. Breadth of Beam 8 ft. 6 in. Depth of Hold 4 ft. 6 in.
Sailed from Gloucester, Mass., June 18th, 1899. Arrived at Gloucester, Eng., August 19th, 1899. Time of voyage 62 days.

Fig. BL-7 "Great Western" as she appeared in a large captioned photograph distributed by Blackburn to his friends back home.

Howard's *Great Western* was by no means a new or untried design (Fig. BL 7) Rather, she was a scaled down version of a well known traditional type of local fishing vessel known as the *"Gloucester sloop boat"*

At the end of May that year, he announced to the newspapers that in three weeks he would set sail alone for England. Reporters and their readers both looked at the big guy, stared at his paunch and his fingerless hands, and wondered if could he possibly be serious? For starters, anyone had to be a bit daft to want to try to sail the Atlantic Ocean by himself, let alone a person in Blackburn's poor physical condition. (Fig. BL 8)

However, he definitely *was* serious. On Sunday, June 18, amid a great celebration and hullabaloo he sailed out of Gloucester with a letter of introduction from the Mayor of Gloucester, Mass. to the Lord Mayor of Gloucester, England!

The first night out the wind was light, but he quickly began to have trouble with his right leg and the right foot that had been frozen at the Burgeo Bank. By the next day both foot and leg were greatly swollen and fearfully painful. For eight days he was extremely sick, while the boat limped along with shortened sail through alternately thick and thin fogs. Finally the pain and swelling began to subside, his appetite returned, and his good spirits as well. With a light westerly wind behind him, he reset all sail and headed off along the shortest route to England, which was the same northern great circle track that was followed by transatlantic steamers. In order to avoid the big ships, he stayed somewhat to the south of the normal steamer track.

Fig. BL-8 "The Fearless Navigator"
Captain Blackburn at the time of his transatlantic voyages.

Gloucester Master Mariners' Association

The prevailing winds over the North Atlantic are normally westerly which would blow him to the east in the direction he wanted to go. Also, the Gulf Stream turns east, becoming the North Atlantic Current which will also carry him to the east, toward England. Initially he took the wheel from 6 PM until noon the next day, so as to be on watch in case he encountered any ships during the night, when he might not be seen by them.

The light westerlies carried him about 500 miles east of Newfoundland before they died, leaving him becalmed for three days. Then the wind came up perversely out of the east. He now made good speed, but had to tack back and forth across his desired course in order to work his way up-wind to the east toward

England. He now changed his schedule so as to take the helm from 4 AM to 8 PM, and he beat his way easterly against the winds for 800 miles before they finally died, leaving him becalmed again for another four days

Now he was at about Longitude 21°W with close to 900 miles still to go. When the wind finally returned it was again out of the east, and this time stronger and accompanied by squalls and rain. Finally on his 60th day at sea, he spotted the Scilly Islands ahead and turned north toward the Bristol Channel. Two days later he was snugly at anchor off a resort town called Portishead, near the mouth of the Severn River where he went ashore to send a cable to the Commodore of the Gloucester Yacht Club (in Gloucester Mass.) to notify him that he had arrived safely after a passage of 62 days The next day Blackburn accepted a tow up the Severn River Canal to Gloucester, England; there to be received by the city officials and a wildly cheering crowd.

Captain Blackburn was an immediate celebrity, and rightly so. True, he was not the first man to sail cross the Atlantic alone. Actually five others, including Captain Joshua Slocum who would continue all the way around the world alone, had preceded Blackburn. But up to then, and up to now as well, Blackburn is certainly the only sailor with no fingers ever to have sailed alone across the Atlantic, or any other ocean.

Fig. BL-9 Blackburn's saloon at 289 Main St. The building is now occupied by the Halibut Point Restaurant.

While in Gloucester, England, Howard was wined and dined, all customs, dock, and canal charges were waived, and he was visited by reporters from all the important newspapers and magazines. Unfortunately, his right knee continued to bother him and he consulted a doctor who advised him that the best remedy would be rest, although this was impossible for a person of his nature. He finally sailed from Gloucester around to London, where he was again cordially received.

He saw the sights of London, then crossed the channel to France and went directly to Paris where he was again lionized. However, his legs were still bothering him, causing him to cut short his foreign tour. He crossed back to Liverpool where he booked passage back to the U.S. on a Cunard steamer.

Great Western had served him well, but he had found she was a bigger and heavier boat than he could comfortably handle. In addition when cruising she did not self-steer very well with the wind abaft the beam. Rather than take her back to the U.S. he sold her to a delighted Mr. Braine, the brother of the Lord Mayor of Gloucester.

His reception back in Gloucester, Mass, was again tumultuous, and he had a wonderful time telling his story to the many reporters who interviewed him. As his leg was now a major problem he intended to spend the winter in Gloucester and try to rest and medicate it. All the while that Blackburn had been wandering off, first on the trip around the Horn to San Francisco, and then building *Great Western* and crossing the Atlantic, his saloon had continued to make money - a lot of money. The saloon had paid for the both trips and a good deal of money was left over.

Howard had by now proved to himself, and anyone else who might still wonder, that in spite of having lost all his fingers, as well as half of his toes, he was still a formidable mariner capable of skippering a sailing ship around the Horn, and could also sail single handed across the North Atlantic. He was a celebrity, and in addition was very well off financially. Many people in such a situation would tend to rest on their hard earned laurels, at least for a while, but not Howard Blackburn.

The coming new year would be 1900. Howard now busied himself with elaborate plans for the new century. He planned and constructed a grand new building for his saloon.(Fig. BL-9) with a splendid second floor residential apartment for himself and his wife (who has not been mentioned thus far, as she figured very little in either his business or his maritime activities).

Incidentally, while researching Blackburns story in Gloucester, I naturally had to stop for a beer in a place as famous as Blackburn's saloon, which I did. The saloon presently bearing Blackburn's name is at #2 Main St. (Fig. BL-10) The beer was good and there were various Blackburn memorabilia about, but the place looked somehow a bit too new. Only several years later did I discover that is not where his original place was located. His saloon had actually been located considerably further down at #289 Main St. The building he built at #289 was still very much in evidence and was then occupied by the Halibut Point Restaurant. Why Blackburn's actual tavern is now Halibut Point Restaurant and

Fig. BL-10 The building at #2 Main St. that is now called "Blackburn Tavern". Although it contains some Blackburn memorabilia his saloon was never here— this building is far too new!

another place entirely is called Blackburn's Tavern, is a mystery.

THE GREAT REPUBLIC

In 1900 Howard also was now planning and building a new boat to replace *Great Western*. His new boat was smaller – 25' long and 7' wide. Her general appearance was similar to *Great Western*, having the same fine clipper bow, flush deck, and wide, high stern. However, her rigging was considerably more simplified. The mast was a single pole with no topmast and no top-sail. The bowsprit was relatively longer and so was the keel, making her steadier on course and better able to self-steer. He named her the *"Great Republic"* (Fig. BL-11) and when asked her purpose, his answer was that he intended to do a bit of coastal cruising.

On New Years Day, 1901 he announced a challenge to the press and to anyone in the world for a single-handed race from the U.S. to Portugal! If no one accepted his challenge he stated he would sail in mid-June, in any event. Partly, he hoped the sea and the sun would help his arthritis, and also he wanted to celebrate the new century.

During the next three months several people came forward, but in the end no one took up the challenge. True to his word, on June 9 Howard set sail alone again to make the crossing to Portugal. His planned course was to be considerably to the south of that followed on his previous trip to England and he would be in the Gulf Stream for a longer period of time, as well.

For the first few days, the winds were very light causing him to make little progress. By the 15th, he ran into gale winds that continued until the 25th. Then the winds began to cooperate. By the 4th of July he had in sight the western islands of the Azores group. He found his navigation to have been absolutely accurate in spite of the fact that for a good deal of the time up to then, he had

Fig. BL-11 "Great Republic" in Gloucester Harbor before the voyage to Portugal.

been unable to get celestial sights.

After a few days in the doldrums, on the 12th of July he was hit again by gales continuing until the 16th. However, by the 18th he had reached the mouth of the Tagus River and docked in Portugal after a crossing of only 39 days! At the time this was the fastest single-handed crossing of the Atlantic ever made under sail, and very few have equaled it since. (Fig. BL-12).

His reception in Portugal was as tumultuous as it had been in England at the end of his previous crossing. He was received at the Royal Yacht Club, he was seated in the box of honor at the bull fights, and generally sumptuously entertained. Initially, he thought of sailing the *Great Republic* back across the Atlantic to Gloucester. But although his health was then quite good he really did not yet feel up to making another crossing alone, so he arranged to ship the boat back on one steamer, and booked passage back to the U.S. for himself on another.

Gloucester again received him with a hero's welcome and great celebrations were held in his honor. Certainly NOW one would expect Captain Blackburn to settle down and enjoy a well earned life of ease - but NO, not Howard Blackburn!

Even before he had started for Portugal he had conceived the idea for another voyage. He wanted to take *Great Republic* down to New York, go up the

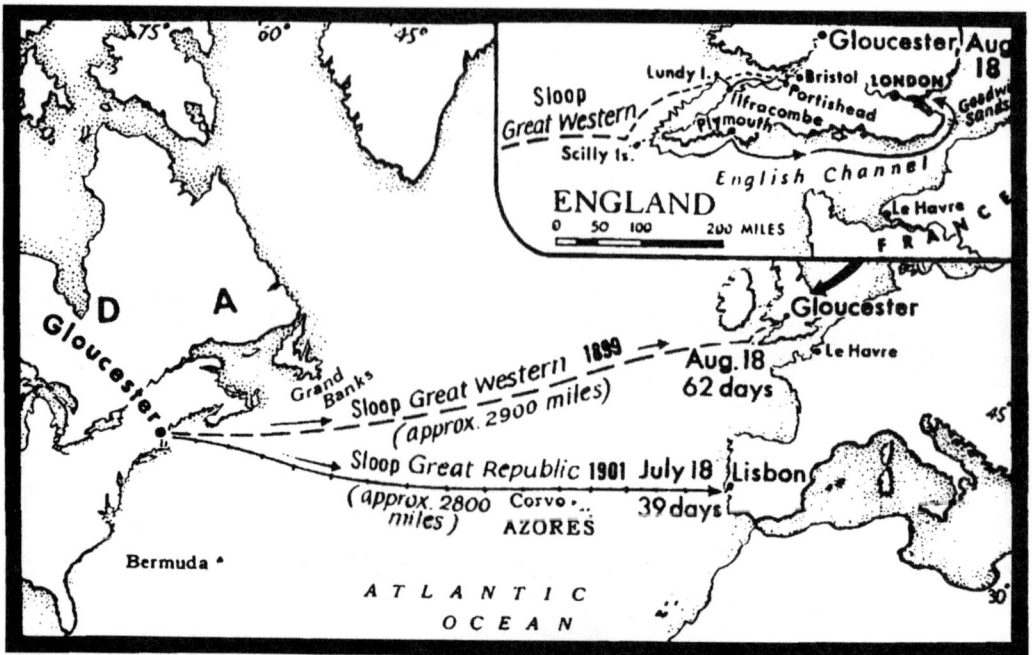

Fig. BL-12 Trans-Atlantic voyages of "Great Western & Great Republic": Gloucester Mass. to Gloucester, England; Gloucester Mass. to Lisbon, Portugal.
from "Lone Voyager" – Garland

Hudson River, then through the Erie Canal to the Great Lakes. When he reached Chicago he would head south and run down the Mississippi all the way to New Orleans. Then he proposed turning east to Florida, then cross to Cuba, continue on to Puerto Rico, then down along the Antilles, and finally sail down the South American coast to Brazil. He would then sail back up to the U.S. east coast, and on north to Gloucester.

He was unable to fully complete this voyage as intended, but the part he did complete was impressive. *Great Republic* had been designed and built to withstand the rigors of the open ocean, and as an ocean going vessel she had been proven superb, but she was not designed to maneuver under sail through the shoals, mud banks, snags, unpredictable currents, and bars of inland rivers and canals. With immense difficulty Blackburn fought her up to the Great Lakes, all the way down the Mississippi, across the Gulf to Florida, and around the Keys to Biscayne Bay. When he went aground there on a sand bar, for the umpteenth time on this trip, his patience finally gave out. Also, his health was now unreliable. He'd had three bouts of malaria, and his rheumatism was also bothersome. He'd had enough and decided to go home. He then sold the boat to a Cambridge resident whom he had known when he summered in Gloucester, but who happened at the moment to be vacationing in Florida. The purchaser gave him a 12' rowboat which he proceeded to *row* a distance of 200 miles up the inland waterway before he was at last convinced to quit, and take a steamer home to Gloucester!

After all he had done up to now Blackburn still had one *more* trip in mind. He wanted to make another solo Atlantic crossing, this time in a 16′ sailing dory. He had the boat built and on June 7, 1903 set sail. This time a combination of age, illness, and the miserable weather conspired to defeat him. A month later on the 8th of July he made it back in to Louisberg on the north coast of Nova Scotia. This, at last, was his final sea voyage.

Now permanently ashore, he lived until November, 1932 when he died at the age of 73. After his death every flag in Gloucester flew at half mast in his honor, and at least 250 old schooner captains and fishermen made up the funeral procession. He was buried there in Gloucester at Fisherman's Rest, among his fellow sailors -- exactly as he had wished.

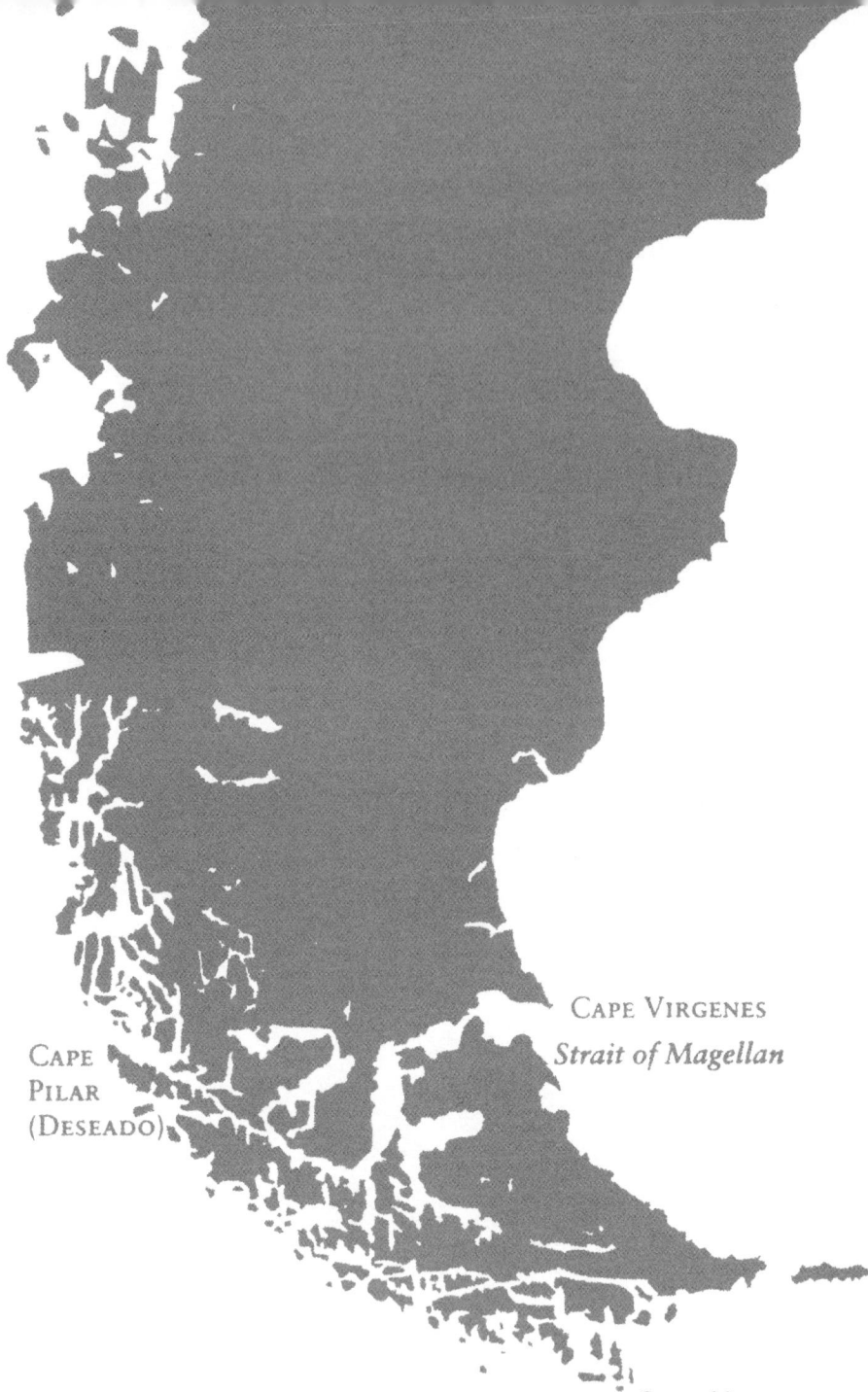

CAPE VIRGENES

Strait of Magellan

CAPE
PILAR
(DESEADO)

CAPE HORN

DIEGO RAMIREZ ISLANDS

Drake Passage

Cape Horn

CHAPTER 4

Two Sail 10,000 Miles in a 20 Foot Boat

"This Dreadful Life", an old chanty bewailing the hard life of the sailor on the old sailing ships

Chorus:
I have sailed across the ocean,
I have rolled upon the sea
And this dreadful life I'm livin'
Is just the life for me

It's haulin' sail and line me boys
*   and pushin' capstan round*
It's workin' pumps and windlass,
*   and prayin' for the sound*
The sound of the bosun callin'
*   to take us all below*
To end the pain of every day
*   a sailor's come to know*

Chorus:
When the mighty ocean tells me
*   with a piece of broken deck*
That life on land's not half as bad
*   as livin' through a wreck*
So I am going home boys
*   to the friends I used to know*
And hoist a pint to every man
*   who has the urge to roam.*
Chorus:

Well, actually *Sopranino* was not quite 20 feet. She was only 19' 8 " with a beam of 5' 4", and with her fin keel in place she drew only 3' 8" of water. This is a *small* boat, a *very* small boat, to carry two people across the Atlantic Ocean. However, two young British sailors, Patrick Ellam and Colin Mudie climbed aboard and did just that. Of course, they first had to develop, design, and build that very small boat in order to make this voyage in her. Their reason for going to all that trouble was to prove that a boat small enough to be moved on a trailer behind an ordinary family car, and stored in the family garage could also make a lengthy passage in open ocean, in safety, if properly designed and constructed.

Back in 1946, Pat Ellam, then an amateur sailing enthusiast, saw all the sailboats that were available in Britain at the time as being divided into two groups: first large brawny, heavily built yachts able to cope with the severe conditions found in the open waters around Britain, and secondly, small, lightly built dinghies and day sailers were safe only in bays and harbors–except perhaps in very mild weather. So, naturally, Pat wanted something that seemed impossible at the time. He wanted a boat of a similar size and weight to that a dinghy, also maintaining its speed and ease of handling, but modified so as to sail safely in open ocean. He, quite correctly, expected this would take some time to develop.

THETA

He decided to start by modifying an existing type of 17' racing boat classified as a "sailing canoe". He approached a boatbuilder familiar with the type and asked him to build a slightly larger version modified to 20' long, with buoyancy tanks and spaces for some navigational equipment and food supplies. By 1948 the boat was completed, and just as Ellam had wanted, she was trailerable and it was from a trailer that she was launched. He named her *Theta*.

By 1949, *Theta* had been taken on a number of sea trials and had performed extremely well, so well that one day Ellam decided to sail her across the Channel to France. On this first cross-channel trip a strong southwest wind blew up, making the notoriously boisterous Channel fully live up to its evil reputation. At the time, his crew was a totally inexperienced stranger he had picked up off the seawall just before leaving. As they approached close to the French coast, bounding along in this tiny 20' boat, Pat remarked to his less than joyful crewman that he guessed half the people watching them from the shore didn't think they'd get there alive. His crewman answered that half the people on the boat didn't think so either. However, they did arrive safely and then sailed safely back to England the next day, by which time an even stronger typical Channel gale had blown up!!

After this trip Ellam made several other Channel crossings in *Theta*, six altogether, in a variety of weather conditions. Many of those trips were again in very heavy weather. This convinced him that a very small boat, properly built and well sailed, could safely survive in strong wind and boisterous sea conditions. He now wanted to expand on what he had learned sailing *Theta*.

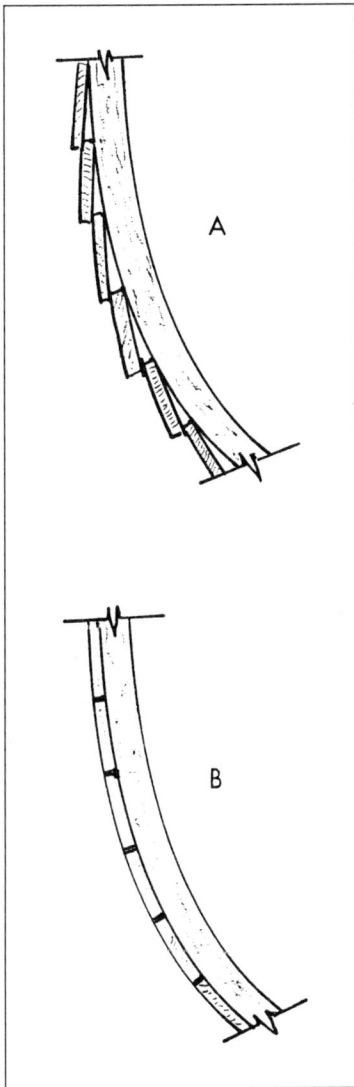

Fig. S-1 A. Clinker Built
B. Carvel Built

This meant graduating to a new boat.

For this he decided to go to none other than Laurent Giles, a prominent naval architect and at the time, the foremost yacht designer in Britain. Pat had no idea as to how this eminent designer of so many of the finest large British sailing yachts then afloat would react to the idea of turning his attention to what was, by comparison, a tiny cockleshell; but he decided to try anyway.

THE BUILDING OF SOPRANINO

Glies received him politely and listened quietly as Pat expounded his theory. He explained what he had done up to then, and the conclusions he had reached as a result of the trips he had made in *Theta*. Pat told Giles he wanted to try a new boat of about the same length as *Theta*, so it would be light and trailerable, but it should be a little broader in the beam and have a small cabin with sleeping quarters, a toilet, and a stove on which to prepare hot meals. This would permit the vessel to stay at sea for longer periods and thus allow for a greatly extended cruising capability. Giles found the idea intriguing. After asking a number of searching questions, and further discussing the project at some length, Giles then offered to design his boat, much to Pat's delight.

The initial design went through several modifications before the final plans were ready to go to a boatbuilder. Since the finalized plans still resembled a racing dinghy far more than they did the traditional sailing yacht, Pat took them to the best builder of racing dinghies he could find, two brothers named Whooton with a yard located on the Thames River, about 40 miles west of London.

It was now 1950, long before fiberglass was to almost completely displace wood in the construction of small sailboats. Consequently, this was to be a wood boat of a type called "clinker built". This type is distinguished by the fact that the planks on the sides and bottom overlap each other (Fig. S-1) rather than being simply placed alongside each other, as in the other common planking method called "carvel planking". Carvel planks are securely fastened to the frames, or ribs, of the boat but not to each other. In clinker building the planks are fastened to each other along the overlaps at intervals of 3" to 5" as well as to the frames underneath. This type of construction requires much more labor due to all the additional fasteners required to connect the planks to each other, but the resulting vessel is vastly stronger. The term "clinker" possibly brings to your mind furnace or fireplace ashes which have absolutely nothing to do with the origin of this term. Rather, it comes from the Old English word "klenken" meaning to "hold fast", which is exactly what the planks do when fastened in this manner.

Sopranino was built of mahogany planking on oak frames. She carried a fin keel terminating in a lead bulb. This fin was bolted outside of the wood keel allowing it to be removed in order to facilitate transportation of the boat while ashore. Both mast and boom were spruce spars - hollow to reduce weight aloft. Below, there were two bunks 6'6" long, stove, washbasin, chart table, and storage spaces for various stores and equipment.

Ellam knew that every two years the Royal Ocean Racing Club ran a race from Plymouth, England across the Channel to Ushant, off the French coast, and then down across the Bay of Biscay to Santander, Spain. This is a long distance race starting on a Friday and ending the following Wednesday or Thursday. The boats that normally enter this event are large cruiser-racers. *Sopranino* was far too small to enter as a competitor, but very shortly after she was launched, the then Commodore of the Club allowed Pat to sail the racecourse with them for a shake-down cruise. *Sopranino* made a remarkable showing by arriving in Santander only a few hours after the big boys.

MIDGET OCEAN RACING

The following winter a group from the Royal Ocean Racing Club formed an organization called the Junior Offshore Group to promote midget ocean racing boats such as *Sopranino*. Two sister ships were built, as well as several other similar midget cruisers. This small fleet then conducted a series of cross Channel races which went a long way toward proving the seaworthiness of these small vessels, since no serious mishaps occurred.

In spite of these successes many of those he knew in yachting circles continued to doubt the safety of these small boats in open water. Consequently, Pat Ellam found himself thinking more and more about doing something that would be a really convincing achievement - making an Atlantic crossing in *Sopranino*. Thinking and pondering gave way to conviction - a trans-Atlantic crossing it would be!!

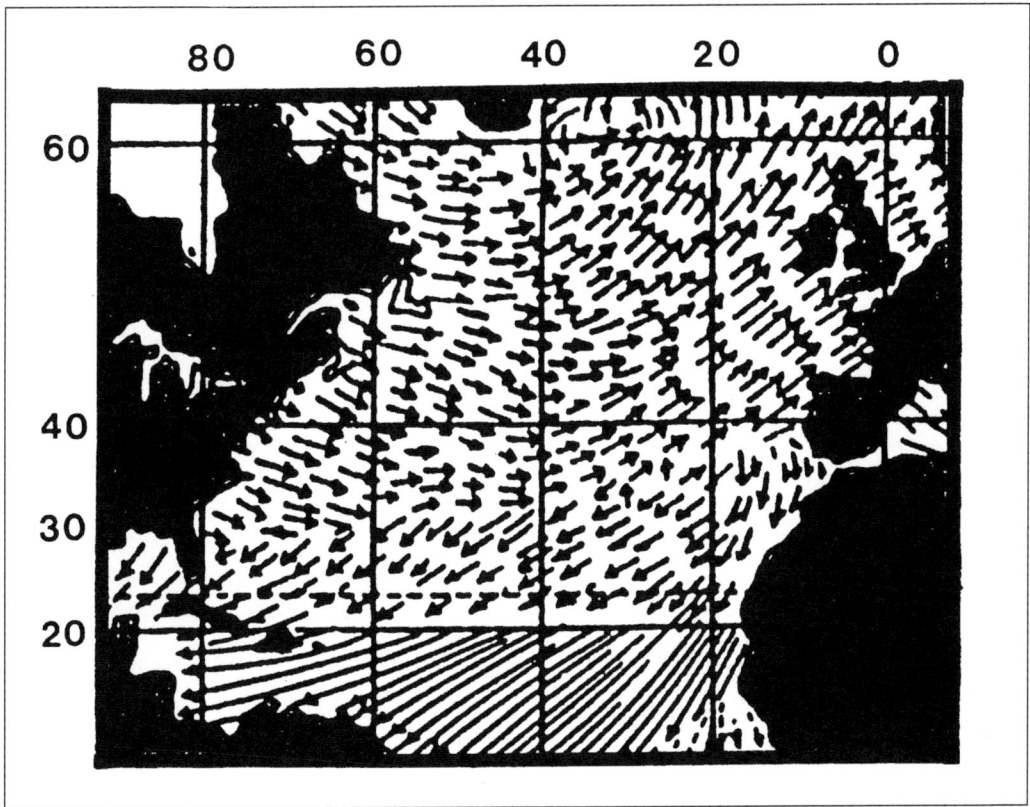

Fig. S-2 Prevailing wind directions, North Atlantic–Winter

PREPARATIONS FOR THE TRANS-ATLANTIC CROSSING

A single-handed passage apparently was never on Ellam's mind because once he decided to do it his first thought was to determine who he would have as a companion. Whoever it was he had to be entirely capable of taking over the handling of the boat in the event Pat suffered illness or injury. He also had to make up for Ellam's lack of maintenance and repair skills, and he must have a temperament and personality such that he and Pat would be comfortable together for extended periods at sea.

After careful consideration of the many sailors he knew, Pat decided to ask a fellow sailor named Colin Mudie to go along. Mudie was 26 at the time and a well known sailing skipper who was familiar with *Sopranino,* as he had often sailed her when Pat was crewing on someone else's boat. He was a competent, coastwise navigator and had worked for a time in a shipyard, so he was also qualified to deal with such repairs as might be needed. As a result of his familiarity with the boat he had become very fond of it. As one of the most highly regarded men in Laurent Giles office, he had also done some of the drawings for the boat. Giles favorable opinion of Mudie was to prove entirely correct, as he has since become, in his own right, one of the finest naval architects in Britain.

When Pat called him at Giles office and asked him out to dinner, Colin was not particularly surprised when Pat asked him if he would like to make the crossing, nor did it take him long to agree to go. The two then started planning how they would proceed. For starters, a division of responsibility was decided upon at once. Pat was in charge of general planning and administrative matters while Colin was to be in charge of the vessel and its maintenance. Two modifications to the boat were needed. The existing racing mast had to be shortened because climbing to the masthead might be necessary under way and with the existing mast height this was not possible without tipping the boat over, which was not a good idea in mid-Atlantic! Also, a foot high safety rail was to be added around the after deck.

Pat went to the meteorological experts at the Royal Geographical Society for advice regarding winds, currents and routing. In accordance with their opinions Pat decided, quite sensibly, to sail down to the Trade Wind belt below latitude 30° N for their crossing, and to time it for December or January so as to miss the hurricane season, and catch the reenforced easterly Trade Winds of winter. (Fig. S-2) By taking this route for the long crossing he would also have the help of the Canary Current first, and then the North Equatorial Current (Fig. S-3).

Another weather consideration was that they needed to get away from England no later than the end of August so as to pass to the south before the start of the September gales in the Channel. This schedule would leave them about three months to dawdle their way down through Spain and Portugal to Africa, and thence to the Canary Islands where they would take their departure for the crossing. From the Canary Islands they would make one long passage of about 2700 miles to Barbados in the West Indies, and then work their way up through those islands to the United States. Altogether, this was a very ambitious plan involving a voyage of approximately 10,000 miles!!

Continuing his homework, Pat went to the Royal Zoological Society to inquire as to what sorts of creatures inhabit the waters they would cross. The Society people apparently told him a great deal more than he really wanted to know about the giant octopus that, he was told, rarely exceeds 80 feet across. He was also informed about some species of large sharks that could quite easily bite right through his little boat - but he was assured they were rather unlikely do so. Both men had medical and dental checkups and assembled a large kit of medical stores along with a book on their use. Meanwhile stores and equipment were being stowed aboard *Sopranino*, then berthed at Falmouth.

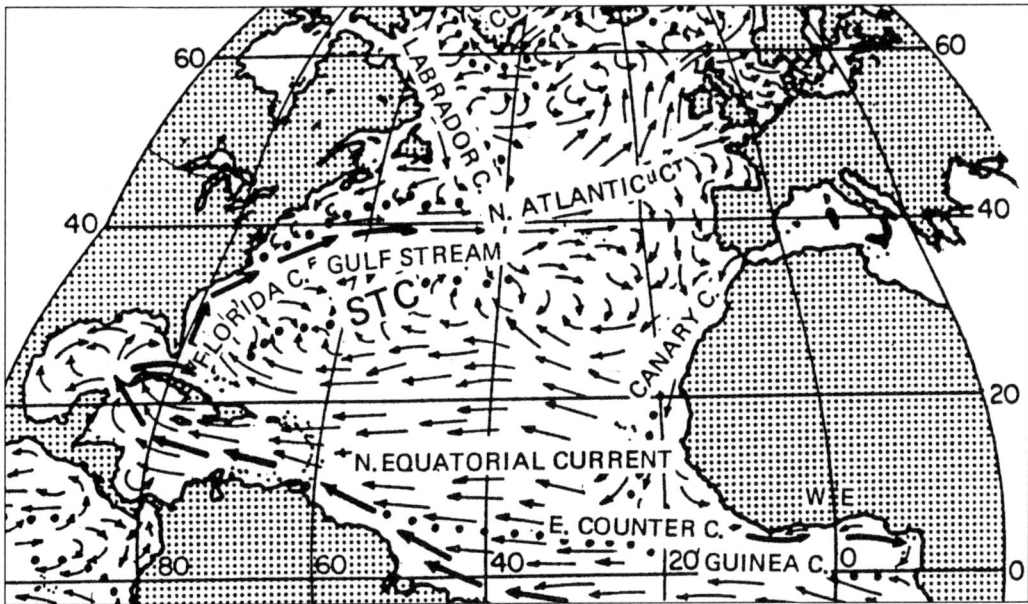

Fig. S-3 North Atlantic Ocean Currents

THE FIRST LEG - FALMOUTH TO LISBON

As it turned out, they departed Falmouth for Lisbon on the 6th of September, just a bit later than the end of August as Pat had intended. Shortly before leaving Pat had talked the Board of Trade into registering *Sopranino* as a British Merchant Ship - probably the smallest vessel *ever* to be registered as such. This authorized her to fly the Red Ensign of the British Merchant Marine, which she promptly proceeded to do on her way out of Falmouth.

Ellam had wanted to be across the Channel and through the Bay of Biscay before the first of the Fall gales arrived, but this was not to be. They departed Falmouth just a bit too late. For the first couple days all went well until they were becalmed in a fog. This lasted another few days, after which it cleared just in time for the arrival of the first gale of the season. Very shortly they had to heave to to ride out the storm. For the next few days they alternately hoisted reefed sail for a while, and then gave up and heaved-to again. During this time the boat held up much better than her crew, both of whom were well battered about by the storm.

By the time the storm had passed they were exhausted and decided that rather than attempt to get all the way to Lisbon, their original objective, they would put in at Corunna, Spain to rest up, check out the boat, and refresh their supplies. They entered the harbor after 11 days at sea proudly flying their Red Ensign and sailed up to dock at the prestigious Real Club Nautico de Corunna.

After identifying themselves they were most cordially received and were given the best of rooms at the club.

After 2 days of R & R they topped off their water tank, bought some food, then moved out and anchored, ready to leave, when Colin became ill. Two days later when he was well, a new gale had blown up. To leave then for Lisbon made no sense, so they moved across to the Naval base at El Ferrol where they waited a few more days until the weather finally cleared.

They left with a light wind, but about 20 miles out the wind died, leaving them drifting for three days. By the fourth day the wind picked up from the northwest, and by the fifth day it was again a gale as they scudded down the coast to Lisbon, 300 miles from Corruna and by then 800 miles from their start at Falmouth, England. Here again, they found a cordial reception at the Yacht Club.

They decided it would be well at this point to take the boat out to inspect and repaint her. The club made its crane available so they unloaded everything, hauled the boat, painted her and put her back in the water. Just when they had everything restowed and ready to go Colin was approached by the owner of an old 12 meter racer who wanted him to design a deckhouse, in order to convert it to a cruising boat. Our wanderers could well use the money, so they stayed an extra week while Colin drew up the design.

LISBON TO CASABLANCA

When they were again ready to depart, of course, there was no wind. A few times they were carried out and then driven back by the tides through the mouth of the Tagus River, where they anchored to wait for enough wind to safely sail out to sea. The following morning a breeze came up, allowing them to up anchor and sail out.

The easterly "trade winds" of the tropics move a considerable distance north and south with the seasons. It was now the end of October and the easterly winds were moving south to their winter latitude, the northern limit being just north of the Canary Islands at around latitude 29°N. This now is where they must go to pick up the following winds needed to make the Trans-Atlantic crossing. Now, in order to get there, they first have to go to Casablanca, French Morroco, and then strike out for the Canaries. (Fig. S-4)

During this season off Portugal and North Africa north of the easterly wind belt, there are frequent southwesterly gales lasting several days. Between these southwesterly gales, the prevailing winds are likely to be moderate, mostly from the north, (Fig. S-2). lasting for about a week before the next gale moves in.

Fig. S-4 England to the Canary Islands
from "Two Against the Western Ocean"– Ellam & Mudie

Luck was with them. They slipped into Casablanca just a day ahead of the next gale so were snugly at anchor when it hit. A photo (Fig. S-5) taken in Casablanca, shows clearly how tiny *Sopranino* actually was to carry the two who made up her crew.

A yachtsman of their acquaintance who had passed by Casablanca in a large schooner about the same time as *Sopranino* arrived, was not so lucky. He apparently had hoped to make it to the next port down the coast. However, after the gale hit he tried to get back into Casablanca, but failed and was wrecked instead outside on the rocks.

A local election was coming up in Casablanca at the time *Sopranino* arrived, and consequently, there was considerable unrest on shore, in the native quarter. For their protection, Pat and Colin were advised to moor close to three French Navy destroyers that were in port, and they did.

While they lingered in port another very strong gale struck. Casablanca has a huge seawall running out parallel with the shore, creating the protected anchorage inside. When the gale was at its height, the seas hitting that wall became quite spectacular. One evening during the storm they decided to walk out there to watch the seas break. Part of the way out, Colin wisely decided to turn back, but Pat wanted to go all the way. Not a good idea! Pat got only a short distance further when a huge wave washed over the wall carrying him down to the rocks on the inside of the wall, and finally depositing him in the bay. Horrified, Colin saw it happen, and got an Arab in a motorboat to help him rescue Pat. After bouncing down over the rocks on the inside of the seawall, Pat was a solid bruise from head to toe, which left him totally useless for about a week.

CASABLANCA TO THE CANARY ISLANDS

It was now the 21st of November as they prepared to leave Casablanca for the Canary Islands. A knowlegable officer from the French Navy told them they now had a good weather window and could safely depart, assuring them that if they hurried straight down to the latitude of Agadir, just a bit north of latitude 30°N, they would then be out of danger from the seasonal southwest gales. They took this advice and set sail.

The first half of this passage was uneventful. They had moderate northerly winds and spent some time practicing sailing downwind with twin spinnakers, and working out the rigging needed to set *Sopranino* up for self-steering. A self-steering arrangement was going to be sorely needed for the long downwind passage from the Canaries to Barbados, in order to free the man on watch from

Fig. S-5 Colin Mudie (left) and Patrick Ellam (right)
on Sopranino in Casablanca

the tedious job of hand continuous hand steering. After several false starts they got it to work properly. Then unexpectedly, Colin had a violent allergic reaction to a detergent solution used for washing some laundry. While keeping Colin on pain killers, they pressed on and finally arrived in Las Palmas on Grand Canaria, where Colin was immediately taken to the British Seaman's Hospital where he recoved in a few days. Meanwhile, Pat developed a brief bout of Canary Fever from the drinking water. They then decided a week for R & R was in order before starting the serious preparations for the long trans-Atlantic run to Barbados.

Everything up to now had been prelude. This next passage is going to be the REAL test!! Every little detail must now be checked. Every possible emergency anticipated and proper responses planned. First, absolutely everything movable must be taken out of the boat so that every detail of the boat itself could be thoroughly inspected and any needed repairs made. This would, of course, require a storage site ashore. They were in great luck when the British Consul put them in contact with a local resident who had a vacant storeroom that he allowed them to use. Then some friendly sailors put them on to a cheap hotel where they could stay while ashore, since the bunks would also have to be temporarily stripped out of *Sopranino*.

They spent all of December and into January removing, checking, testing, and re-stowing everything. One evening, after everything had been stripped out of the boat, and while she lay at anchor in the harbor, Pat and Colin got a severe jolt. A chap rushed into the hotel where they were staying to tell them their boat was gone! They rushed down to the harbor, and sure enough when they looked where they had left her – no boat. After much frantic rushing around the harbor, word came that a local fisherman had found the boat drifting up against a seawall. The anchor line had been cut and the anchor stolen. Next day, they received a message from the "thieves union" of Las Palmas apologizing for the unacceptable behavior of one of their number – but they never did get the anchor back.

ACROSS THE ATLANTIC TO BARBADOS

Finally, everything that could be done, was done. They were as prepared as they possibly could be. The time had come to show what they and their boat could really do!! On January 11 they cleared from Las Palmas with a light easterly wind behind them and headed across the Atlantic for Barbados. (Fig. S-6)

Lying between the westerly wind belt of the middle, or temperate latitudes, to the north, and the easterly Trade Winds of the tropics, lies a narrow band of very light winds called the *subtropical high,* centered at about 30°N. The Canary Islands

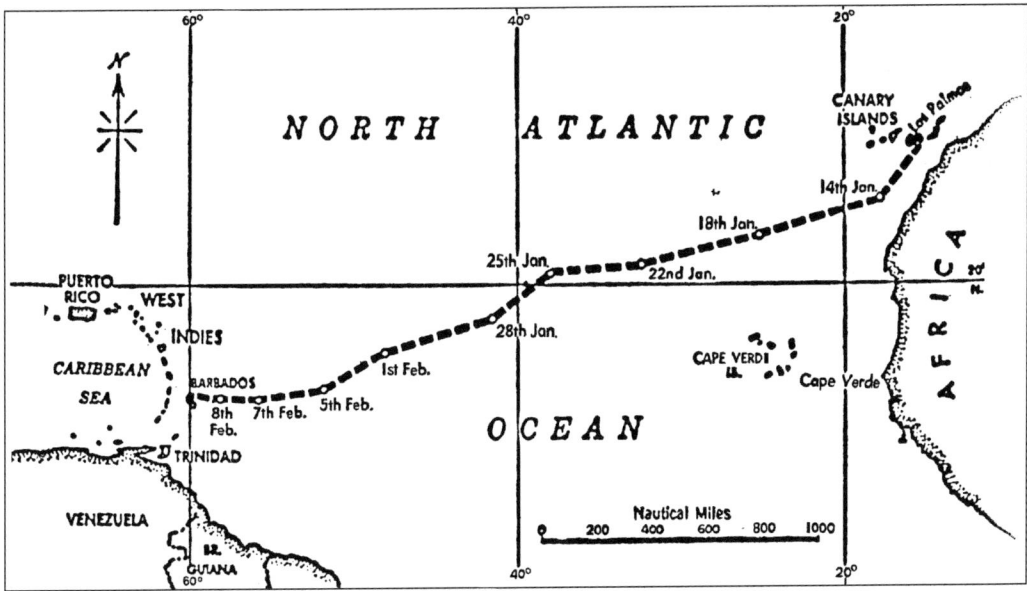

Fig. S-6 Atlantic Crossing
from: "Two Against the Western Ocean"– Ellam & Mudie

are located within that band so *Sopranino* had to sail southwest for two days in order to reach the latitude of the strong northeast Trade Winds (Fig. S-2). They could now set their twin spinnakers and attach the self-steering rig they had devised. This proved continually to be an immense help; the weeks it took to make the crossing, the self-steerer, nicknamed Harry Lime, held their course, day and night, freeing them both from endless hours of holding the tiller. They continued to stand watch, although, the man on watch was also free to do various other chores since he only had to make a check on deck every 15 or 20 minutes.

In the Trade Wind belt the steady day and night winds build up regular swells of 8 to 10 feet. Just as they had hoped *Sopranino* bobbed easily over them making for a very bouncy, but safe ride. Both sailors were subject to seasickness for the first day or so at sea, however after it had persisted for about three days they knew something was wrong. Pat thought it was because of the paint he had put on the outside of the packages of some porridge they had been eating. He threw the rest of the packages overboard, but they continued to feel poorly for some days afterward. Meanwhile, the boat was barreling along, smoothly doing about 100 miles a day.

They had started with food rations for 40 days, and water for 50 days with the water ration figured at 1 quart per person per day. These stores were based on a projected crossing time of 35 days. Of the supplies aboard, water is the most critical item since a person can live for between a week and two weeks with no food, but only 3 to 4 days without water. Once under way they found that the liquid in their canned vegetables was providing the equivalent of nearly a pint of water per person per day so their water supply would be more than adequate.

By the time their log registered 500 miles they discovered that Pat had made a major blunder by failing to wind their chronometer, which had now stopped. Since celestial navigation requires accurate time, it then took them several days to pick up a reliable time check by radio. Then they discovered that while they had sextant, chronometer, and navigation tables aboard, and both of them had done coastal navigation by sights, dead reckoning and RDF, neither one had done any more celestial navigation than a few noon sun sights for latitude. Since this was before the days of Loran and GPS, it is a mystery as to why they started out on this passage without insuring that at least one of them was competent at celestial navigation. Happily, a bit of on-the-job training and practice working with the RAF Tables for air navigation produced wonders. They found they were soon able to fix their position to within a few miles, which is an entirely satisfactory level of accuracy on such a long voyage, in a small boat. No mention is made of their taking anything other than sun sights, although Pat mentions on one occasion clearly seeing Polaris. This being the case he may well have used it to crosscheck his latitude, since essentially no calculations are required to take latitude by Polaris.

As they forged ahead in the steady winds and swells of the northeast trades day after day they settled into an easy, relaxed routine. At last this was the pay-off for the weeks and months of hard work devoted to preparing themselves and their boat for this passage. Most of the time the weather was clear and sunny with the typical tropical scattering of small fair-weather cumulus clouds. The trade winds normally slacken somewhat at night, only to pick up again the following morning. Every so often they were overtaken by brief, but intense, tropical rain-squalls which are also a typical feature of the weather in those latitudes. These squalls are frequently preceded by an intense gust of wind and then often followed by a short calm.

At sea, the barometer and the passing cloud trains were the the best indicators they had of oncoming weather changes. Hurricanes do not occur in late winter in the North Atlantic Trade Wind Belt which is why they chose to cross at that time. During winter in the middle latitudes, north of 30°N, the North Atlantic Ocean is extremely rough and stormy, but in the tropics, the warm air of the Trade Winds flowing steadily over warm water, discourages the formation of major weather disturbances. Even so, they kept a constant eye on the passing cloud trains so as to be prepared for a passing squall.

About 3:00 AM one morning, when they were 11 days out, they were passed by a large ship at a distance of about a mile. Since this was the first sign of civilization they had seen since leaving Las Palmas, they tried to signal it with their lantern, but as might be expected, received no response. From a mile away at night, they were a very small target for the ship's lookouts who certainly would not be expecting to see anything that small.

On a boat this small, a month's provisions for two people made up a significant part of her total sailing weight when they departed Las Palmas. Consequently, as water and canned stores were used the boat grew appreciably lighter and hence sailed faster. Their daily runs edged upward from about 100 miles a day, now getting to closer to 120 miles. Accurate navigation was by no means a high priority. They were no dangers to navigation along the way toward their destination, so frequent checks on their location were not necessary. They took sun sights every third day to check their position - unless it happened to be cloudy. If so - no problem - tomorrow would do.

One night, and into the following day, they were overtaken by a weather disturbance that, from their description, sounds very much as though it was a very weak, winter easterly wave. The barometer dropped sharply, a heavy overcast moved in, accompanied by a series of rain squalls closely following each other. The squalls then moved on, the barometer rose and the sky cleared. A week or so later they ran into another, somewhat stronger one lasting about two days. Later on, when they were about 2,000 miles out of Las Palmas with about 700 miles yet to go, they hit a two day dead calm - clear and hot, but with no wind and the sea completely flat. The winds then gradually returned to normal, pushing them on westward toward their objective, the island of Barbados.

As they advanced they decided to head for a point about 300 miles due east of the island, and then revert to a method commonly used in the early days of sail, before accurate timepieces made it possible to accurately determine longitude. They planned to "run down the latitude" to their destination. After the distance they had sailed, the island they sought was a very small target. Running down its latitude was a good way to be sure it wouldn't be missed.

They reached their target latitude at about 350 miles out of Barbados and changed their course from southwest to due west. The twin spinnaker/self-steering arrangement now had to be changed. One spinnaker came down, the main went back up and they returned to hand steering. Their average speed now increased to over 130 miles a day for those last few days. Finally, after sailing 2700 miles in 29 days they rounded North Point into the shelter of Maycock Bay,

Barbados. At this point, they stopped to clean up both the boat and themselves, so as to make a neat, trim appearance when entering Bridgetown harbor to report their arrival at the yacht club.

When first going ashore they ran into some of the officers from the British cruiser *HMS Devonshire,* which happened to be in port. These Navy people were sufficiently impressed with Pat and Colin's achievement and offered to take *Sopranino* aboard to clean and paint it for them, which was done most promptly. During this time, the Royal Navy also gave Pat and Colin lodging in the Captain's sea cabin!! With their newly cleaned and painted boat back in the water, they moved to the yacht club for a few weeks of playtime in Bridgetown.

BARBADOS TO NEW YORK

There were still several thousand miles to go before the voyage of *Sopranino* would be complete. The complete voyage consisted of three basic parts: first; Falmounth, England to Las Palmas, Canary Islands, second; Las Palmas across the Atlantic Ocean to Barbados (Fig. S-6). The third part still to be done was Barbados to New York. (Fig. S-7)

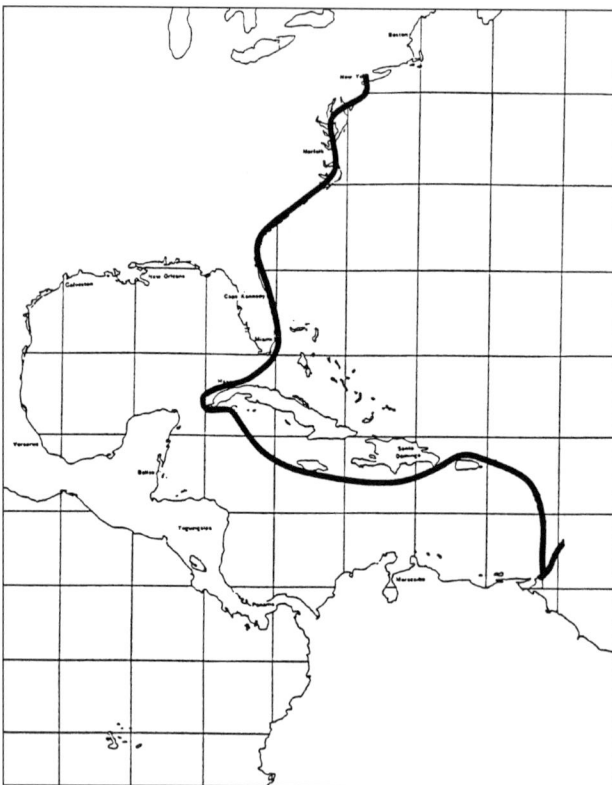

Fig. S-7 Route of Sopranino from Barbados to New York

From Barbados, *Sopranino* went south to Trinidad, and in the Gulf of Paria were almost to the South American coast, They then turned north through the Lesser Antilles past the Grenadines, Martinique, Dominica, and Guadeloupe toward Antigua. During this time, they had to battle the northeast Trades until reaching their next destination. From Antigua they turned west, passing the Virgin Islands, Puerto Rico, Hispaniola, and Jamaica to reach Cuba.

There Colin had to leave the boat to fulfill prior commitments. From there, Pat carried on, taking the boat across to Florida and on northward up the U.S.

east coast, to finally arrive in New York.

While Parts one and three of the voyage were interesting and important in themselves they were really only necessary to get to and from part two – their Atlantic crossing. By making that uninterrupted single passage of 2700 miles they conclusively proved their point, that a properly designed, very small trailerable sized boat can safely sail offshore, and survive a major passage in open ocean.

CHAPTER 5

The Odyssey: Was It Fact or Fiction?

The opening of Homer's Odyssey as translated by Robert Fitzgerald

Sing to me, Muse, and through me tell the story
of that man skilled in all ways of contending,
the wanderer, harried for years on end,
after he plundered the stronghold
on the proud height of Troy.

He saw the townlands
and learned the minds of many distant men,
and weathered many bitter nights and days,
in his deep heart at sea, while he fought only
to save his life, to bring his shipmates home.
But not by will nor valor could he save them
for their own recklessness destroyed them all.

Since the fifth century BC there has been lively argument and discussion, and frequently, furious disagreement as to whether the Iliad and the Odyssey of Homer are history, myth, fiction, or some combination of all of these. Also, there is a widespread belief in academic circles that stories which have become myths are actually based on real events having been elaborated and idealized in the course of many re-tellings.

Certainly it has become much more difficult to dismiss the Iliad and the Odyssey of Homer as pure myth since Heinrich Schliemann, at the time merely a wealthy amateur archeologist, confounded the professional historians and archeologists of his day by finding the real Troy, as described by Homer, under a mound at Hissarlik, in Turkey, using local traditions and the works of Homer as his guide. More recently, in the early 1960s, a British sailor named Ernle Bradford, also using Homer as his guide, retraced the Mediterranean Sea voyages of Odysseus on his return from Troy, as chronicled in the Odyssey, to see if they could have been based on stories of real voyages by real people. Using what we know now about winds, weather systems, sea currents in the Mediterranean area, and the construction and speed of oared vessels, both ancient and modern, again there appear to be too many similarities between the Odyssey and Captain Bradford's findings to dismiss the Odyssey as pure fiction. After we look at some of these areas of agreement, you can be the judge!

GREEK SHIPS OF THE PERIOD OF ODYSSEUS

To begin retracing the wanderings ascribed to Odysseus it is necessary first to develop an understanding of the sort of vessels that would have made up his squadron. Homer provides little detailed information regarding those vessels, but other sources allow us to reconstruct classical Greek ships of the period in a reasonably accurate manner. They were propelled by a square sail when the wind was favorable, and by oars when the wind failed or was contrary. How big were these boats, how many rowers did they carry, and what speed was normal for them? It is necessary to put together several sources of information to answer these questions.

Many naval historians have researched the subject of the oared vessels used by the ancients, with somewhat differing results. Rear Admiral Paul Serre of the French Navy took a novel approach, proposing to work backwards into the past by starting with what is known today by both seamen and naval architects. He felt this data would be valid since the weather, climate, and sea conditions in the Mediterranean, as well as the physical dexterity and strength of sailors today are not materially different from what they were in Homeric times. This being so, a rowing arrangement that works successfully today would also have worked for the early Greeks as well.

The oar, as the propelling power of a vessel, must be our central starting point. We know at present that a man of average weight comfortably uses an oar between 10 and 14 feet long. About a third of that length is inboard of the thole pin or oarlock. When two men are to share the same seat on opposite sides of a boat, each one using–let's say a 12 foot oar–this arrangement requires that the distance across the boat between thole pins cannot be *less* than 6 feet. The distance between a rower and those seated in front and behind him must be at least 3 feet to allow him to swing his oar freely without hitting either of them. Clearly, there must then be at least 3 feet fore and aft between oar thole pins, and the same spacing between the rower's seating thwarts. Archeological investigations have found that ample evidence exists showing that these spacings had been used by the early Greeks and adopted as their standard.

The length of a wooden rowing vessel should be no more than 8 times its

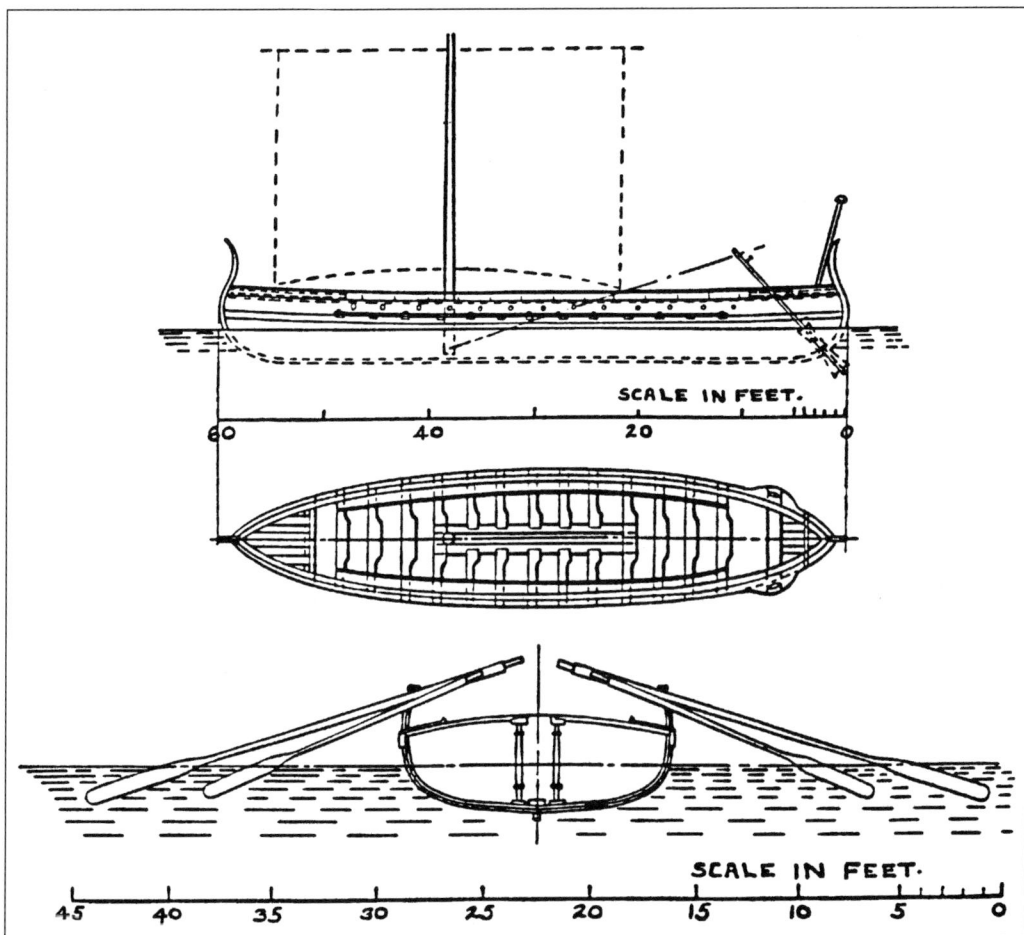

Fig. O-1 An Early Pentekonter from Serre
from "Greek and Roman Naval Warfare"– U.S. Naval Institute

beam, preferably less. Otherwise, it becomes too narrow for its length, making it impossible to adequately reenforce internally making it subject to breaking apart at sea. Remains of the Greek dockyards at Piraeus indicate that they were also aware of these proportions. Thus, a vessel with a 6' beam could measure up to 48' long. As we shall see, since the Greeks normally beached their boats in port rather than docking them, as they were of shallow draft. The standard ratio of draft to beam then used was 1:3. Our 48' x 6' boat will thus have a draft of 2'. This boat could have had up to 12 oars per side requiring 36' of its 48' length. This gives a rowing crew of 24, plus the helmsman, and leaves only 12' in the cramped bow and stern for supplies and weapons.

Again, referring to contemporary research, we find that for very short spurts this crew of oarsmen could possibly reach a speed of over 7 knots, but over a period of 4 hours or more they could not maintain a speed of more than about 3 to 3.5

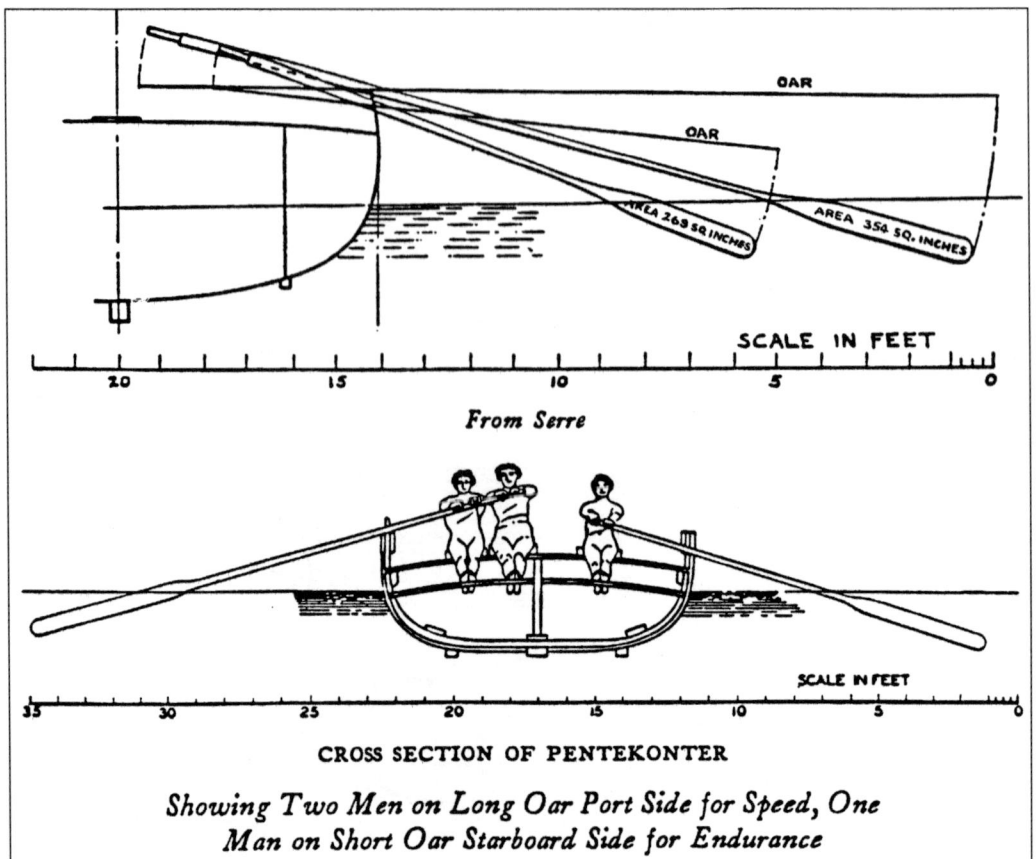

OAR

OAR

AREA 269 SQ INCHES

AREA 354 SQ. INCHES

SCALE IN FEET

20   15   10   5   0

From Serre

SCALE IN FEET

35   30   25   20   15   10   5   0

CROSS SECTION OF PENTEKONTER

Showing Two Men on Long Oar Port Side for Speed, One Man on Short Oar Starboard Side for Endurance

Fig. O-2 Pentekonter cross section
from "Greek and Roman Naval Warfare"– U.S. Naval Institute

knots. For a sustained trip of any distance a second relief crew of rowers is needed in order to keep moving at even that speed. By reducing the number of oars per side to 10, another 6′ of boat length is now available for the off-duty crew. The rowers now occupy 30′ of the boat length leaving 18′ for additional off-duty rowers, supplies, etc.

Captain Bradford envisions the Greek boats as being about this size. Where locations, times, and distances are given he sees the voyages of Odysseus at an average boat speed of about 3 knots to be consistent with the Homeric accounts This speed is also consistent with what we now know about vessels of the type used at that time.

Admiral Serre reconstructed a design for the Argo of Jason, whose voyage in search of the Golden Fleece included Odysseus father, Laertes, as one of the crew, hence this design would have been close to the period when the Greeks attacked Troy. This vessel, called a *penteconter* (Fig. O-1), could have been close to the type used by Odysseus, although it is somewhat larger than the one envisioned by

Capt. Bradford. It is about 60' long, with a 9' beam and a 3' draft. He shows 13 oars per side and allows for either two men (Fig. O-2) per 20' long oar for maximum speed, or one man per 13' oar for endurance. Both maximum sprint speed and ordinary cruising speeds remain about the same as for the smaller boat, but carrying capacity has been considerably increased.

In either case, the sail was a simple square sail set from a yard raised on a short mast (Fig. O-1). The actual sail was probably made of either papyrus or linen. They had no fabric for sailmaking at that time with anything like the strength we are accustomed to having in today's sails made of cotton, dacron, or nylon canvas. Consequently, they could use sail only when two conditions were met. First the wind had to be abaft the beam, and second, that wind had to be quite moderate, otherwise the sail would blow out. As we shall see, this is exactly what is mentioned as having happened in a storm after Odysseus and his people left Ismarus. In a strong wind and a correspondingly rough sea these vessels were very quickly in real trouble, and while the *hurricane* is unknown over the Mediterranean Sea, some very boisterous conditions caused by extratropical frontal and cyclonic storms frequently occur. The Mediterranean Sea is a comparatively small, almost totally enclosed body of water; huge, long-period storm waves of open ocean cannot develop here. Instead, very steep, short-period waves develop very quickly as the wind picks up. These can be much more difficult and uncomfortable to sail through than the long rollers of open ocean. Having sailed for about a day and a night through conditions of this type in the Eastern Mediterranean, aboard a modern sailboat about 46' long, the author can testify as to how extremely uncomfortable it can become aboard present day boats, and it probably was far worse on the primitive, flat bottomed vessels of Odysseus' time.

MEDITERRANEAN WEATHER

The Odyssey mentions numerous winds and storms that Odysseus encountered during his voyages around the Mediterranean, storms for which Homer makes the gods Poseidon and Zeus primarily responsible Although ancient mythology gave these gods the power to raise storms of the types described whenever they felt so inclined, similar storms continue to occur in that area today. Modern meteorology now gives us considerably clearer explanations, although they are certainly less colorful.

The Mediterranean is an enclosed and fairly shallow body of water and considerably warmer than the Atlantic Ocean, where most of the major traveling weather systems affecting it, originate. Ocean surface temperatures over the vast North Atlantic vary from near freezing up to about 52° F; over the Mediterranean

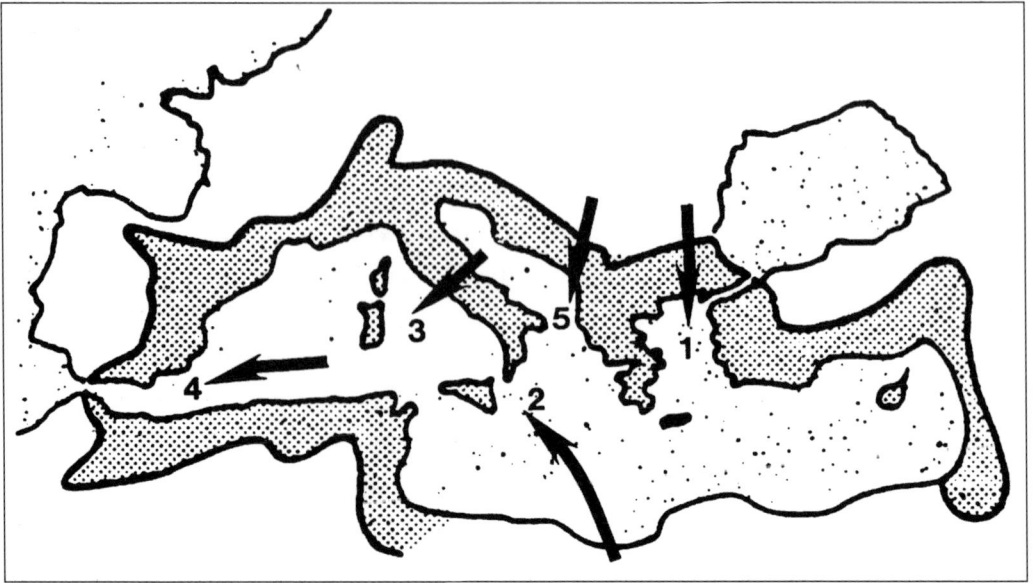

Fig. O-3 Some of the Localized Mediterranean Winds that Helped or Hindered Odysseus Travels
1. Etesian Wind   2. The Sirrocco   3. The Tramontana   4. The Levanter   5. The Bora
(Mediterranean Weather Dominates in Shaded Areas)

they run from about about 50° to 60° F. This temperature differential between the open ocean and the enclosed sea strongly affects the traveling air masses moving in over this sea, producing what is termed the *Mediterranean Climate*. This climate is dominant over the Mediterranean Sea and for a considerable distance inland around its shores (Fig. O-3).

Most of the traveling air masses dominating the Mediterranean area originate in one of three sources. In winter, *maritime Polar* air originating over the North Atlantic either sweeps in from the northwest over France, or curves down north of the Azores and then comes in from the west. This maritime air is cool and humid. As it reaches the comparatively warmer Mediterranean surface its lower layers are warmed, causing a lifting movement. This moist air cools as it rises, forming great banks of heap-type cumulus clouds bringing squally winds and rain.

The second type of traveling air mass reaching the Mediterranean in winter is *continental Polar* air that forms over the European land mass to the north, and moves directly south. This air arrives cool and dry. Again, the lower layers are warmed, and rise, but large cloud decks do not form until this air has lingered over the sea long enough to pick up considerable moisture from it.

In summer, incursions of *maritime Polar* air from the Atlantic are infrequent. When they do occur, the air mass has been considerably warmed en route over the summer North Atlantic, and is very unstable, producing stormy conditions. In summer, the *continental Polar* air tends to remain as a substantially stationary mass over northern Eurasia. This produces a steady wind flow from the north of warm dry air over the central and eastern Mediterranean, known as the *Etesian winds*. (Fig. 0-3) At this point the sea surface is cooler than the incoming continental air, producing great stability and steady winds. Depending on temperature and pressure differentials there can be a great variation in the strength of these winds.

The third source of incoming air masses affecting the weather over the Mediterranean Sea is the *continental Tropical* air that moves in from the Sahara, mainly during the spring and summer. The air is very hot, dry, and dusty. Like the Etisian air, this hot Saharan air is quickly cooled by the sea below, becoming very stable with steady, persistent winds, and at times, unpleasant cloudy conditions. These are called the *Sirrocco* winds (Fig. 0-3).

The west to east expanse of the Mediterranean Sea causes significant changes in the traveling air masses passing over it. In addition, its irregular shape, as well as the wide variations in height of the land around it, results in a very wide variety of local wind and weather disturbances having strong effects, but over very limited areas. This variety of strong, but localized winds (Fig. 0-3) helps to explain the accounts of Odysseus being blown so far out of his way, so many times, keeping in mind the fact that his ships could only *sail* with the wind and could only row against the wind with great difficulty. In case of a strong wind they could not make *any* progress against it at all, even under oars, as we shall see.

ODYSSEUS DEPARTS TROY TO RETURN HOME

As we now begin our attempt to track the wanderings of Odysseus, we can conclude at the outset that regardless of whether his vessels were about 48' long or up to 60' long, or somewhere in between, in any case, by present day standards they were *small* vessels. For example, most of the yachts that have raced for the "America's Cup" over the years have been larger.

When the Greeks burned their camp in front of Troy and put to sea, leaving the wooden horse before the gates, they sailed to a small off-shore island named Tenedos lying about 2 miles away. This island is only about 3 miles long but a large fleet of vessels, the size the Greeks then had, could easily hide behind it, particularly since Galileo had not yet invented the telescope.

After the Greeks returned and sacked Troy, a disagreement developed between Agamemnon and Menelaos, after which part of the fleet, including Odysseus, went back to Tenedos, with the rest staying with Agamemnon. At Tenedos there was a second disagreement, after which part of that group left with Odysseus and the rest split off with other commanders. Odysseus tells King

Alkinoos in Book Nine of the Odyssey that he and his group left Tenedos with a wind that carried him west to Ismaros on the coast of the Kikones. To get there he actually had to go northwest, as this city was in southern Thrace (Fig. O-4). Bradford was able to duplicate this trip in a small sailboat driven by the same local wind off the Turkish mainland that Odysseus probably would have used.

The Greeks of this period really admired heroes who sacked and plundered when there was an opportunity to do so. Consequently, Odysseus and his men considered it a rule of war to sack and plunder Ismaros, after which Odysseus ordered his men to put to sea at once before the main army of the Kikones showed up, but his men refused. They were having too good a time feasting, drinking the local wine, and raping the local women. They made the mistake of feasting too long and the main army of the Kikones showed up and gave them a severe drubbing. Finally they got their boats out to sea but many of their men were lost in the fight. Odysseus comments, "Six benches were left empty in every ship".

After escaping from Ismaros they apparently stopped for the night because the Odyssey states that no ship made sail the *next day* until rites were performed for their lost shipmates. After setting sail, a strong Etsian wind (mentioned previously) blew up, driving them south until their sails "cracked and lashed out in strips in the big wind". Remember, they had only comparatively weak fabrics with which to make their sails.

They had no choice but to ship their oars and pull for the nearest shelter where they stayed for two days until the gale died down on the third day. They then reset sail, and with a following wind, ran south and then southwest to Cape Malea (Fig, O-4). Again, Captain Bradford repeatedly sailed from north to south down the Agean Sea with a following Etesian wind.

THE LOTUS EATERS

Odysseus wanted to go west to Cape Taenarus, then northwest to Ithaca, and home. Instead, a combination of current and a resumption of a gale out of the northeast drove him southwest for nine days. The dominant wind in this part of the Mediterranean is called a *Levanter*, which is a wind that blows over that area with gale force, usually for not more than five days, but may continue from the same direction for several days more after the gale has died down. On the tenth day they reached the land of the Lotus Eaters. Based on ancient sources, Captain Bradford locates this as either the island of Jerba or the Libyan coast close to it. From Cape Malea to Jerba is about 650 miles. Assuming Odysseus vessels traveled at an average speed of 3 knots, which we know can be expected from them, in nine days and nights he would have gone 648 miles, which is close enough!

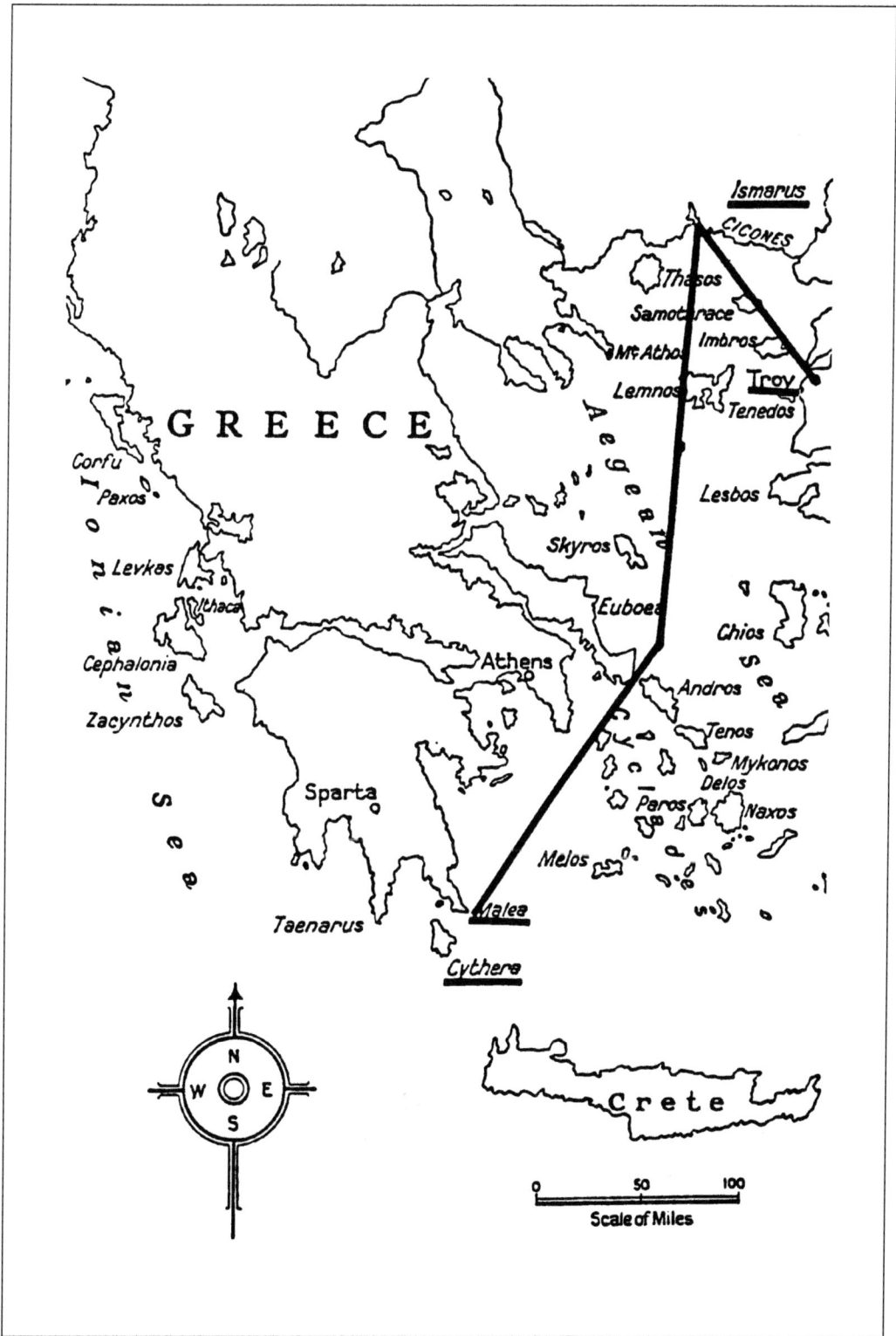

Fig. O-4 Odysseus travels from Troy to Ismarus then Cape Malea
from "Ulysses Found"– Bradburn

A mariner named Scylax of Caryanda wrote a handbook for sailors about 350 BC and identified the Jerba area as the land of the Lotus Eaters. Herodotus agrees with him. In fact there is a fruit growing in that area that while not containing any drug producing happy lethargy, was used in ancient times to make a type of staple bread. Could that have been romanticized into the Lotus? No one knows, but after nine mostly stormy days bouncing about at sea in an small open boat, nearly any local food was likely to be remarkably attractive.

A scouting party of only three men went ashore and they were the only ones to eat the Lotus. When they indicated that they wanted to desert and stay on the island, Odysseus took decisive action to prevent any possibility of mutiny These three were then taken aboard and the fleet was ordered to sail at once.

THE LAND OF THE CYCLOPS

Odysseus knew that after leaving Cape Malea he had gone far to the south of Greece and was now well outside the area where Greeks normally sailed and with which they were familiar. He may also not have been aware of how far west he had gone, but he did know he had to go north to reach his destination. He is quoted as having said, on leaving Cape Malea "the current took me out to sea and from the north a fresh gale drove me past Cythera." Cythera is an island south of Cape Malea still bearing the same name as it did in Homer's time. (Fig. O-4).

The ancient Greeks had no compasses, but were familiar with some astronomical signs. They knew the sun rose in the east and set in the west, but may not yet have known that due to seasonal changes the sun moves north and south far enough so what seemed an east or west wind varied with the seasons over a very wide angle.

The Greeks also knew that the Big Dipper, Ursa Major rotated around north. Today, Polaris is very close to true north, but at the time of Odysseus the closest star to true north was the one now called Kochab, which at that time was about $7°$ east of north. With no other reliable guide available Odysseus may have used Kochab to steer by. Also, he knew that in addition to being south of where he wanted to be, he was also too far west. Therefor, upon leaving the Jerba area it is logical that his next landfall would be to the northeast.

"The next land we found was the Kyklops" (Cyclops), a people he describes as ignorant, uncivilized giants. He then states, "across the wide bay from the mainland there lies a desert island - - - Wild goats in hundreds breed there - - -". He then goes on to describe the harbor in detail. Off the west coast of Sicily is an island generally fitting this description called Favignana (Fig. O-5) In classical

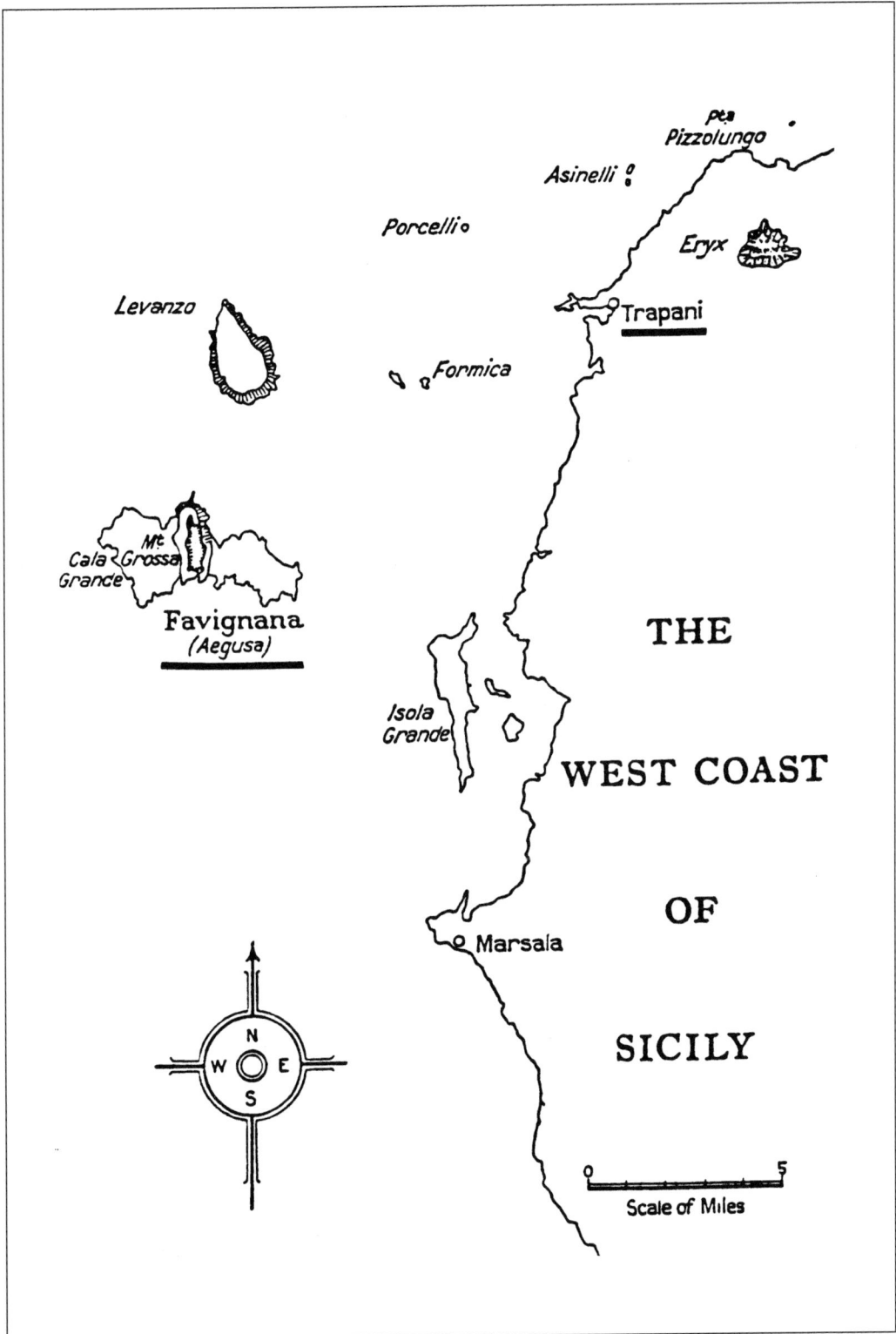

Fig. O-5 Sicily West Coast
from "Ulysses Found"– Bradburn

time, this island was called Aegusa, Goat Island, and it is certainly northeast of Jerba. Also, after cruising over that entire area it was the only Sicilian offshore island that Bradford could find with a harbor fitting Homer's description.

A time period for the run from Jerba is not given, but they arrived under sail as the "furling of the sails on arrival" is specifically mentioned. They probably left Jerba with the southwest wind off the Sahara, the Sirrocco, behind them. The ships arrived at Aegusa at night and Odysseus says, "Some god guided us that night for we could barely see our bows in the dense fog". Bradford notes that sea fogs generally are not common over the central Mediterranean, however, it is interesting that he notes he has encountered them repeatedly in this area at the west end of Sicily.

Next morning they went goat hunting and spent the day having a feast, washed down with some of the wine they had "liberated " at Ismarus. Then, the following day Odysseus decided to cross over to the Cyclops side of the channel with his one boat and crew. Not a good idea. They ended by being trapped in the cave of a giant Cyclops who ate two of his crew for supper, two more for breakfast, and two more for dinner the second evening. That second evening they got the Cyclops drunk and blinded him so that the next morning when he opened the entrance to the cave the ones who were left were able to escape. In the process, they also stole the Cyclops flock, and were able to have another feast back at Aegusa, before setting out again.

As mentioned earlier, when the fleet was driven far to the southwest of Cape Malea they were then in waters completely unknown to the Greeks at that time. In addition, they had no way of dead reckoning to tell how far they had come. All they knew was the Land of the Lotus Eaters was well southwest of where they wanted to be so they figured they needed to go northeast. Now, when they had reached Favignana they knew they had made back considerable distance to the north as well as some distance the east, but they did not know how much. They guessed they had better continue toward the northeast which they did.

THE ISLAND OF AEOLUS

The morning after feasting on the sheep they put to sea again. This time Odysseus specifically mentions that they started out by rowing, but it does not not mention, as to how far or how long, or whether the sails were raised. All that is said is that their next landfall was the island of Aeolus, King of the Winds. Northeast of Favignana Bradford found two possibilities on the map (Fig. 0-6). One of these is the lone island of Ustica lying about 65 miles northeast of Favignana, and the other would be one of the Lipari islands further to the east.

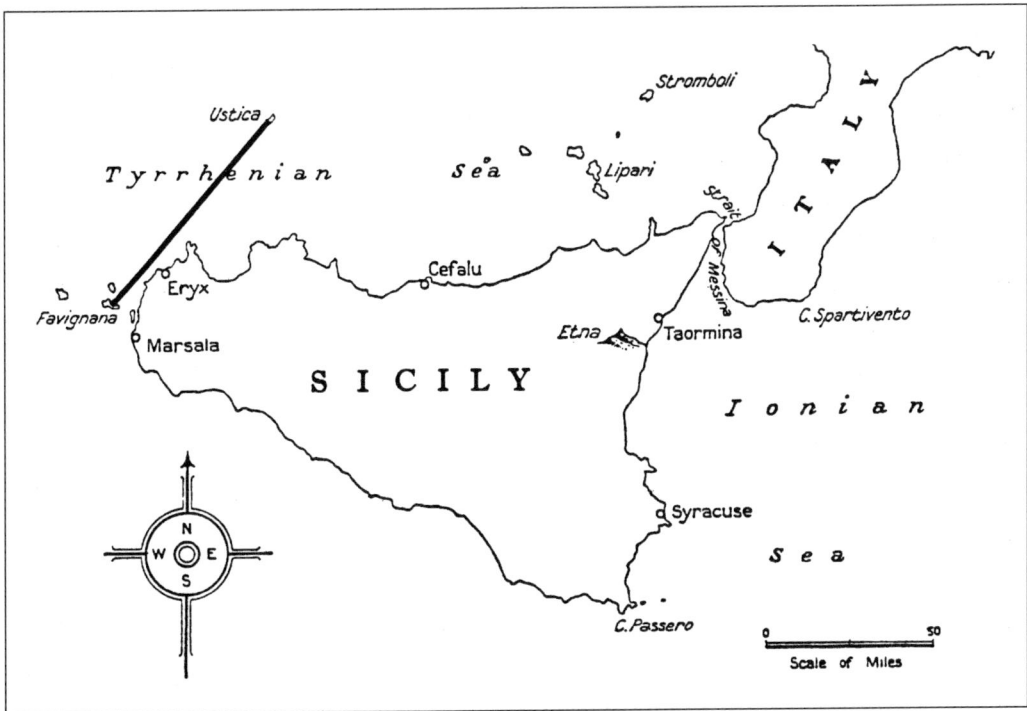

*Fig. O-6 Land of the Cyclops to the Island of Aeolus
from "Ulysses Found"– Bradburn*

Their landfall is referred to as "an isle adrift upon the sea". Ustica is alone, while the Lipari group is made up of seven main islands as well as a number of protruding rocky islets, many spaced within sight of each other. If the landfall was at one of these islands, why was only that one island of Aeolus mentioned? Ustica also fits better as the island of Aeolus, as we shall soon see, when the departure of Odysseus is described.

His squadron is hospitably received and royally wined and dined. Aeolus keeps Odysseus around for an entire month to hear him tell the complete story of the siege of Troy. When they finally prepared to sail again, Aeolus "stinted nothing" in provisioning the vessels, and also had them store aboard a great bag made of a bull's hide. The crew did not know that it contained all the winds except the West wind, which was the only one needed to blow them home to Greece. This was to assure them of a safe, smooth passage and no contrary gales.

If we go along with the idea of Ustica as Aeolus's island, and accept that a "west wind" is likely in that area to be somewhat north of west, then they started out with about a beam wind until rounding the west end of Sicily, and then would have had a following wind all the way back to Greece. Odysseus says "nine days we sailed without event till on the tenth we raised our land". Again, by sailing at an average of 3 knots for nine days with no gales, they would have covered about 600 miles, taking them from Ustica back to the Greek coast. On the other hand, had the Lipari Islands been the land of Aeolus, a west wind would have been a head wind all the way along the north coast of Sicily.

With their homeland in sight, Odysseus, who has been at the steering oar most of the time, finally takes a well earned rest. His crew now falls to speculating and squabbling over what is in the bag Aeolus gave their captain. Deciding it contains gold, silver or other valuable gifts, they open it. Another very bad idea! Immediately, the howling gale winds that Aeolus had tied up in the bag begin to blow, and they are now blown all the way back to the island of Aeolus.

THE LAND OF THE LAESTRYGONIANS

They again appealed to Aeolus for help, but he was disgusted with them. He did everything he could to make it easy for all of them to get home, but the greed of the crew made them altogether too curious and they got themselves into serious trouble. Aeolus wanted nothing further to do with them and drove them away.

They left, and with no wind at all rowed for 6 days and nights after which they reached the land of the Laestrygonians. A detailed description of the harbor is given as "a sheltered bay with high stone cliffs on either side of an entrance so narrow that the bay inside is completely calm." All the other ships entered this sheltered harbor and moored inside, while Odysseus alone tied up just outside. After a small shore party alerted the local inhabitants to their presence the entire squadron inside the bay was attacked and totally destroyed. Having wisely tied up outside, Odysseus was able to get away in a great hurry!

Trying to locate this land at a suitable distance to be reached in 6 days and nights of rowing presents a major difficulty. Bradford sailed extensively in the area north of Sicily looking for a bay that is at a suitable distance from Ustica, and fits the detailed description given in the Odyssey for the Laestrygonian harbor. He cruised all along the coasts of Sicily, Italy, and even Sardinia checking every place that could have been reached in six days and nights by the squadron of Odysseus. Nothing could be found that came close to the description given, and he had just decided that this was one place that existed only in Homer's imagination, when, purely by chance he was asked to help a friend deliver a boat to Corsica. When they arrived at Port de Bonifacio near the southern tip of Corsica (Fig. O-7), Bradford realized upon entering it that he was looking at a harbor exactly as Homer had described the Laestrygonian bay—"a curious bay with mountain walls of stone to left and right and reaching far inland"!

The distance of Bonifacio from Ustica is about 240 miles, again an appropriate distance for a rowing vessel to have gone in 6 days, arriving on the seventh.

However, there is an odd inconsistency here. The eminent classical scholar Professor C. F. Herberger has pointed out to me that Homer also states "In that land the daybreak follows dusk, and so the shepherd homing calls to the cowherd setting out".

Professor Herberger sees that as a description of a Scandinavian fiord or at least somewhere at a very high latitude where summer nights are very short. Early Greeks are believed to have sailed outside the Pillars of Hercules (Straits of Gibralter) and may have gone as far north as Scandinavia - but whether they had done so by Homer's time is unknown, and they certainly couldn't do it in 6 days!! Is this Homer's description of "daybreak following dusk" or is it the addition of a later scribe?

THE ISLAND OF CIRCE

Leaving the island of the Laestrigonians, Odysseus has been reduced to his one ship. The crews of all his other boats had been set upon by the man-eating Laestrigonians, and slaughtered.

What kind of navigational error caused him to row all the way up to Corsica in the first place, is not explained. No indication is given that he was forced there by adverse winds or currents; in fact, Homer states that on the way up there was no breeze for 6 days.

Upon leaving the land of the Laestrigonians, Odysseus apparently is aware that Greece is off to the east, so when he leaves, he sails east. He is going in essentially the right direction, but apparently does not realize the entire Italian peninsula stands between his present location and Greece. His next landfall is Cape Circeo, which is referred to as Circe's *Island*, although presently it has a narrow neck of land connecting it to mainland Italy.

Circe turns part of his crew into swine but Hermes shows Odysseus how to avoid this fate himself. Odysseus then convinces Circe to remove her enchantment from his men, and everyone settles down again to "feasting long on roasts and wine". It seems that throughout this entire voyage, when not in some kind of trouble, these fellows have done a great deal of feasting on "roasts and wine" and will continue to do so.

Odysseus is quite happy with Circe, and his men are equally happy with Circe's attending ladies, so they lingered here for an entire year. Eventually, the crew suggested to Odysseus that it was time to head for home. He asked Circe for her help since she had promised long ago to help him whenever he wanted to leave. She now informs him he cannot go directly back to Ithaca. He must first go to the Land of the Dead which is at "the bourne of Ocean", and make appropriate sacrifices to call up the shade of Teiresias, who will give him instructions

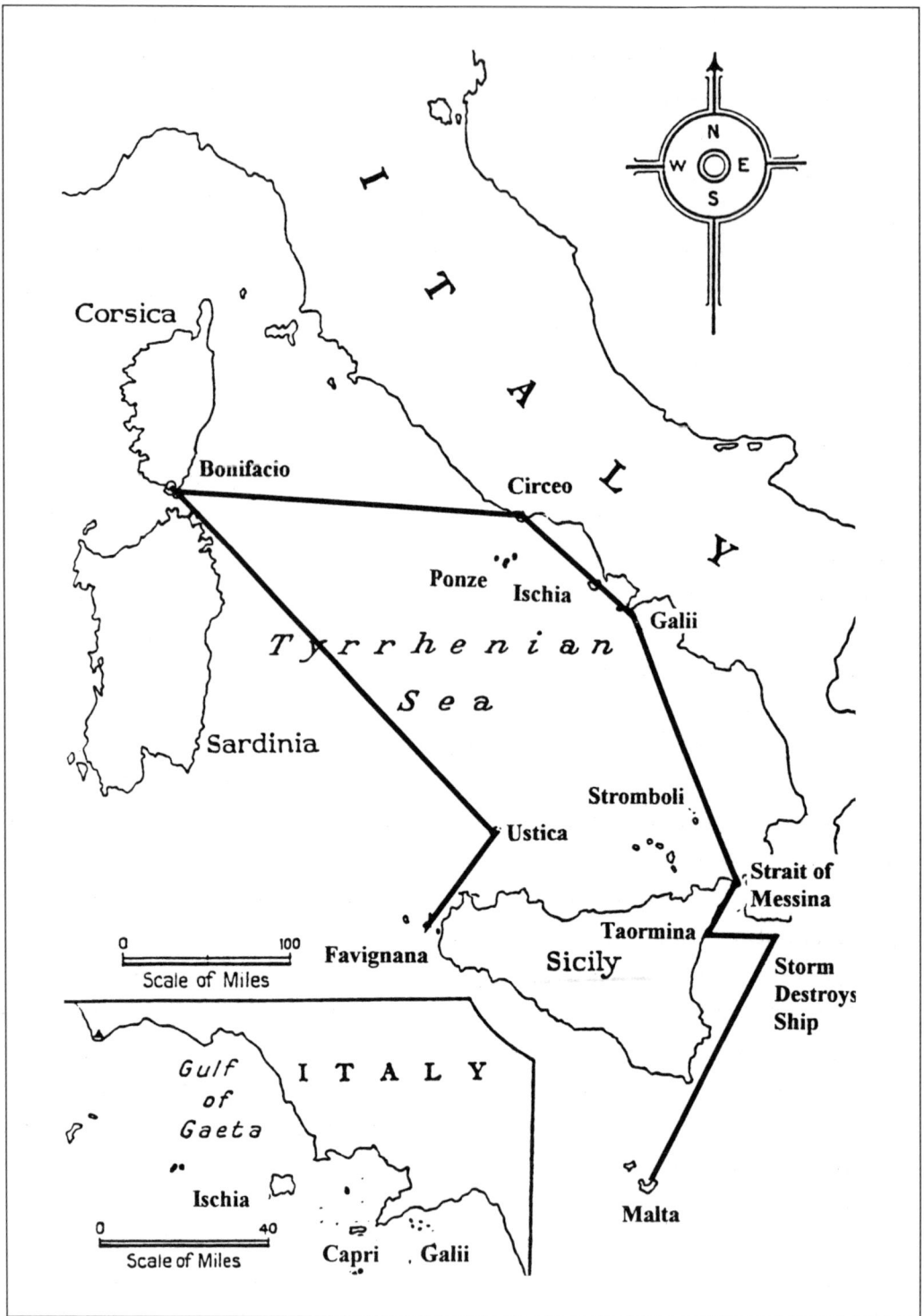

Fig. O-7 Cyclops, to Aeolus, to Laestrigonians, to Circe
Circe, to Sirens, to Scylla and Charybdis, to Land of the Sun God,
Zeus destroys Ship, Odysseus drifts to Calypso
from "Ulysses Found"– Bradburn

regarding the course he must take. Circe tells him " set up your mast and haul your canvas to the fresh blowing North. Sit down and steer, and hold that wind, even to the bourne of Ocean".

THE PILLARS OF HERCULES AND THE LAND OF THE DEAD

The night before they leave, they, of course, have a farewell feast accompanied by considerable wine. One of the crew named Elpenor has a bit too much wine, falls asleep on the roof, and when he wakes up walks the wrong way, falls off and is killed. They cannot wait to give him a proper burial, and sail off.

Curiously, things now become rather confused. "Ocean" is well off toward the west – just beyond the Straits of Gibralter, known in classical times as the Pillars of Hercules. In this case, how long they sailed is not mentioned, nor is any description given of the place where they finally landed. Previously, where sailing times and harbor descriptions have been given it has been possible to find reasonably similar locations for Odysseus' landings. This time, Homer gives us nothing to go on except that they go to "Ocean". Did they land on the African side or the European side? Did they land inside east of the Straits, or did they land outside on the west? Curiously, Homer is silent regarding these details.

Because of this vagueness a number of Homeric scholars feel that this voyage from Circe's "island" to Ocean and back again comes from a different source than the rest of the poem. Captain Bradford notes this, but also indicates that Homer could well have based this section on a story he had heard of a Phoenician voyage to the west, since by this time Odysseus and his crew are believed to have reached the Straits and beyond, although the Greeks had not. In any event Bradford himself made the same trip from Italy most of the way to the Straits in a heavy deep draft sailboat at an average speed of about 3 knots, blown by a steady and persistent northeast wind called, in that area, the Tramontana. He showed that this part of the Odyssey *could* have happened, but even so he doubts it due to the sudden complete lack of detail of the sort marking so much of the previous part of the story.

According to the versions of the Odyssey available to us, after reaching Ocean and making a landing somewhere, Odysseus completes the proper sacrifices. He then communicates with the shades of a number of his former comrades, his mother, and Teiresias as well. Odysseus now learns that he is to go back to Circe's land. When he leaves there, he may reach Ithaca with his crew if no one kills any of the Sun-God's sacred cattle. However, if any of the sacred animals are injured, the ship and the entire crew will be lost and Odysseus will return alone, and in dire straits in a foreign ship to Ithaca.

THE RETURN TO CIRCE

He now leaves the Land of the Dead heading back to Circe's realm. The normal current through the Straits of Gibralter sets to the east and the prevailing wind is from the west with both helping him on his way. Once he has returned to Circe's land the details of his movements from there again become accurately trackable.

The first thing they do upon arriving at Circe's island is to give their dead comrade Elpenor a proper burial. Then, of course, comes the obligatory feast. While the crew sleeps near the ship, Odysseus goes back to the palace with Circe to hear from her what he is to do next. She tells him he must first sail past the Islands of the Sirens. There, he is to keep well offshore, have his crew plug their ears with beeswax so as not to hear the songs of the Sirens, and have himself securely tied to the mast so he cannot leap overboard.

THE ISLANDS OF THE SIRENS

Bradford has sailed south from Cape Circeo and notes passing the islands of Ischia, Procida, and Capri, but picks the Galli Islands at the mouth of the Gulf of Salerno as the Islands of the Sirens because they are the last group of islands on the west coast of Italy, and there are three of them close together. True, Homer only mentions two Sirens by name, but other classical writers have come up with the names of many more. The Fitzgerald translation of Homer does not specify anything about where the Sirens were located, except that they are on an island, and the notation that "There are bones of dead men rotting in a pile beside them."

If the Sirens were not on the Galli Islands, as Bradford believes, they must have been on one of the others nearby to the north, because looking south there is nothing between there and the Straits of Messina (Scylla and Charybdis) except the Prowling Rocks or Drifters.. Of these rocks Circe tells Odysseus that "Not even birds can pass them" and she describes "boiling surf" and "high fiery winds". Heading from Cape Circe directly toward the Straits of Messina (Fig. 0-7) anyone on this course first must pass Stromboli which is a 3,136' high volcano. Close by it lies Strombolicchio, a steep sided rock 164' high with a fairly narrow, and often rough passage between it and Stromboli. Stromboli was then, and still is, a very active volcano with lava and cinders constantly sliding down its steep sides into the sea. Since it is an active volcano the statement that "Not even birds can pass" makes perfectly good sense.

To get from Cape Circeo to Stromboli and thence to the Straits of Messina, Odysseus had to pass across the Bay of Naples. This being the case, you may wonder why the volcano at Stromboli is described while no mention is made of the much bigger Vesuvius. The answer is that in Homeric times Vesuvuis was completely dormant and remained so until 79 AD!

PASSING SCYLLA AND CHARYBDIS

Circe had explained to Odysseus that he should pass by the Prowling Rocks and go on to run between Scylla and Charybdis (through the Straits of Messina Fig. 0-7). She also told him that Scylla will kill and eat six of his men. This, he was told, is unavoidable, but still he should stay close to Scylla's side of the channel because the whirlpool on the Charybdis side poses yet a worse danger.

THE LAND AND THE FLOCKS OF HELIOS

After doing as Circe has directed, Odysseus emerges on the south side of the Strait and starts down the east coast of Sicily. This is the Land of Helios, the Sun God, where both Teiresias and Circe have cautioned him, on pain of disaster, that no one from his ship may injure any of the cattle of Helios, the Sun God. Consequently, Odysseus wants simply to keep going and not stop here. Unfortunately, some of the crew grumble and complain that they need a rest. Odysseus finally agrees to stop with the provision that they use only the supplies Circe provided, and absolutely do not touch any of the cattle or sheep ashore. They arrive at a half moon bay with beach and water nearby, and with everyone swearing they will leave Helios's flocks alone, they anchor.

Captain Bradford has sailed along that part of the Sicilian coast many times and found that about 25 miles down from the end of the Strait is a small cove with a sandy beach, now called Taormina that meets the Homeric description. Bradford has stopped there several times because it is the only sheltered cove in the entire area. Odysseus would have reached it in 6 to 8 hours from Scylla, and by now about nine days after leaving Cape Circeo assuming again an average speed of 3 knots.

Once they had stopped, the weather turned on them. They had a month of onshore gales blowing continuously so they couldn't get out of the bay. These onshore winds were undoubtedly what is now known as the Sirrocco; a hot, humid wind blowing in from the south to southeast onto eastern Sicily. This is strongest and most persistent in August, September, and October.

The supplies with which they had started on their cruise had given out and they scoured the area for fish and birds and whatever they could find. As the storms continued, their supply situation became progressively worse. One day, Odysseus slipped away to plead with the Gods for help, but ended, unfortunately, by falling asleep. While he was gone, his crew decided to kill some of the sacred cattle, and to appease the gods they would make a sacrifice of the best ones, and proceeded to do. Word of this got back to Helios at once and he angrily appealed to Zeus who assured Helios that he would destroy the ship and its crew. By the time Odysseus woke up and returned, the damage was done. His reprimands to his crew came too late.

As the Greek gods of myth were wont to do, Zeus played with Odysseus and his crew for a few days. For 6 days he let them feast on beef from Helios's herds. The onshore gales stopped. Then an offshore breeze sprang up so they stepped the mast and set sail, putting the island astern. This is significant since it means they started off toward the east which was the right direction to sail to reach Greece. Zeus then let them get well offshore before hitting them with a furious gale that destroyed the ship and drowned the crew. This was exactly what had been predicted as their fate if they harmed the flocks of Helios. Only Odysseus survived on a raft improvised out of pieces from the broken ship.

THE ISLAND OF CALYPSO

The renewed Sirrocco blows him back into the Straits and this time to Charybdis. After a hair-raising escape from both Charybdis and Scylla he came out of the Strait and drifted for nine days in the open sea before arriving at the Island of Ogygia, the domain of Calypso, on the tenth day.

Finding this island requires another careful look at the Mediterranean Sea. The island of Calypso is described as "alone in the sea" and "well wooded". Leaving the Strait of Messina, Odysseus is drifting along the east coast of Sicily where there are only rocks, and on repeated passages Bradford could find nothing that qualifies as an island.

Since there is a weak south flowing current in this area it would seem that in nine days Odysseus would have drifted south well beyond Sicily. Malta and Gozo lie almost directly south of Sicily (Fig. 0-7), with Malta about 150 miles from the Messina Strait. At a speed of one knot for nine days and nights plus one day, he would have drifted 228 miles. At a speed of half a knot the distance would be 114 miles. At an average varying speed somewhere between the two he could easily have reached Malta in the stated time. Malta is not "alone in the sea", as Homer notes regarding Calypso's island. It is one of a small group of islands, but it does fit the time frame and direction for Odysseus having drifted from the Strait to the Island of Calypso, plus it also fits the time frame for his subsequent homeward raft trip from the Island of Calypso back to Scheria, off the coast of Greece.

Odysseus is forced to stay with Calypso for seven years at the end of which time Zeus decrees that he shall be allowed to return to Greece. To make that return he must first build a raft, and rig a mast and sail on it, which he completes. Calypso supplies him with food, water, and wine for the trip and raises a fair wind when he starts. He sails for 17 days at which time he is in sight of Scheria, the land of the Phaecians, a "land that looked like a shield laid on the misty sea". Sailing from the heel of Italy, Captain Bradford says that is exactly how the Island of Corfu appears when approached from that direction. Corfu is about 330 miles from Malta, and if Corfu is actually Scheria, this would mean that the raft sailed at an average of just under 20 miles a day, or at an average speed of .75 knots. This is quite slow, but remember this is a raft not a boat, so his speed probably varied from a top speed of up to 2 knots or more, down to practically nothing. Seventeen days for a 330 mile trip on a mere sailing raft becomes is reasonable.

When he is just in sight of Scheria, his implacable foe Poseidon spots him and raises a sudden strong storm destroying the raft, and forcing Odysseus to swim to land. A local wind called the Bora that blows down the Adriatic could account for that storm. In any event, after Odysseus lands among the Phaecians his wanderings are ended. They take him home to Ithaca where he kills off the band of freeloaders who have taken over his palace, and takes back his rightful place as king.

Of course, we shall never know whether any, or all, of Homer's tale is based on fact. However, Captain Bradford's extensive voyages through the area, as well as detailed studies of Mediterranean winds and currents show that many places conforming to Homer's descriptions do exist, and at such distances from each other that classical Greek vessels could travel between them in the time periods mentioned. Is the Odyssey fact, or fiction, or some combination of the two? What do you think?

CHAPTER 6

Arther Piver Rediscovers the Ocean Going Trimaran

On both his trans-Atlantic and trans-Pacific voyages in order to decrease weight Piver kept his galley equipment to an absolute minimum. He used a single burner Primus stove and all stores were dried or canned to eliminate the need for refrigeration, so we all can sympathize with those who sailed on those long voyages with Piver. The following Chanty harks back to an earlier day when food at sea normally left a good deal to be desired.

THE COOK'S CHANTY

The devil take the cook, that greasy, bearded fellow
Way! Hey, heave away, a hundred miles today.
He feeds us mouldy bread , and meat that's turnin yellow
Way!Hey, heave away, heave away home

And what we gwt to drink is chick'ry soaked in water
Way! Hey, heave away, a hundredmiles today
Each man aboard the ship has marked the cook for slaughter
Way! Hey, heave away, heave away home

The divil take the cook, the spuds we git is rotten
Way! Hey, heave away, a hundred miles today
And 'vittles from a tin that's seven years forgotten
Way! Hey, heave away, heave away home

The divil take the cook. When his gally days are over
Way! Hey, heave away, a hundred miles today
May he roast in Hell gnawing salted junk foreever
Way! Hey, heave away, heave away home

During the late 1950s and early 60s a lively interest in multi-hulled sailboats developed among sailing enthusiasts in the U.S., primarily in twin hulled racing *catamarans*. By now, small racing catamarans have become commonplace, but at that time these were the first multi-hull boats most U.S. sailors had ever seen. Many were a bit afraid of them, but still vastly impressed by their tremendous speed. For those who had been sailing and racing in *Sabots*, *Lidos*, *Lasers*, *Snipes* and various other small racing sailboats, the catamaran heralded a revolution. The instant acceleration and fleetness of the catamaran were tremendously exhilarating compared to sailing any of the small conventional mono-hull racers, and for that matter, the larger ones as well.

In the South Pacific and Indian Oceans multi-hulled sailboats have been in use for thousands of years. A wide variety of outrigger sailing canoes had been developed all over that area varying in size from small dugouts used for fishing in the lagoons, to large seagoing multihulled vessels capable of journeying across thousands of miles of open ocean. The people who first settled on the far flung islands scattered over these immense oceans, traveled to and between them on large multi-hulled sailing vessels. It was the discovery of these vessels that provided the inspiration for modern day naval architects and designers to venture into building multi-hull vessels.

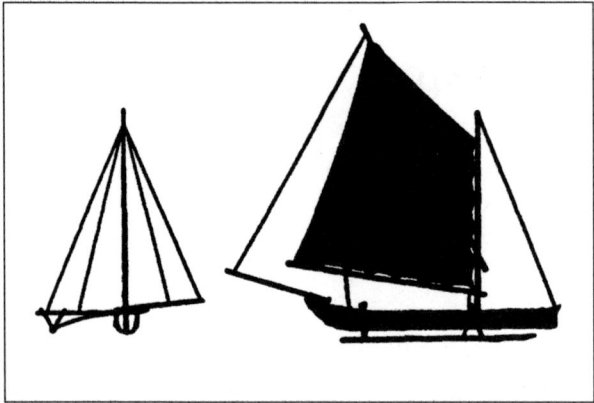

Fig. P-1 Pahi–Single Outrigger Canoe–Society Islands from "Sailing and Small Craft Down the Ages" – E. L. Bloomster–Navel Institute Press, 1940

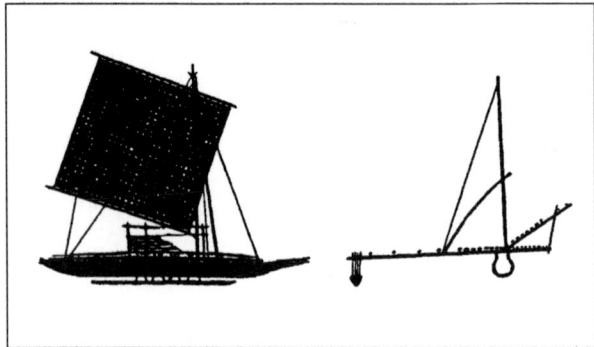

Fig. P-1 Pahi–Single Outrigger Canoe from the Admiralty Islands from "Sailing and Small Craft Down the Ages" – E. L. Bloomster–Navel Institute Press, 1940

The Pahi (Fig. P-1) and the Endrol (Fig. P-2) are examples of the smaller outrigger canoes. Each has a very long, narrow main hull carrying a mast and sail with a light outrigger for balance well off to one side. The Tahitian Pahi (Fig. P-3) with two equal sized hulls is an obvious precursor of the catamaran, while the double out-riggered Gul (Fig. P-4) is already a prototype for the later three hulled trimaran that subsequently captivated the Californian sailor and designer, Arthur Piver.

Piver was an avid amateur pleasure boat sailor from a very early age. An interest in sailing was to be expected since his father before him, had owned a schooner that had sailed in trans-Pacific races. His fascination with speed under sail led him to investigate the fast outriggers of the South Pacific islanders back in the 1950s, when the small racing catamarans that were soon to become immensely popular in the U.S., were first being introduced and developed. His stint flying P-38s in WW II may also have helped to spur his lifelong interest in speed.

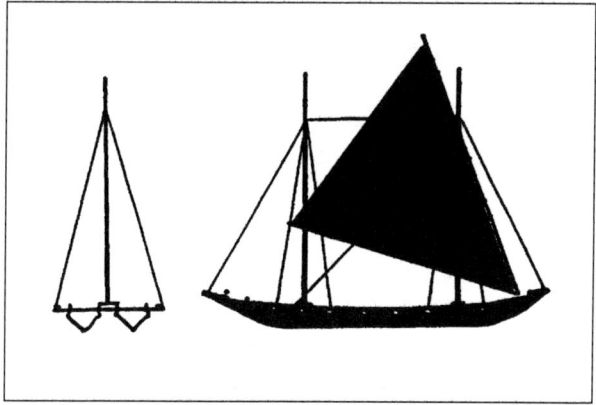

Fig. P-3 Pahi–A Type of Tahitian Sea-Going Double Canoe from "Sailing and Small Craft Down the Ages" – Navel Institute Press, 1940

Arthur Piver was not a formally trained naval architect as were Rudy Choy, Roland Prout, Dick Newick, Hobi Alter and others who were early modern multi-hull designers. Most of these recent and present multi-hull designers had no way of knowing that their invention of

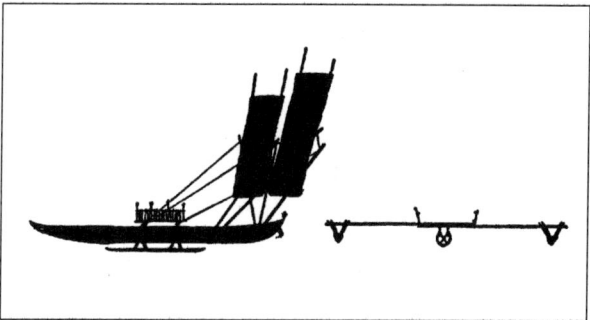

Fig. P-4 Gul–Type of Double Outrigger Sailing Canoe from Torres Straits from "Sailing and Small Craft Down the Ages" – Navel Institute Press, 1940

the catamaran had been preceded in Europe more than 300 years ago. Although this fact is now almost totally forgotten, in 1662, a British inventor and amateur naval architect named Sir William Petty, designed and built a sailing catamaran the *Simon & Jude* (Fig. P-5) that may well have been inspired by descriptions of South Pacific island multi-hulls. This vessel was the first of a series he designed and built that eventually reached 128 tons. Although they were fast, they were difficult to handle. Lacking present day light weight materials and understanding of fluid mechanics he was unable to solve that problem, therefore, his revolutionary idea died fairly quickly.

Actually, Piver's occupation was the rather unglamorous one of publishing a business journal in Mill Valley, California. He started designing boats as a hobby which gradually grew to become his primary occupation. His early designs were racing dinghys and catamarans.

Another designer named Victor Tchetchet believed that the double outrigger

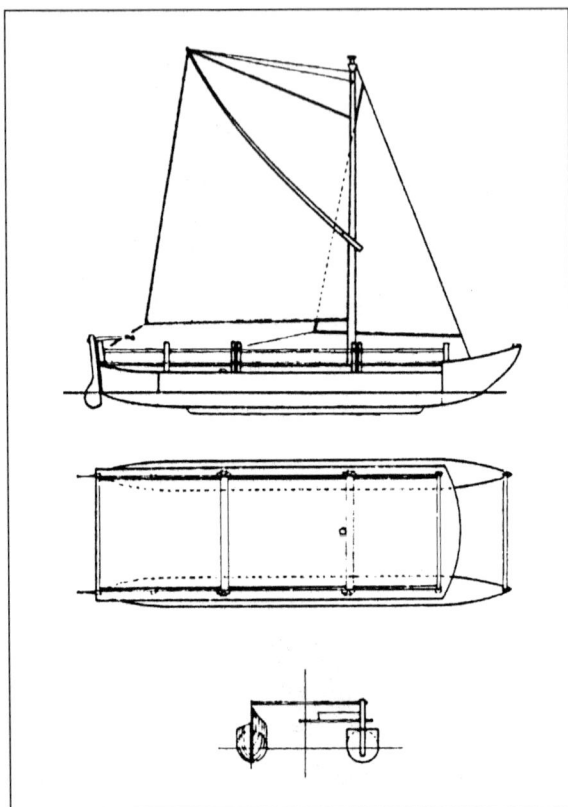

Fig. P-5 The 1662 catamaran "Simon & Jude" the first of a series of catamarans designed by Sir William Petty from "The Story of Sail"– Navel Institute Press, 1999

similar to the Gul (Fig. P-4) was inherently faster, as well as much more stable than the catamaran. He is believed to be the first to use the term *trimaran* to identify this type. When Piver saw the trimaran he was particularly interested in its vastly superior stability over the catamaran. In strong wind gusts a twin-hulled catamaran can be capsized if not handled correctly, at which point it can be very difficult to right. The trimaran with two outriggers on either side of a central hull will heel very little and is virtually impossible to capsize.

Initially, Piver designed several catamarans, but because of this factor of greatly increased stability, variations in the design of the trimaran became Piver's primary interest. He designed trimarans ranging from daysailers of about 16' up to ocean cruisers of over 60'. He proceeded to prove the seaworthiness of his cruising trimarans to the many skeptics of the time by making ocean crossings in them himself. He first crossed the Atlantic in a 30 foot trimaran he called *"Nimble";* then later crossed the Pacific in a 35' tri he called *"Lodestar"*. A second Atlantic crossing several years later was thwarted by a gale that blew out his sails, but as the boat itself sustained only minor damage, he succeeded in returning safely to Bermuda.

NIMBLE

Piver's first trimaran designs were a series of day sailers. His main aims were speed, ease of handling, and safety, as well as ease and inexpensive construction. By the time he got to his 6th trimaran he was up to a 24 footer (Fig. P-6) he called *"Nugget"*. This was the first one he had done that went beyond the daysailer/racer size. It could be used for limited cruising, albeit with very primitive accommodations. As we shall see, luxurious living aboard was not one of

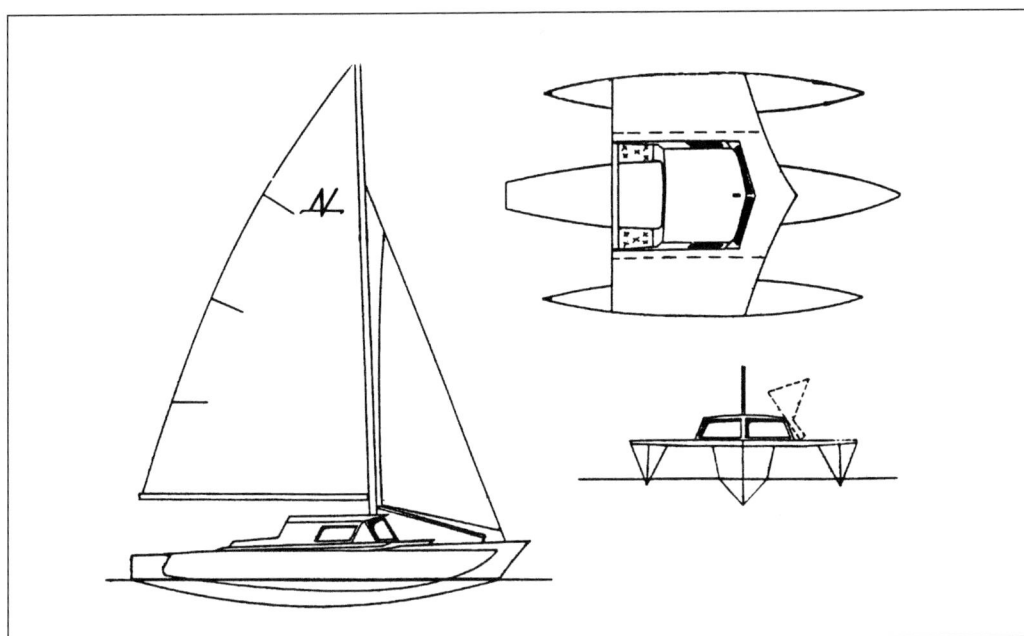

Fig. P-6 24x14x18" Trimaran "Nugget" from "Trans-Atlantic Trimaran"– Arthur Piver

Arthur's major concerns. He was willing to cruise very long distances under very spartan conditions.

There was, of course, a calculated reason for this. By limiting the facilities aboard that were devoted to crew comfort, he greatly reduced the initial cost of building the boat, which was one of his primary aims. In addition by limiting facilities assigned primarily to comfort he greatly reduced the vessel's loaded weight - which he correctly considered a major factor in achieving high speeds with multi-hulls.

After he had tested *Nugget* on San Francisco Bay, a very severe testing ground due to its frequent strong and gusty winds, he cruised in it down the coast of California, down the Baja coast, and across to Acapulco. He then decided he wanted to build an ocean cruising trimaran large enough to compete in the 1960 Slocum Single-Handed Trans-Atlantic Race. This one had to be large enough and strong enough to make an ocean passage while at the same time small enough, and with a sufficiently simple rig that could be sailed by one person. In addition to all that, the design had to be simple enough to construct so it could be built in his back yard because he was not in a financial position to farm the job out to a boatyard. He wanted to design a boat that was large enough to use as a cruising boat, but that was both simple enough and inexpensive enough to build so an ordinary person of limited means and limited experience could build one. The result was a boat 30' long, with an 18' beam,

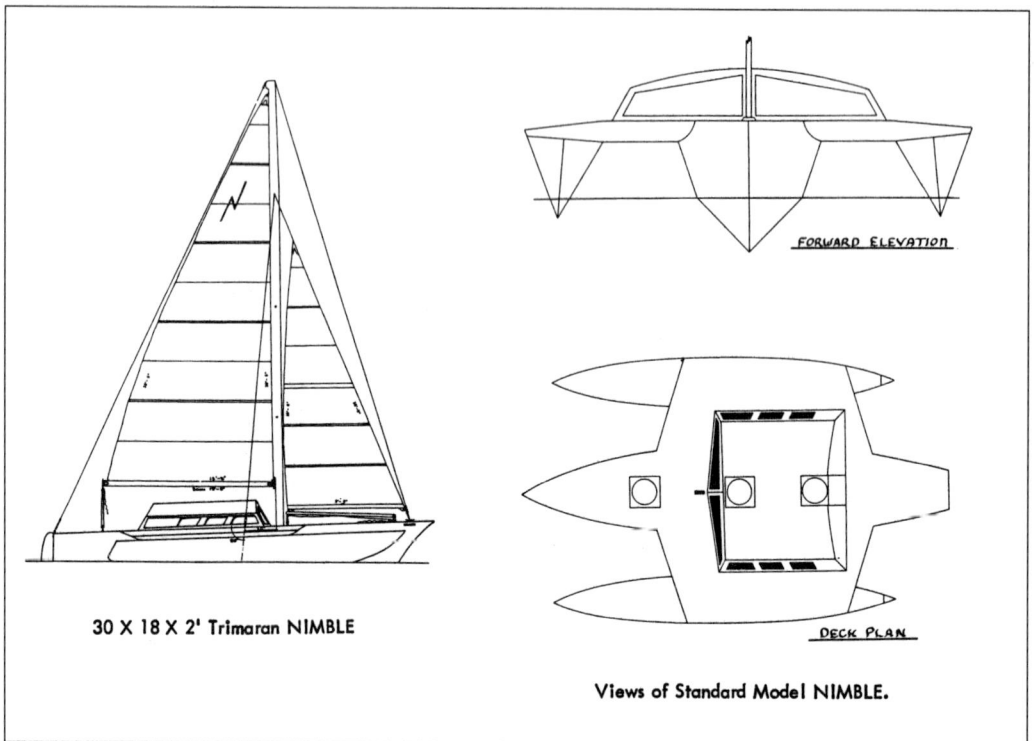

30 X 18 X 2' Trimaran NIMBLE

FORWARD ELEVATION

DECK PLAN

Views of Standard Model NIMBLE.

Fig. P-7 30x18x2' Trimaran "Nimble" from "Trans-Atlantic Trimaran"– Arthur Piver

and drawing only 2' of water - the *"Nimble"* (Fig, P-7).

The hull, or more accurately, the hulls were built of fiberglass covered sheet plywood nailed and glued to interior frames. Fiberglass covered plywood was a common and accepted small boat construction method at the time. As with all his previous smaller boats, Piver was acutely cost conscious on this project. As a result he did some curious and unusual things. For one, he used galvanized nails to fasten the plywood to the internal frames. This is not normally acceptable in boat construction particularly when the boat will be used in salt water. His thinking was that since the hulls were to be sealed inside a fiberglass skin there should not be a problem because the nails would be sealed away from salt water corrosion.

A 36' mast is normally quite an expensive item. Piver built his mast by scarfing together 5 pieces of 2 x 8 clear fir cut from ordinary lumberyard staircase stringers (Fig. P-8), and strengthened by three spreaders with diamond stays. This saved him a great deal of money because in 1960, the mast material he used came to only $21!! A 36' marine grade one piece spar was, at the very least, several hundred dollars at that time. While unorthodox, Piver's mast stood up through fair weather and foul, as we shall see.

He also seemed to take considerable pride in the fact that the cabin ports and many of the fittings for the boat came not from marine suppliers but rather from military "surplus" stores, again considerably reducing costs.

Long before roller reefing was available, Piver also devised a remote reefing system for the jib, (Fig. P-9) making it unnecessary for anyone to go forward in foul weather to reef it. This system later worked admirably in quite blustery weather at sea. He used full length battens on the jib, then from the cockpit by slacking the halyard and taking up on the reefing lines port and starboard that run from A to B to C to D, the sail could be reefed and secured from flogging in the strongest winds. It seems likely that the full battens in the jib would have prevented it from assuming the most perfectly possible aerofoil shape, but the ease of reefing would more than offset that disadvantage on a cruising boat, where safety and convenience are more important than the last tenth of a knot of speed.

With the new boat completed it was time to launch her and put her to the test. Due to her extreme width of 18′ to it was necessary to take the two side hulls off in order to get her from Piver's yard to the water, and reassemble her there. When finally reassembled, launched, and rigged she was test sailed on San Francisco Bay for two months, under varying weather conditions. Her performance was everything Piver had hoped. She was fast, maneuverable, stable, and easy to handle in the often gusty conditions found on that bay. She was so fast that on one occasion he clocked her doing 24 knots in a 30 knot wind!!

THE TRANS-ATLANTIC PASSAGE

Now that he had his boat, the next problem was getting it from California to England. for the race. The cost of simply shipping it was unacceptably high to the economically minded Arthur Piver. So, he

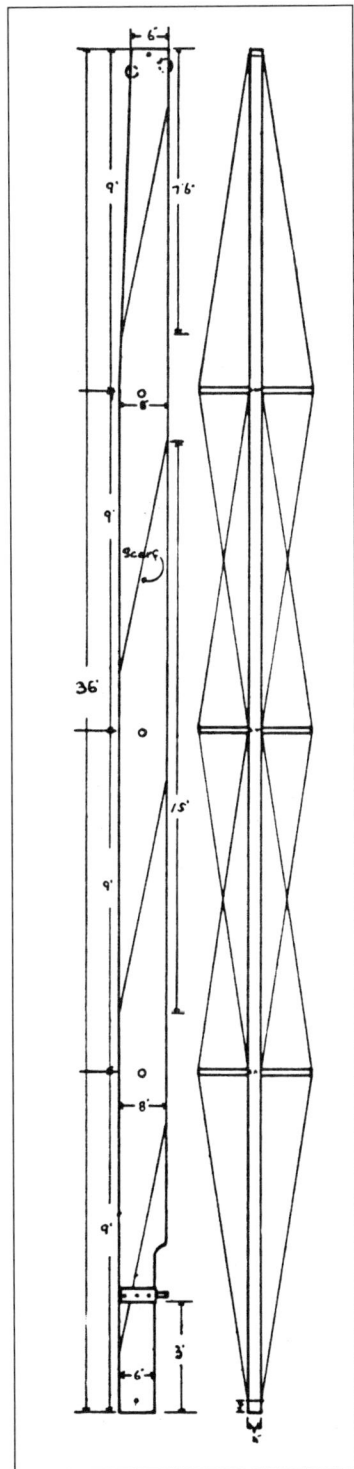

Fig. P-8 Scarfed mast used on "Nimble" from "Trans-Atlantic Trimaran"– Arthur Piver

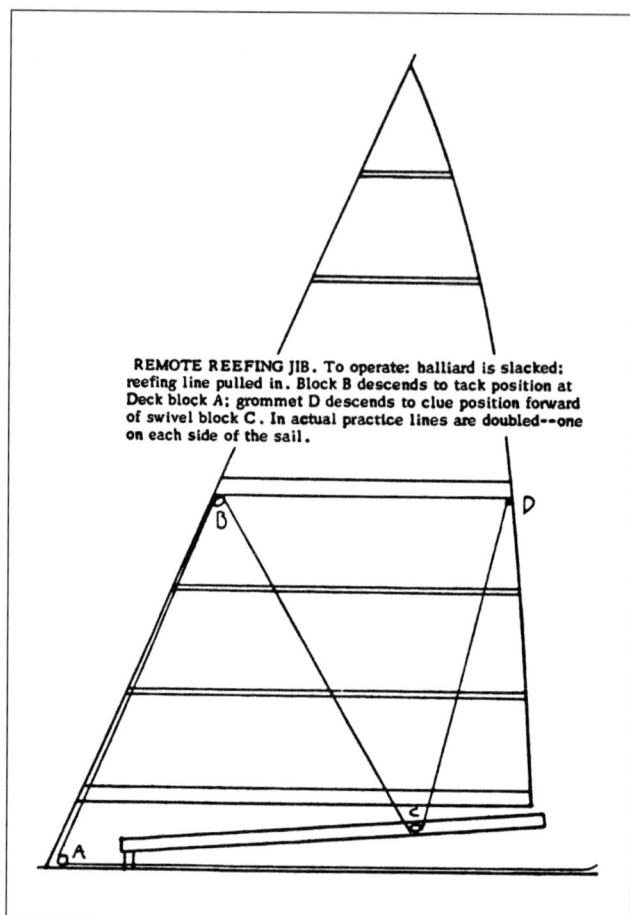

REMOTE REEFING JIB. To operate: halliard is slacked; reefing line pulled in. Block B descends to tack position at Deck block A; grommet D descends to clue position forward of swivel block C. In actual practice lines are doubled--one on each side of the sail.

Fig. P-9 Remote jib reefing system used on "Nimble" from ""Trans-Atlantic Trimaran"– Arthur Piver

decided to take it apart again, put the side hulls on one trailer, the center hull on a second trailer and tow it across the U.S. to Swansea, Mass. There he would reassemble it and sail it from there across the Atlantic to England.

Through the Amateur Yacht Research Society, of which he was a member, he had located two men who signed on to make the Atlantic crossing with him. One was George Benello, a college instructor who was building one of Arthur's 24' designs. The other was Bill Goodman who had already made an Atlantic crossing under sail on a conventional single hulled boat, and who had become interested in Piver's design ideas. These three recruited a fourth man to make the cross country drive and they started on their way.

In Swansea, they reassembled the boat, rerigged it, and after completing their sea trials were ready to load their equipment and supplies for the trip. Rather than use tanks, which would add weight and require hoses and pumps, fresh water was stored aboard in 1 gallon plastic bottles. This also allowed the considerable weight of the fresh water supply to be strategically scattered so as to to help trim the boat. Since there was no refrigeration aboard their food choices were limited to dried and canned stores. Cooking was done on the one burner Primus stove mentioned earlier.

Nimble carried no auxiliary engine and no generator - both heavy and costly pieces of equipment - so there was no renewable source of electric power to operate electronic gear. They had a home-built dry cell powered radio direction finder, an Army "surplus" hand-crank emergency radio which would be of little help

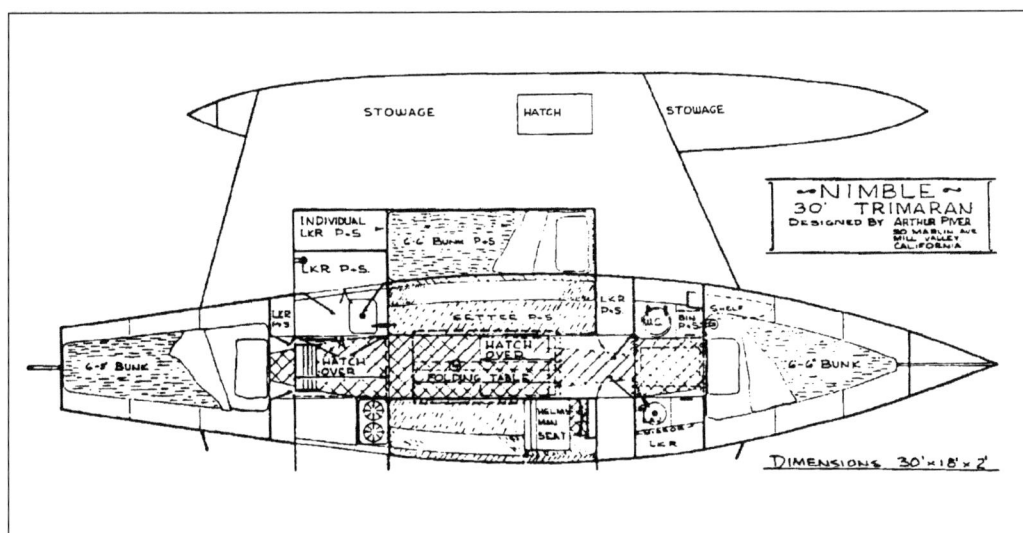

Fig. P-10 Accommodation plan on "Nimble" from "Trans-Atlantic Trimaran"– Arthur Piver

in any real emergency, and a self-winding wrist watch for a chronometer. What George, the navigator, had for a sextant is not mentioned in Piver's account, but judging by the quality level of some of their other equipment one might be excused for wondering. He also does not identify what they had for a compass. They had a pitot tube type marine speedometer that died very shortly after departure, and for a radar reflector they had painted the mast with aluminum paint. Of course, they had no radar, Loran, or GPS.

All in all, as one can readily see (Fig. P-10) crew accommodations were very simple, Crew comfort definitely was not Piver's primary interest.. The helmsman's position was inside the main hull and thus protected from weather and spray and being midships provided far better visibility than the aft cockpit position of the helmsman in most conventional sailboats.

They set out from Narragansett Bay on May 11. It being late spring they hoped, with the help of the normally prevailing west winds, to make a fast passage across the Atlantic. No such luck - by the dawn on the 14th, due to very light winds, they still had not passed Narraganset Light Ship. *Nimble* could sail happily in winds far stronger than many other sailboats her size, but when the wind died she could make little headway. Finally a roaring Nor'wester blew in and they took off running before it. They quickly shortened sail and threw out a long rope astern as a drag to keep the boat from racing down into the troughs between waves, which soon built up to over 25'.

Fairly soon, the stern rope snarled, reducing its drag, so that as the next wave steepened and was about to break–much to their surprise, the boat simply surfed down the wave front ahead of the breaking crest. They then found they could do this regularly in heavy seas. The boat reached speeds of close to 20 knots running down a wave under these conditions. This was the first time Piver had been in open ocean with *Nimble* in gale conditions, so he was more than pleased with the way she handled. His theory of keeping everything as light in weight as possible was certainly being vindicated. The boat rode *over* stormy seas like a cork and was undamaged. A conventional heavy displacement boat crashing through those heavy seas would be more than likely to take a severe beating.

The NW gales continued for ten days, by which time running before them toward the SE, *Nimble* had reached a point about 1000 miles east of the U.S. eastern coast but several hundred miles south of their intended track.

It was now late spring and they had expected the normal SW winds of that season to push them toward the NE so they could to follow the Gulf Stream toward England. Instead, they were now well south of the Gulf Stream about 800 miles west of the Azores, and in light, variable winds. Their hope for a fast passage had evaporated The food supply was beginning to run low, and there were signs of wear on a few pieces of the standing rigging, so it appeared that heading east to the Azores would bring them to the nearest place where they could resupply and make minor repairs. With the light winds now present it took them another eight days to get there.

Since they originally had no intention of going to the Azores, they had no detailed charts for either of these islands, or of their ports. Their first landfall was the island of Flores, after which they passed Corvo on the way to Horta, the major seaport on the island of Fayal. Horta is one of the few major ports in the Azores, and is also a most beautiful and picturesque place built on a sloping hillside. Piver mentioned, only briefly, a detail I personally found particularly impressive about Horta. Nearly all the sidewalks in this town had been laboriously surfaced with beautifully inlaid patterns in mosaic tiles and each street had a different and distinctive tiled design.

They initially intended to stay only a day or two in Horta, but a strong Northeaster blew up while they were there. To sail while it blew meant going directly against the wind in open ocean - not an encouraging prospect, so they waited five days until it blew out. By then it was June 6 and the Slocum Race was due to start June 11. With 1300 miles yet to go they obviously were going to miss the race, but having come this far they opted to complete their crossing anyway.

They left Horta intending to sail north to the latitude of Plymouth and then run down that latitude to their destination. Three days out of England the last gale of the trip hit them, but this time it was from the SW, speeding them on their way. For the final 450 miles of the trip they were in fog and overcast, making it impossible for George, their navigator, to get a sight. In addition, to make his life more challenging, they had no radio receiver, the direction finder had died, they had no log, and no fathometer. His entire equipmentation consisted of his sextant, an ordinary wrist watch, and a shrewd guess.. Up to that time, obviously, Piver had not considered navigational equipment to be of primary importance. Oh well, as we all know, people get in sloppy habits when things are made too easy. Piver apparently didn't want this to happen to George.

Ten days out of Horta, while still in the fog, they met a small Dutch freighter on the same course as theirs. When hailed, the Dutch vessel told them they were only a few miles from the Lizard which, Piver claims, was exactly where George had thought they were. How George determined, this Piver does not say.

At this time they were in fog with very little wind so it took them several hours to finally reach their landfall, and when they did, the lack of wind kept them offshore overnight. However, their Atlantic crossing was successfully completed. They had sailed 3800 miles in 28 days giving them an average of 135 miles a day. Under favorable conditions *Nimble* could sail vastly faster than this, but they had run into long periods of very light wind where no sailboat can go fast. They also went through gales and heavy seas which repeatedly forced them off their intended course. While Piver had not chalked up a speed record he had definitely more than proved the seaworthiness of his design.

They had arrived at Plymough too late for the Slocum Race, and as it happened business problems at home required Piver to return to California as quickly as possible. This being the case, he would not have been able to complete the Slocum Race, anyway.

They were most cordially received in Plymough and the boat aroused considerable curiosity and interest. After a short stay in England, Arthur flew back to Boston, picked up his truck and trailers and drove back to California well pleased with the performance of *Nimble* on the Atlantic crossing. She had broken no speed records, but her speed was quite respectable given the weather and wind conditions she had encountered. Her performance under gale conditions proved that Piver's extreme emphasis on light construction to achieve light weight was practicable, since it allowed the resulting boat to ride high over rough seas rather than punch through them.

LODESTAR

Even before embarking on the trans-Atlantic crossing in *Nimble,* Arthur had already envisioned a 35' trimaran that he called *Lodestar* (P-11) He wanted to use

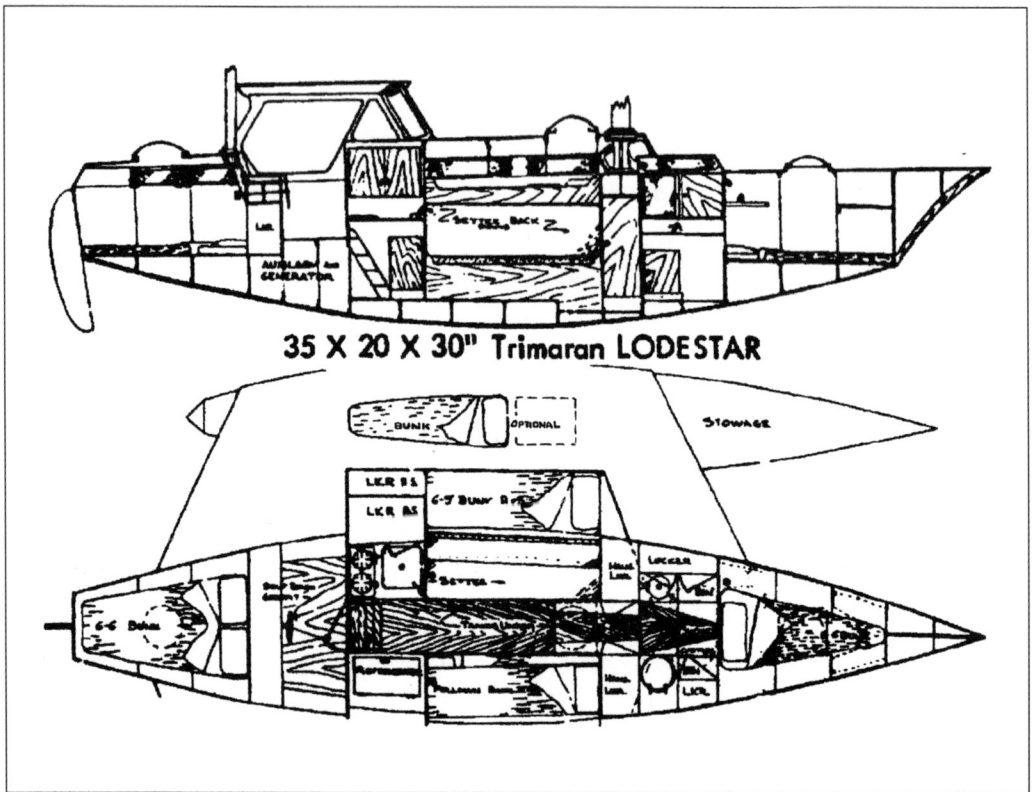

35 X 20 X 30" Trimaran LODESTAR

Fig. P-11 Lodestar Plans: by Arthur Piver

this one for a trans-Pacific crossing. To non-sailors the 5′ difference between a boat 30′ long and one 35′ long may not seem particularly significant. However, by the time the other dimensions of the boat have been enlarged proportionally to the addition in length, the difference in its internal volume becomes huge. This provides space where many additional facilities could be installed to offer far more comfortable accommodations for the crew than were available on *Nimble,* as well as supply improved navigation and communications capabilities. Of course, the fact that more space was available did not mean that Arthur filled it with equipment - far from it!! He continued to carry primitive radio receiving sets and no transmitter. He didn't want the weight of a battery bank and its generator.

Lodestar now carried a small outboard engine that fit in a well in the after part of the central hull. When not in use, which was most of the time, the engine was removed and a plug dropped in its slot to fill the well, and produce a smooth outside hull surface.

A conventional single hull sailboat sailing in strong winds tilts, or heels, to the side allowing part of the wind to spill from the sails, thereby reducing the strain on the sails and on both the standing and running rigging. A trimaran heels very little even in strong winds so Piver devised an ingenious sheet release mechanism (Fig. P-12) so that in a strong wind, the sail would be automatically released before the pressure on the sail and rigging could become great enough to cause damage. Safety, as mentioned earlier, was one of Piver's primary concerns. While he was extremely interested in speed he was by no means reckless. Remember, he intended to be on this boat at sea.

While Arthur was building the *Lodestar*, again at his house, he was helped by a young nearby neighbor, Rich Gerling, who, at the same time was building a 24' *Nugget* (Fig. P-5). The *Lodestar* was finished first and launched. Then, like *Nimble*, test sailed in San Francisco Bay under its varying wind and weather conditions. She performed well and drew considerable interest among local sailors during her shakedown runs. Although by now there were several other trimarans in the area, the entire concept was still a very new one. Not long after the launching of *Lodestar* Rich Gerling finished, launched, and test sailed his *Nugget*, also in San Francisco Bay.

THE CROSSING TO HAWAII

In July 1961, not long after these two trimarans were launched in San Francisco, a sailboat race for conventional single hull cruising racers was scheduled to run from San Pedro in Southern California to Honolulu, Hawaii. Some Southern California sailors had issued a challenge for a simultaneous multi-hull race to Honolulu. This struck Arthur as an ideal way to initiate the Pacific Ocean cruise he had in mind. He assembled a crew of four - one was the same Bill Goodman who had made the Atlantic crossing with him, plus two other local sailing buddies. Meanwhile, Rich Gerling had just finished the *Nugget* and decided to go with his own boat as well, and had picked up a student surfing friend to go with him. Remember, the *Nugget* is only a 24' boat with very minimal accommodations, but Arthur had already sailed one from San Francisco to Acapulco proving it could be used as a cruiser in open ocean.

By the time they both left for the coastal run down to San Pedro, they had received word that all but one of the catamarans which had intended to enter the multi-hull race had dropped out. Rich and the *Nugget* left San Francisco three days ahead of Arthur, but because he made a stop along the way, he arrived at San Pedro only two hours ahead of *Lodestar*.

After their arrival they discovered that the lone 35' catamaran that was going to join them had also dropped out. There were now 42 conventional racers registered for the formal Honolulu Race, so Rich and Arthur decided to sail with them anyway to see how the boats would compare. The trimarans carried no

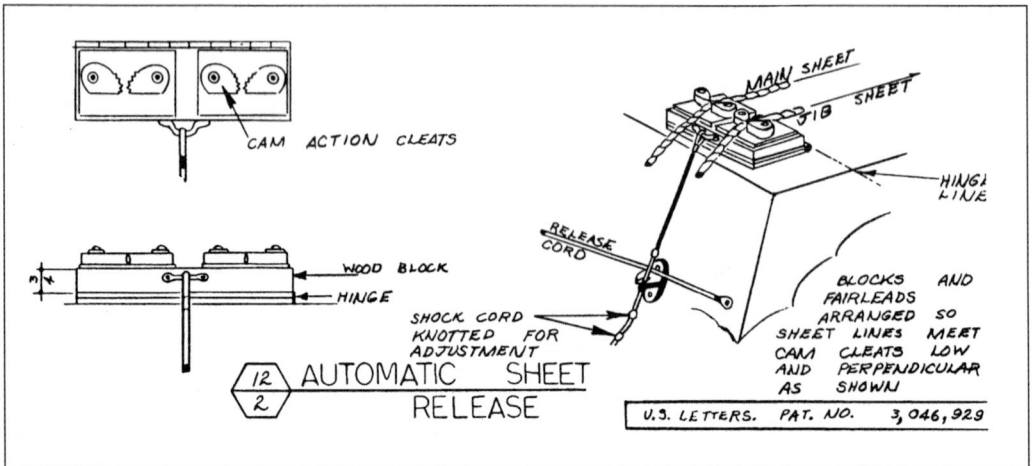

Fig. P-12 Automatic Sheet Release designed by Arthur Piver

spinakers or other light canvas, and since it was mid-summer, winds along this route could be expected to vary from very light to moderate. Only if the winds were fairly strong could the trimarans expect to keep up with racers that were able to hoist acres of light canvas when little wind is available.

The trimarans started a few minutes after the formal start of the racing fleet. *Nugget* had a serious problem the first night out. Rich was driving his boat hard and not noticed until later – the deck hatch cover on the lee outboard hull came off, leaving that hull open to the seas which quickly filled it. He and his crewman decided to return the 60 miles back to San Pedro to repair it properly, rather than continue with a makeshift cover. Two days later they again departed for Honolulu.

Meanwhile, at first there were good winds allowing *Lodestar* to clock 660 miles during the first three days keeping her up with the leaders in the race. The crew on *Lodestar* knew this because they kept up with the progress of the race through radio reports. They had two dry cell powered receivers aboard this time: a radio direction finder built from a kit (Arthur's eagle eye on cost again), and a small transistor multi-band receiver. But they still had no transmitter. Why Arthur never carried a marine transceiver aboard is a mystery he never adequately explained.

The wind died and without light air sails, their progress slowed at this point considerably. With the fleet running away from them they lost interest in the race, shut off the radio, and concentrated on enjoying the trip. As they approached Hawaii they set the RDF on Makapuu Point, Oahu and deliberately set a course that would put it a bit to their starboard. They overdid the offset, and during their last night out darn near barked up on Molokai instead. When they sailed into Alai Wai Yacht Basin most of the racers had already arrived. However, to their delight they found that although it had taken them all of 15 days to get there six of the racers, although well equipped with proper light air sails, had still not arrived

Since neither boat carried two way radios, Piver had no way of knowing when he arrived in Honolulu that *Nugget* had lost two days because of the hatch cover accident. He had expected *Nugget* to show up about 5 days after *Lodestar*, and when the five days had come and gone, there was considerable nervousness on *Lodestar* until *Nugget* finally appeared two days later. Except for the hatch cover incident they'd had a slow, but uneventful passage.

Arthur's wife and children had come out by ship so they all enjoyed a Hawaiian vacation for several weeks. Arthur then decided he wanted to cruise to some of the other Hawaiian islands before returning to the Mainland so both boats went to the Big Island, and then to Maui. On returning to Honolulu, Piver decided that rather than sail *Lodestar* back home he would leave it there for the winter so he could then start from Honolulu for Tahiti, the following spring. He wanted first to go south to Tahiti and then turn southwest, to complete his Pacific crossing at New Zealand.

By now his trimaran designs were beginning to receive widespread acceptance among sailors in the U.S. and also in various foreign countries, as well. By now not only small daysailers and small cruisers were being built, but also larger boats ranging from 40' to 60. Some problems were now arising with the larger ones because any sailboat in the 40' to 60' range definitely needs an auxiliary engine, if only for manoevering purposes. At the same time, Piver wanted no permanent propellers and shafts installed. He had designed fast, light *sailboats* and felt the drag from these projections would ruin the sailing characteristics of his hulls. Consequently, he favored outboards that could be pulled or tilted up out of the way, or inboard-outboard installations that again allowed the propeller to be tilted up out of the way when sailing. To his dismay, several larger trimarans were built with standard marine inboard engine installations with fixed shafts and propellers. He was horrified - and as he had feared, they did not perform well. The combination of propeller drag and the added weight of the engine and fuel tanks defeated the main purposes of his design - speed based on light weight and smooth hull surfaces.

SOUTH TO TAHITI

When he returned to San Francisco, Piver found a good deal of trimaran building was under way, including some very large ones. One of these was 55' long with a 30' beam. Not many yacht clubs could find a berth for that one!!

One of the boats under construction, the *Nimble*, was being built by a doctor who lived quite close to Arthur's home so Arthur observed and probably helped out from time to time. It became apparent that the doctor expected to be taught sailing as well, because when he heard Arthur was about to leave for the South Pacific he asked who would teach him how to sail his boat. Arthur answered, "OK I'll teach you - lets take a cruise - to Hawaii." They signed on a third fellow and that was exactly what they did. They had a smooth passage, the doctor learned a good deal about sailing, and Piver came back to his *Lodestar* in Hawaii.

The first job was to clean *Lodestar's* bottom where a heavy growth of seaweed had built up in his absence. That accomplished, Piver then turned to completing the interior of the boat which had been rather sketchily done before departing from San Francisco the previous year. When exterior and interior were finished to his satisfaction, it was time to take on stores for the trip to Tahiti. His crew from the previous summer rejoined him.

The run from Hawaii to Tahiti would be in the vicinity of 3,000 miles because it was necessary to detour outside the area of upcoming atomic bomb tests. Piver estimated that even under adverse conditions they should be there in no more than a month's time. As a standard procedure he started every voyage with food and water for twice the estimated time at sea. He still carried his fresh water in 1 gallon plastic jugs, rather than install a tank. These jugs allowed the very considerable weight of the fresh water supply to be distributed through the center hull at the start and adjusted as the voyage proceeded. In addition, the empty jugs could be capped and kept in the side floats for emergency flotation.

By the time they put out to sea the winds had deserted them, and they drifted more than they sailed to their favorite Hawaiian harbor, Lahaina on Maui, to wait for the Trades to pick up. They were there a week before the Trades came back in earnest to start them on their way. The wind then picked up in force. The boat was now fully loaded and they started driving it as hard as they could, which turned out to be too hard. They were on the verge of reefing the main when it tore loose from the boom. Rather than put back in to Maui, Piver decided to press on and repair the sail as best he could himself.

They first worked their way east avoiding the atomic test area, and then turned south across the doldrums. There, they ran into severe squally conditions that continued for five days. On the sixth day, the wind died and the Equatorial Current pushed them 50 miles back to the west. When they finally pushed through to the south of the doldrums, they were in the belt of the Southeast Trades which meant they had to sail against the wind toward Tahiti. Although they were now out of the doldrum belt of severe squalls, they ran into a lot of cloudy, rainy weather along with head winds and seas. This was not a very comfortable run.

Finally, as they approached the Tuamoto Archipelago they were well off toward the west end of the island chain. Their first landfall there was Rangiroa Atoll. As they sailed down along the lee side of the atoll they briefly found calm seas and a fair wind. All too soon they passed the south end, emerged from the shelter of the atoll, and were again hit by both wind and sea. Since they now had enough easting they were able to turn their course more to the south which considerably eased conditions. As luck would have it, they arrived off Tahiti in late afternoon and reached Papeete that night. The town is on the west side of the island, the lee side, so as they approached, they entered the wind shadow of the island and ran out of wind. They finally made their entrance using the trusty little outboard motor and found a Bastille Day celebration in progress, so that first night, even though anchored, they got little sleep.

At that time, Papeete was an inexpensive place to go ashore and play so they spent 2 weeks doing a few repairs and playing. Arthur then received word that the first 45' boat of his design was due to be launched in the U.S., so he took a flight home to check it out. When he arrived he found to his dismay that it had a marine diesel engine installed with a standard strut, shaft, and 3 blade propeller. This was exactly the type of engine installation he had said should NOT be used, and as he feared, the boat was sluggish under sail. A week later he returned to Papeete.

ON TO NEW ZEALAND

Arthur now found that his crew had to return home. After a delay due to French Polynesian government objections, his crew were finally able to return home, and he looked around for someone to continue his cruise with him. About that time, a large U.S. schooner, the *Wanderer* which had formerly been owned by Sterling Hayden, the actor, pulled into port and discharged five of its crew. After further fussing with the French authorities, Arthur finally signed on one of the young crew members from *Wanderer* and was then ready to leave for Raritonga. He'd had enough trouble getting permission for his original crew of two to leave Papeete, and then to sign on his new crewman, that he had had quite enough legal problems with the French Polynesian authorities, and couldn't get away fast enough.

Piver and his new crewman, Johnny, had good wind for all of the first half hour after departing Papeete. Then the wind died. Light winds then doomed them to a slow passage, six days to go about 600 miles. After having previously endured so much really bad weather at sea, he decided he wouldn't complain.

When reaching Raritonga they decided to motor into harbor since the wind was so weak. The little outboard started on the second pull, but from lack of use the throttle had frozen. They could not advance the engine speed beyond idle, so they slowly crept in to port.

They spent several days relaxing, shopping for stores, exploring the island, and making friends at the local sailing club. Raritonga is one of the Cook Islands under the control of New Zealand, and they had better relations with the authorities here than they had with the French in Tahiti. Since New Zealand controlled this island they had expected to be able to obtain current charts here of the waters around New Zealand. No such luck. The only chart available was a duplicate of the one they already had of Auckland so they had no choice but to make do with it.

They decided to leave as soon as the Trade Winds blew up again. Piver had cleaned the outboard throttle so when they left–under engine–it operated perfectly this time. The Cook Islands are well within the Trade Wind belt so they thought they could expect several days of E to SE winds to help them on their way. That hope was a bit optimistic. They had a few good days, then, as before, they ran into all kinds of weather from calms to gales. One day at noon, after a nightlong gale, they found they had covered 215 miles since the last noon sight. Since they had been surfing large following seas for most of the night, Piver felt they had covered most of the distance in only about 10 hours. This meant that their average speed during those hours was over 20 knots, which is more than phenomenal in a sailboat.

On arrival in Auckland, *Lodestar* was met by John Malitte, who was editor of the New Zealand yachting magazine "Sea Spray". Malitte was really enthusiastic about trimarans. He had long been in correspondence with Piver and had given trimarans considerable publicity in his publication. Also, he had a 30 footer himself. Because of Malitte's publicity, Piver found several trimarans of his design in the water, and many more in the process of construction.

A boat show was in progress when Piver arrived in Auckland, and because of the local interest in trimarans he was asked if they could put *Lodestar* in that show. Piver agreed, and that same day the boat was hauled, transported across town, and placed on exhibition where it was the center of a great deal of interest, as was Piver himself.

By this time a good many trimarans had been built in New Zealand based on his designs. He was horrified to find that a number of those built by professional boatbuilders had not properly followed his specifications. They apparently thought the construction looked too light, so they beefed it up. The lively performance of Piver's designs was based on the light weight of his boats. This added weight thus degraded their performance. On the other hand, the ones built correctly by following his designs performed beautifully.

THE ROARING FORTIES

After about a month in a place where a happy Arthur Piver could feel his boat designs and his basic multi-hull philosophy were really appreciated, he and his crewman, Johnny, decided they would continue their cruise by heading out across the Roaring Forties to South America. As every mariner well knows this is certainly one of the most inhospitable and dangerous areas on the entire planet for any vessel particularly a small sailboat. However, in these dangerous conditions Piver saw a unique opportunity. The very strong prevailing westerly winds behind him would raise huge seas. Piver expected to be able to surf these swells at 20 to 30 knots. This, he hoped, would allow his boat to set a new sailboat record for a 24 hour run.

Fig. P-13 Johnny and Arthur depart Auckland for the "Roaring Forties" on "Lodestar

The plan was to sail SE from Auckland deep into the Roaring 40s to the Chatham Islands. There they would await the development of the kind of seas Piver wanted to use to surf from there to South America—a truly formidable prospect!

After extensive preparation they departed Auckland (Fig. P-13) on a day with a fine, moderate breeze. That night the weather turned windy, squally, and rainy. During the night they suddenly found themselves in the midst of an area of off-shore rocks where none were supposed to be. The next morning, after clawing their way out of this rocky area, Arthur discovered the 18° navigational error he had made that put them there. After two more days of pounding in high winds and seas, the jib club broke. Since they had no idea what might be available on the Chathams they decided to put back to New Zealand to repair it.

At this point, with the prospect of another delay, Arthur seriously began to wonder whether he hadn't already been away too long from his California business. He decided to return home and leave the boat to "Captain" Johnny, who wanted to go ahead and try for the record on his own. Johnny found two eager fellows to go with him, but their try turned out to be rather anticlimactic. They started in early December, summer in the southern hemisphere, and had mild weather almost all the way.

CONCLUSION

Although he was never formally trained as a naval architect Arthur Piver was an original, inventive, and ingenious designer. His boats were relatively inexpensive to build, light in weight, non-capsizable, non-heeling, non-rolling, with shallow draft, and fast. In addition, since they sailed upright the crew would be far more comfortable in a seaway than in a conventional single-hull cruising sailboat pounding along and heeled at 20 or 25 degrees.

In general, sailors are a very conservative lot and very suspicious of unproven innovations. As a result, many experienced mariners initially viewed his boats as utterly unsafe. They were far too lightly built. However, Piver had absolute faith in the soundness of his designs. and had the courage to prove his point by sailing them through whatever wind and sea conditions both the Atlantic and Pacific Oceans could throw at him. His boats were eminently seaworthy as Piver showed by making both ocean crossings in them.

By the mid 1960s, many hundreds of Piver's boats had been built by amateur builders based on the plans he sold. He deliberately kept the plans as simple as possible so that an average amateur, who was not a trained shipwright could build his boats. As long as they didn't insert too many of their own ideas into the project the amateur builders came out OK. When the private builder, or worse yet a professional boatyard, decided the framing or the plywood skin looked too light and obviously should be heavied up they defeated Piver's emphasis on light weight, and the boat's performance suffered.

The trimarans enjoyed a period of considerable popularity in the 1960s, but gradually fell out of favor. Unfortunately, they had several disadvantages. Due to their huge beam, few marinas or yacht clubs could offer them dockage. In addition, the average cruising sailor had become accustomed to a good deal more creature comfort than Piver's light weight allowed: such as two-way radio communication, elaborate electronic navigational equipment and entertainment gear, and refrigeration, all of which require a heavy battery bank, plus generating capability. Next, add the weight of propane cooking facilities: a stove and a propane tank plus hot and cold fresh water capability which means a sink, tank, hoses, and pump—a lot more weight. All that added weight defeats Piver's emphasis on lightness.

Furthermore, except for very small sailboats, an auxiliary engine is necessary to get in and out of most marinas and small boat harbors. For this purpose the small and mid-sized trimarans successfully used an outboard motor that could be tipped up or removed when under sail because Piver wanted no permanent propellers, shafts, or struts under his hulls. Unfortunately, a completely successful solution to the auxiliary engine question for the larger trimarans—50 to 60 footers—does not appear to have been found.

As the popularity of trimarans has faded Arthur Piver and his innovative work have been largely forgotten. Also, unfortunately forgotten, is the fact that by making both Atlantic and Pacific Ocean crossings in what the establishment viewed as his "dangerously lightly built" trimarans, he was able to prove conclusively that they were entirely safe after all!!

CHAPTER 7

A Voyage of 17,000 Miles Around "The Horn" in a 25' Sloop

The light described in this chanty lies a short distance west of Sparrow's home port of New London.

FAULKNER'S LIGHT

The island known as Faulkner's sits stately in the Sound
Mas san com mock was her name back then a place where hawks abound
They put a light upon her in eighteen oh and two
To guide through storm and fog so thick to save a ship and crew

Chorus
The Sound is cold as a place can be when the wind she blows a gale
It'll take the beat right from your heart when you're workin under sail
Don't let the light go out, my friend, as they cry with all their might
Keep lookin through the sleet and rain, for sure it's Faulkner's light

Captain Brooks was a family man who looked to settle down
He took his wife and children out to that rocky crown
He labored there for thirty one years with life and limb at will
He was praised by friends and presidents, his legend lingers still

Many a man has come and gone, but Faulkner's she still stands
A monument to the history of those who worked off the land
But time is now her enemy, as nature takes its toll
It must be saved. It must be done!! is the crying of her soul

When tied up at a marina in her homeport of New London, Conn., or when out under sail anywhere nearby where small sailboats normally go, there is nothing strange or unusual looking about *Sparrow*. (Fig. SP-1). Her hull has the lines of a very traditional full keeled sailboat scaled down to a length of 25'. Her compact sailing rig looks entirely traditional as well. (Fig. SP-2) What is extraordinary about *this* particular small boat is not how it looks, but where it has been.

Why on earth would two *seemingly* normal fellows, living *seemingly* normal lives in the quiet old seaport of New London, Connecticut even think of taking

Fig. SP-1 Sparrow under way at sea

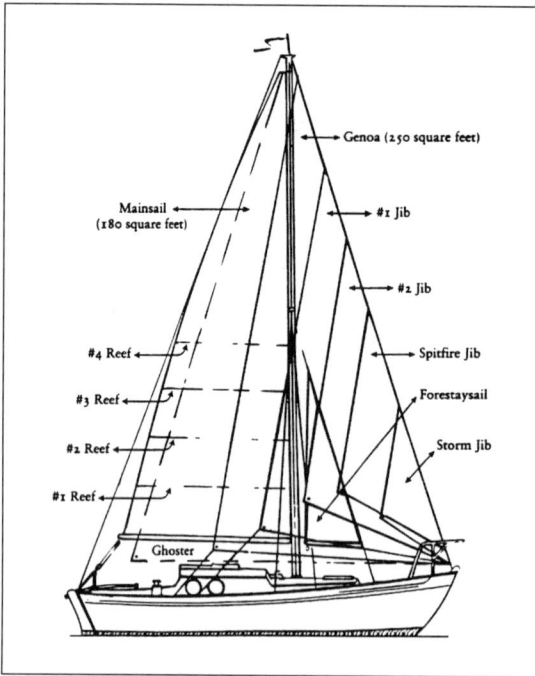

Mainsail (180 square feet)
Genoa (250 square feet)
#1 Jib
#2 Jib
#4 Reef
Spitfire Jib
#3 Reef
Forestaysail
#2 Reef
Storm Jib
#1 Reef
Ghoster

Fig. SP-2 Sail plan for Sparrow

this tiny 25' sailboat down to the most miserable latitudes on earth, the Roaring 40s and Screaming 50s of the Southern Ocean, to then sail it around Cape Horn? Why would they even *think* of it, much less go ahead and *do* it?

The voyage of the *Sparrow* around Cape Horn is particularly extraordinary because this unquestionably exceptional feat was accomplished by two, up to then, rather unremarkable men. The pair were David and Daniel Hays, a father and his son. At the time, the dad, David, was a Harvard graduate and a college instructor. His son Daniel was a recent college graduate who admits to a rather mediocre academic record, and at that time, no very clear idea as to what he wanted to do after he was out of school.

At the opposite extreme, David was well established in his field professionally. However, his father before him had been an enthusiastic yachtsman, and had succeeded in infecting him with the same enthusiasm. Consequently, David had been around boats since childhood, and grew up reading many of the famous sea stories. Since childhood he had been particularly fascinated by tales of passages around "The Horn" under sail. He read not only of Magellan and Drake, but the many others who came after them, and he dreamt often of what it must have been like to make that grueling passage on the early square-rigged sailing ships. That fascination finally had matured into a determination to some day make that passage himself. Both David and his son Daniel had built up quite an extensive range of experience in sailing small boats for many years. On one occasion the two had sailed a 22′ catboat back to New London from the Bahamas so they also had experience both at making a run in open ocean on a small boat, and in doing it together. Critical to this project was the fact that David had previously owned a 38′ sailboat designed by the eminant British naval architect Laurent Giles. He had sailed it from Britain to the Canary Islands, and from there across the Atlantic to New York. During this experience of making an ocean crossing under sail he had come to particularly admire the sailing qualities of Laurent Giles′ designs.

Neither David nor Daniel had anything in the way of extensive professional nautical training prior to deciding to sail a small boat down into the "roaring forties" and "screaming fifties" of the Southern Ocean. On the other hand, although David and Daniel were not highly trained professional mariners, they certainly had considerable amateur experience on small sailboats, and subsequently proved themselves, in the course of this voyage, to be thoroughly competent as both sailors and navigators.

Prior to sailing they wisely and carefully did their homework by studying the winds, currents, and weather conditions they would encounter, and very sensibly decided to make their passage around the Horn from west to east so as to have the ferocious winds and seas of the screaming fifties behind, rather than ahead of them. Also, they timed their arrival at the Horn for the middle of the southern hemisphere summer so as to encounter the mildest possible weather conditions when they got there. Of course, "mildest possible" in those latitudes can still be quite boisterous.

THE BOAT

David says the idea of making the trip started with him. According to his story he suggested it to Dan one day out of a clear sky, and Dan quickly answered, "It sounds like a great idea—let′s do it."

The very first decision the Hays′ had to make was the selection of the boat they would use for their voyage. The design they finally picked was a slightly modified version of a 25′ midget ocean cruising boat Laurent Giles originally designed in 1936. David′s previous experience with owning and sailing a Giles designed boat gave him the greatest confidence in anything Giles had designed.

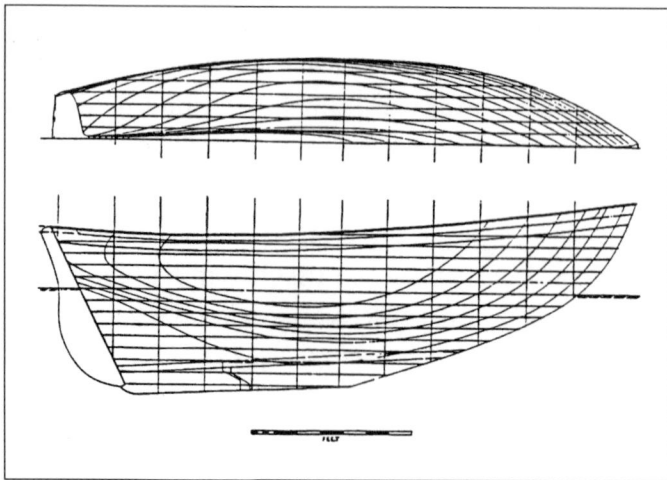

Fig. SP-3 Sparrow's *Traditional workboat hull lines*

Why a midget ocean cruiser to go around the Horn? In the first place, with their modest finances there was no way they could afford a large ocean cruiser and all the elaborate equipment that would go with it. Furthermore, they decided that even if they could afford it they did not really want a large boat. Rather, what they really wanted was a vessel small enough so that either one of them could readily douse the sails and manage the boat single handed if necessary in an emergency.

The Giles design they settled on was a class called the *Vertue*. She was 25' 7 1/2 " in length and had a draft of 4' 6". The lines of the hull were a scaled down version of a full keeled, well proven traditional working sailboat design (Fig. SP-3). By 1982, when the two decided to get a *Vertue,* that design had already built up an extremely impressive ocean cruising record. Back in 1938, shortly after the first boats of the class were built, *Vertues* made a number of open sea passages around the British Isles and across the Channel to Spain and back, an area noted for very changeable and boisterous weather and sea conditions.

In 1950 a stock *Vertue* with only slight modifications made a trans-Atlantic crossing the hard way, from east to west against the prevailing winds. She went from the Lizard, at the southern tip of England, to New York in 47 1/2 days, 23 days of which were bucking head winds. In addition, 200 miles north of Bermuda she was hit by a hurricane. In spite of all this she finally arrived safely in New York. This voyage certainly tested the seaworthiness of the design.

In 1953 a *Vertue* built in Hong Kong was sailed from Singapore to England via Cape of Good Hope. That voyage took 140 sailing days and covered about 14,000 miles. Then in 1963 a boat named *Cardinal Vertue* was sailed from Auckland to Buenos Aires around Cape Horn, so by 1982, when the Hays' father and son got the notion to sail a 25' *Vertue* around the Horn, the idea wasn't as foolhardy as it might at first appear.

By then the *Vertue* design had been proven repeatedly on long ocean passages, and although at that time it was not well known among U.S. yachtsmen, it definitely was known to David Hays because of his personal experience with Giles' work. He also knew that although it was an old design, *Vertue* boats were still being built at a yard in Portsmouth, England, so he took his son Dan there to see it. When they arrived they found the yard was having financial difficulties, but they did have an unfinished hull available.

The original *Vertue* hulls were of wood construction, however, by this time, the hulls were being made of fibreglass. Compared to fibreglass constructing a wood boat took too long and was too labor intensive. In addition, ship's carpenters capable of building such a hull were, by then, difficult to find. Another advantage of fibreglass, in addition to ease of construction, is that it is totally impervious to shipworms, or teredoes, the marine wood borers that were the bane of the great wooden ships of old, and are still the bane of wood boats today. In addition, fibreglass is also impervious to the other major enemy of wood boats–rot.

After seeing the unfinished hull they decided to go with the *Vertue*, partly because they could afford it, partly because it was small enough to meet their size criteria, but as much as anything else, because they simply fell in love with it. Those of us who have put to sea in small sailboats know the feeling that a particular boat is *the* right one, and that was the feeling they had about this hull. After the decision was made they ordered an unfinished fibreglass hull to be delivered to them at New London. They then spent two years of work completing, refining and fitting her out.

At the time they ordered the hull they were also given the plans for the boat so they could begin to make parts for her interior even before the hull arrived in New London. After she arrived they kept her tied up in a small marina where they worked on her nights and weekends in order to fit her out exactly the way they felt it should be done, for the voyage they intended to make.

In the process they had to remove some parts of the interior work that had already been installed by the manufacturer. This was necessary in order to reenforce the connections of the deck to the hull, and also the deck attachments for the shrouds supporting the mast because they felt these original connections were not sufficiently strong. Although the hull, as delivered, had a Lloyd's rating, meaning that everything as supplied was warranted to be of the highest quality, they found that these and a number of other items had been glossed over and/or entirely omitted. Whether the manufacturer's financial troubles had anything to do with these defects was never made clear.

Undismayed, they persisted. The type, size, and placement of every winch, cleat, and deck fitting was carefully thought out for maximum safety and convenience, as was the size and location of every storage locker and access opening. Here, all of the extensive knowledge gathered during their prior experiences sailing on small boats came into play, plus whatever they could learn from other sailors they knew. Many lively discussions and arguments occurred before the boat was finally declared complete (Fig. SP-4).

Early on, they had decided not to install an engine but to rely entirely on sail. An engine plus its fuel tanks would take up far too much badly needed space, and even if they had an engine it would only be of use entering and leaving port. It is almost impossible for a boat this size to carry enough fuel to motor any distance in open ocean.

Solar panels and a storage battery bank were installed to power radios, but high tech navigational electronics were not included. Radar is not a big navigational help on a small boat in open ocean and Loran C covered very little of the route they intended to take. Today's worldwide GPS system was not yet available. Celestial navigation and dead reckoning had guided the many others before them around the Horn, and they were certain it would be entirely adequate for them as well. Both men knew how to do celestial navigation, but from their record of the voyage Dan appears to have been the primary navigator.

The amount of time David could take off from his work for the voyage was limited so it was decided that with help from various friends, Daniel would sail the boat as far as Jamaica. There, David would join him and the two would then proceed on together.

NEW LONDON TO JAMAICA

On July 14, 1984 Dan put to sea from New London accompanied by a totally inexperienced aspiring playwrite friend from New York, and a kitten handed to him just as they left. Prior to this, *Sparrow* had only been sailed for a few hours around the harbor so this first sail south along the U.S. East Coast would actually be her shakedown cruise.

Between changeable, and at times boisterous, weather plus intermittent seasickness, the first few days running south along the coast were by no means comfortable. Dan and his crewmate Glenn worked their way slowly south to Swansboro, N. Carolina where Glenn, not at all reluctantly, left to return to New York. From there, Dan worked his way down to Charleston where he picked up another friend, this time an experienced sailor, who helped him take the boat the rest of the way to Florida.

They put in at Cape Canaveral where Dan knew some friends who had a house and dock where he could tie up. Up to now the cruise had shown that a few

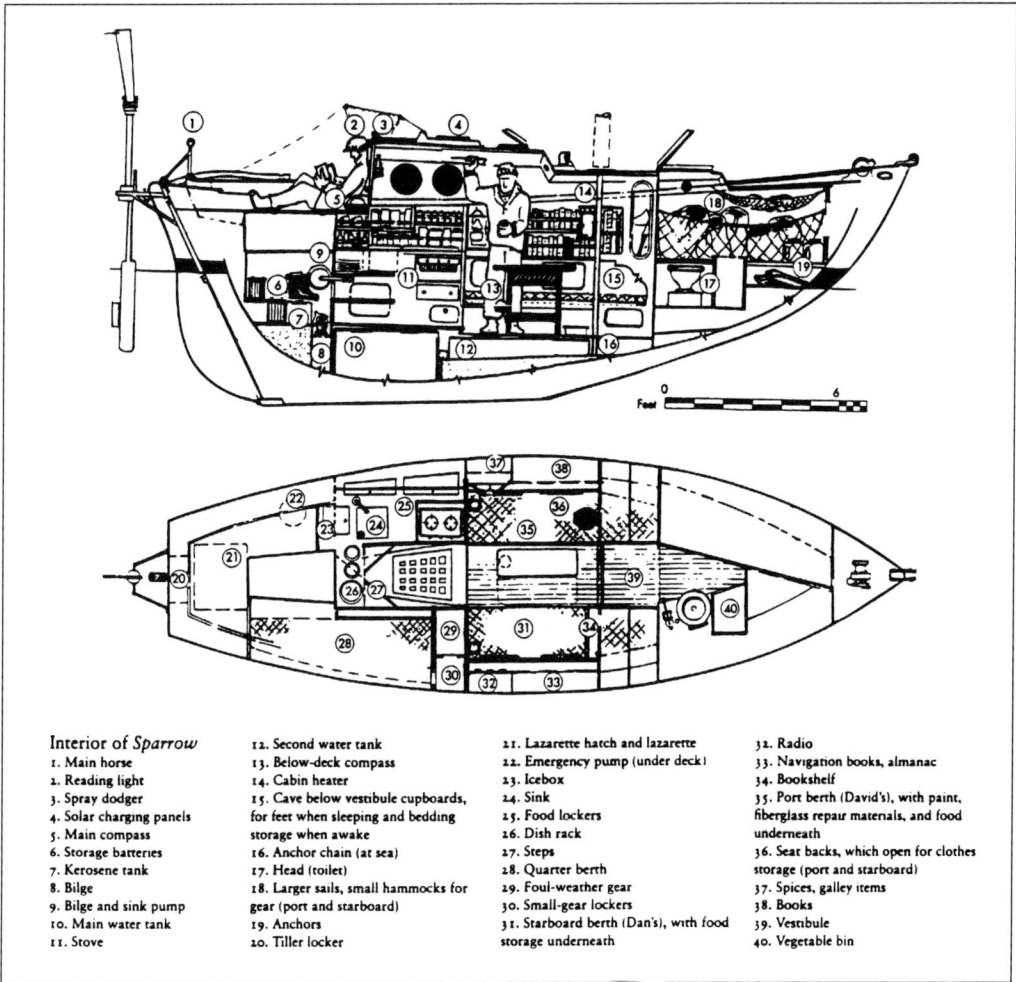

Fig. SP-4 Interior Layout of the Sparrow
from "My Old Man and the Sea"– D. & D. Hayes

Interior of *Sparrow*

1. Main horse	12. Second water tank	21. Lazarette hatch and lazarette	32. Radio
2. Reading light	13. Below-deck compass	22. Emergency pump (under deck)	33. Navigation books, almanac
3. Spray dodger	14. Cabin heater	23. Icebox	34. Bookshelf
4. Solar charging panels	15. Cave below vestibule cupboards,	24. Sink	35. Port berth (David's), with paint,
5. Main compass	for feet when sleeping and bedding	25. Food lockers	fiberglass repair materials, and food
6. Storage batteries	storage when awake	26. Dish rack	underneath
7. Kerosene tank	16. Anchor chain (at sea)	27. Steps	36. Seat backs, which open for clothes
8. Bilge	17. Head (toilet)	28. Quarter berth	storage (port and starboard)
9. Bilge and sink pump	18. Larger sails, small hammocks for	29. Foul-weather gear	37. Spices, galley items
10. Main water tank	gear (port and starboard)	30. Small-gear lockers	38. Books
11. Stove	19. Anchors	31. Starboard berth (Dan's), with food	39. Vestibule
	20. Tiller locker	storage underneath	40. Vegetable bin

interior refinements would be helpful so a few days were spent getting them done. A girl named Carol who he refers to as a "California Valley Girl" then showed up to accompany him as far as Nassau.

Their first objective was Miami. Leaving there they went past a waterspout and through several periods of dead calm before they managed to inch across the Gulf Stream to the Bahamas. As they were entering the harbor at Nassau the wind died, so for a time they were sailing at 3 knots, against a current of 3 knots making them almost completely stationary. Most sailors have encountered the contrary demon that causes this wind, fair and steady out at sea, to suddenly fail when you sail into port without an engine. In this case a powerboat saw their predicament and finally helped them in to the anchorage.

Dan then dropped his "Valley Girl" at the airport and returned to take *Sparrow* single-handed on down through the Bahamas toward Jamaica where he was to pick up his father. On the way while he was drifting becalmed in the Windward Passage between Cuba and Haiti, he was spotted by the U.S. Coast Guard who apparently thought this lone sailboat was highly suspicious A helicopter circled overhead while a 150' cutter charged up and put over an inflatable with a boarding party of 6 armed crewmen who came storming onto little *Sparrow,* looking for drugs. When they failed to find any contraband they settled for giving him a citation because he had no bell aboard. According to the Rules of the Road, U.S. vessels are required to carry a bell to be rung while at anchor, in a fog. The fact that there was absolutely no possibility of his anchoring in a fog anywhere in that area wasn't the point! When I sailed in that area we used to have a saying "If you see fog - clean your glasses!"

FROM JAMAICA THROUGH PANAMA TO GALAPAGOS

Not only did David appear on schedule in Jamaica but also Leonora Hays, Dan's mother, and an aunt, plus his sister and her boyfriend all showed up. Several days were spent exploring Jamaica and doing various last minute jobs on the boat. After the family had flown out, it was finally time to get under way. Just what these family members thought about David and Daniel's intention of sailing that small boat around Cape Horn remains unreported.

The trip from Jamaica to Panama was David and Daniel's first leg together, and was uneventful except for David's various bouts with seasickness and sunburn. After they finally had the isthmus in sight, it took them another three days to finally creep into Cristobal at the Atlantic end of the Panama Canal, due to extremely light and variable winds. Again—almost no wind and, of course, no engine as they attempted to enter port. Once inside, with the help of a friendly live-aboard, they found a slip where they could tie up.

Cristobal is by no means a scenic tropical paradise. It is a hot, dirty, and rather seamy tropical port town with several rather poor restaurants, some suppliers catering to passing boat people, and a number of bars and establishments of the evening catering to canal workers and local Panamanians. It is a place most people would just as soon get in and out of as quickly as possible. In David and Dan's case "as quickly as possible" turned out to be about a week.

Taking a small boat through the Canal becomes rather complicated with a great many forms and regulations involved. After the paperwork is finally completed the small boat will, of course, have to lock through with one or more large ships. Furthermore, there is no way *Sparrow* will be allowed to hoist sail anywhere in the Canal, so they had to rent an outboard motor and work out a tem-

Fig. SP-5 Entering the first of the Gatun Locks from Cristobal at daybreak.
Passing through the Canal will take the rest of the day.
(Illustration: Author)

porary bracket on which to mount it. When they transited the canal there were six people aboard: the helmsman (David), the required Canal Pilot (an employee of the Canal Authority), three linesmen (Dan and two others), plus the owner of the outboard who also operated it. The Canal (Fig. SP-5) is approximately 50 miles long from the Atlantic to the Pacific side and on average vessels make the transit in approximately 8 1/2 hours. so it took just about a full day for *Sparrow* to get from Cristobal to Panama City, another port that leaves a good deal to be desired. After two uninspiring days there, they finally headed out into the Pacific, bound for the Galapagos Islands.

Sparrow now headed down into the equatorial doldrums where winds are generally light and variable, with frequent heavy rain squalls. By working their way down the coasts of Colombia and Equador to a point a bit south of Guayaquil they planned to turn west and pick up the west-flowing South Equatorial Current to help them on their way.

The run south along the coast turned out to be both difficult and uncomfortable with both winds and seas against them. By the time they were six days out of Panama they were still over 100 miles north of where they had planned to turn into the west bound current, but they were so tired of fighting their way south that, in exasperation, they turned west.

By now, understandably, you are wondering if their objective is Cape Horn, why on earth did they go way out west to the Galapagos Islands instead of simply sailing south down the coast of South America? As mentioned earlier the Messers Hays had done their homework and among other things, had studied wind patterns and ocean currents. If they continued down the west coast of South America the strong, cold, north flowing current variously known as the Peru Current or the Humboldt Current (Fig. SP-6), would be against them all the way. Close to the Equator off the coast of Equador, that current turns west to become the South Equatorial Current. By coasting south from Panama they can meet this current where it turns west and use it to help them out to the Galapagos.

From there they planned to sail further on out to the southwest to Easter

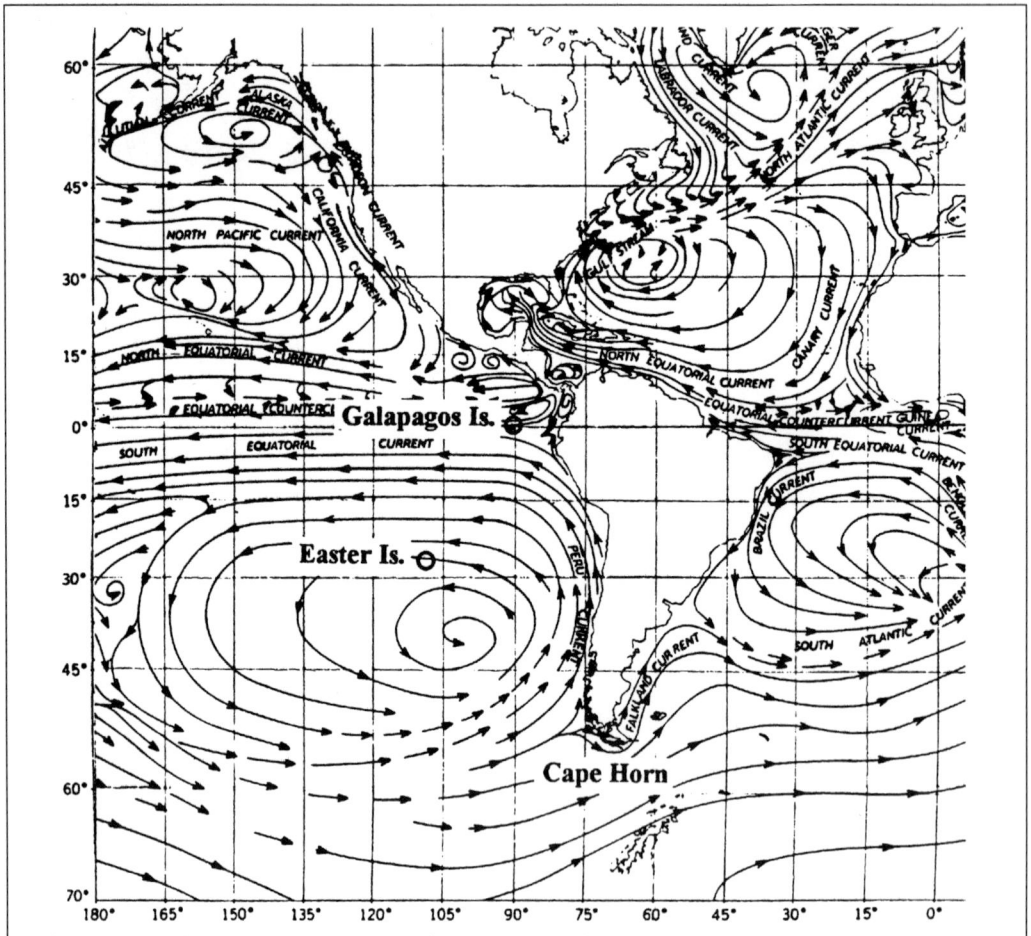

Fig. SP-6 Ocean Currents
from "The American Practical Navigator" – Bowditch

Island using the southeast Trade Winds and the help of ocean currents that will be fairly weak and from the east. Then when they leave there to go southeastward toward Cape Horn working their way southward, they should get help from the increasingly stronger winds and currents from the west.

Close to the Equator, on the way to the Galapagos where winds are normally light and variable, *Sparrow* appears to have run into a bit of good luck. After they turned west toward the Galapagos they had good, steady easterly Trade Winds enabling them to clock about 145 miles a day. They made the run from Panama to the Galapagos island of San Cristobal in 12 days. Luckily, heading west at a slightly higher latitude than they had originally intended turned out to have been a good move.

GALAPAGOS TO EASTER ISLAND

In an attempt to minimize ecological damage to these islands the Equadorian Government has put a 3 day limit on yachts visiting the Galapagos, although enforcement of this limit turned out to be rather "flexible". Between stays at San Cristobal and Santa Cruz Islands, *Sparrow* managed to delay a week before setting out for Easter Island. During that time they were able to do some sightseeing as well as replenish both their food and water supplies.

David and Daniel characterized the sail from the Galapagos to Easter Island, a distance of about 2,000 miles, as "The Perfect Passage". They had the steady, dependable southeast Trades on the beam. In open ocean these Trades blowing at 20 knots or so build up some quite large swells, which coming from the side made for a rather bouncy ride in their small vessel, particularly when squalls built the seas up to as high as 12 feet. However, for about 16 days most of the time they read, played music, played cards, talked, ate and generally had a beautifully smooth, relaxed sail.

When cruising at sea a normal routine with a two man crew is usually to stand watch 4 hours on and 4 off. During this run Dan proposed they change it to 6 on and 6 off allowing the person off watch to get a more restful sleep. Since their Navik self-steerer relieved the on-watch person from the need to stand constantly at the helm, this watch system worked so well that they continued to follow it for the rest of the voyage.

Dan's navigation on this leg was absolutely accurate and he hit Easter Island dead ahead. After making landfall at Easter Island they sailed around to the west side of the island in order to anchor off its only town, Hanga Roa. Getting ashore from the anchorage into the small landing area at the town turned out to be just a bit tricky The anchorage is by no means a protected one, and the only way to

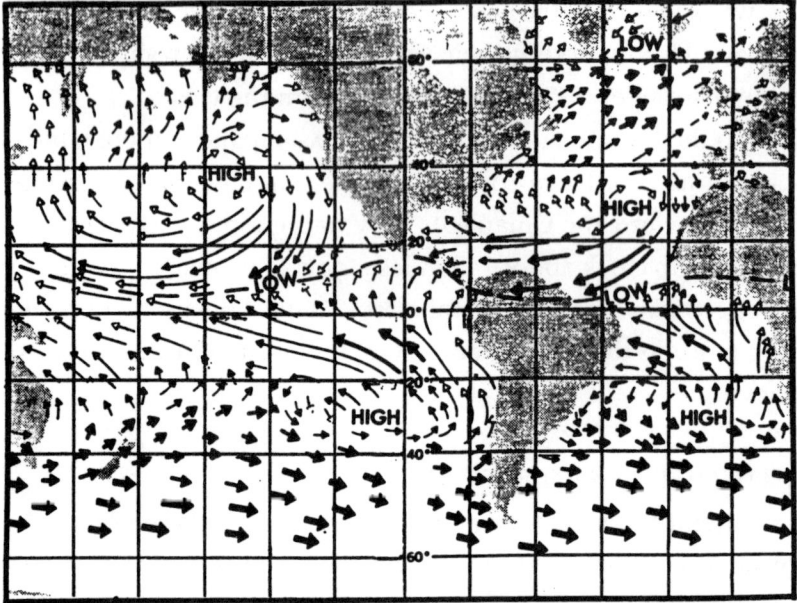

JULY AND AUGUST

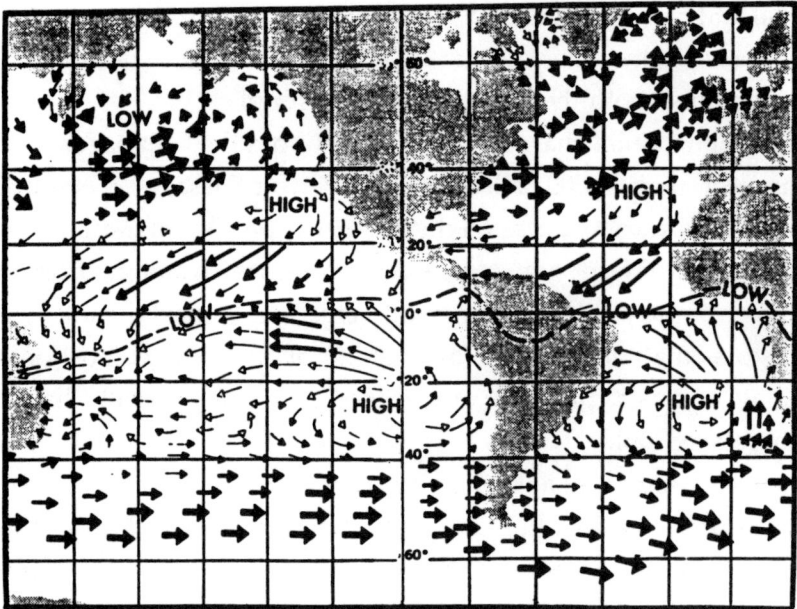

JANUARY AND FEBRUARY

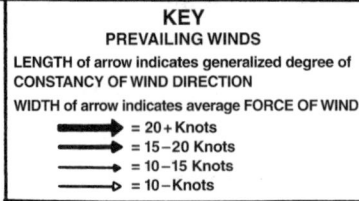

KEY
PREVAILING WINDS
LENGTH of arrow indicates generalized degree of
CONSTANCY OF WIND DIRECTION
WIDTH of arrow indicates average FORCE OF WIND

= 20+ Knots
= 15–20 Knots
= 10–15 Knots
= 10–Knots

Fig. SP-7 Surface Wind Patterns
from "The American Practical Navigator"– Bowditch

get into town is by dinghy. The channel in from the anchorage is narrow, and if they strayed a bit outside of it their inflatable dinghy could easily get flipped over by the waves swirling around the entrance To Dan's great embarrassment after they had been in port for a few days, this happened to him at an awkward time. He was bringing a most attractive girl he'd happened to met in town, back from a visit to *Sparrow*. Fortunately, although well soaked, she was not at all upset.

When they first arrived, David called home. He and Leonora decided that she really should see the island so four days after *Sparrow* arrived she showed up at the airport. Since planes only come in to Easter Island twice a week an aircraft arrival is a major local event since the stop at Easter Island is basically for refueling. This is not a resort destination so Leonora was one of very few passengers to deplane here. The rest of the passengers picked up a few trinkets, got a quick look at a nearby giant stone head and took off again.

As David expected, Leonora was delighted with the island which they explored for several days after which she returned to New York. After her departure, a final cleaning and arranging was done aboard the boat. Laundry was done ashore, and the final shopping for stores was completed. Everything was now ready for the assault on "The Horn".

ON TO THE HORN

Two years of building, fitting out, and refining the the boat, then close to five months sailing it from New London to Easter Island was all preliminary preparation for the next step. It was now finally time to set sail for what the old-timers called "Cape Stiff".

It was now mid-December, the start of the Southern Hemisphere summer, by far the best time to round the Horn. Since they will pass from west to east, the strong prevailing westerly winds of the high southern latitudes will be behind them. Also as they pass the Horn, the West Wind Drift—the ocean current that circles entirely around the Antarctic Continent, will be with them, as well. That's the *good* news! The bad news is that at *any* season gale winds of 35 to 40 knots and full storm winds up to 55 knots are likely to be encountered in the high latitudes of the southern ocean, where Sparrow is now headed. The "roaring forties" and "screaming fifties" were so named in the days of the full rigged sailing ships for very good reason. It is light winds in that area that are the rarity (Fig. SP-7).

They had light winds for several days after leaving Easter Island, after which the winds picked up. The Chanukah and Christmas holidays came and went while they made good progress with strong winds and large seas, but they were not hit by a true "roaring forties" gale until the 14th day. From then on for the next

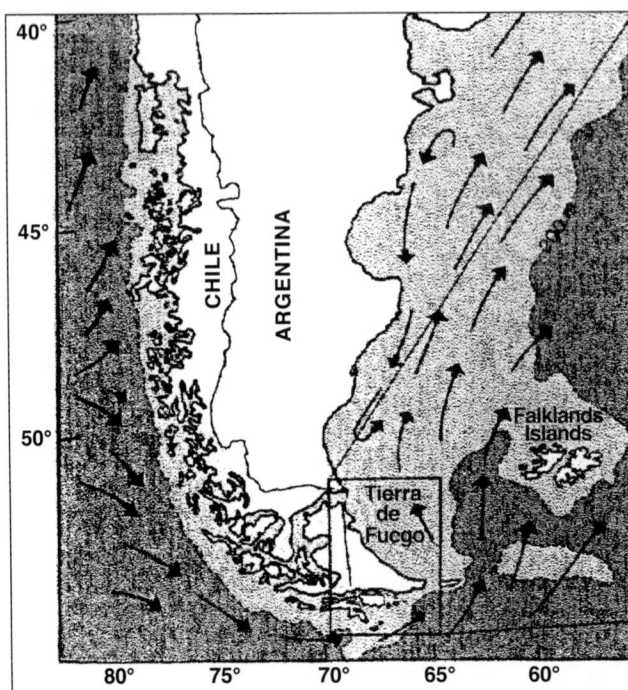

Fig. SP-8 Ocean Currents - Vicinity of Tierra del Fuego
from "Oceanus"–Vol. 32 No. 1

ten days they sailed through almost constant gale winds and huge seas.

They had decided early on to go outside around the Horn rather than risk the rocky and dangerous passage through the Straits of Magellan. Here they would be subject to erratic wind shifts around the islands in the Straits, and erratic tidal currents as well. By staying outside they were assured, in addition to the likelihood of following winds, of helpful ocean currents as well all the way to the Falkland Islands (Fig. SP-8).

On the 7th of January at about 0100 the gale let up and they found they had the Horn in sight! At that point it had been 36 hours since it last was clear enough for Dan to take sights, so that, at the end, he found the Horn by dead reckoning –and as it turned out he was within about two miles of where he wanted to be. The sight of the Horn has to have been both a moment of supreme triumph, and in a way perhaps somewhat of an anticlimax. as well. The fabled, famous, infamous, and awesome "Horn" appeared from *Sparrow* as no more than a mere hump of land on the distant horizon which is doubtless the way it appeared to many of the others who had passed that way before them.

By January 8, the next day, the Horn was still in sight but they had rounded it and shifted course to the north toward Port Stanley in the Falkland Islands. Two days later they made landfall at Port Stanley and after four hours of tacking back and forth to reach the entrance channel in winds of about 40 knots the harbor master sent out a launch to tow *Sparrow* in. They were now safely in port with the fearsome Horn behind them!

FROM THE FALKLANDS BACK TO NEW LONDON

Before the building of the Panama Canal this port was normally the last stop for vessels making the east to west passage around the Horn, and the first stop for vessels having made the west to east passage. Since the opening of the Canal, traffic at Port Stanley had slowed to a trickle until the recent unpleasantness between Argentina and Britain over possession of the islands. There were still live mine fields carefully fenced off at the time *Sparrow* arrived. Other reminders of the recent fighting were still apparent as well as grenades, jet drop tanks, and shallow graves frequently being found.

Port Stanley is a cold and extremely windy outpost, but *Sparrow's* crew received a warm welcome and took a well deserved two week rest before heading north toward Montevideo. While they were in Port Stanley several other yachts made port, either coming from or heading to the Horn.

David and Dan now realized that since leaving the Pacific end of the Panama Canal they had circled all around South America without ever setting foot on the mainland since all their stops had been on islands. Now Montevideo will be the first time they will actually stand on the soil of the South American continent.

After 2 weeks of rest ashore in Port Stanley, they both became miserably seasick for the first few days back at sea. One night, a few days out of the Falklands, their cat Tiger, apparently fell overboard. This was the little cat given to Dan when he shoved off at New London, and been a constant companion all the way up until then. He had been in and out and all over the boat for months in good weather and bad, in calm seas and rough. They never did find out what happened, but he was sorely missed by both of them. He disappeared the night they passed the 10,000 mile mark of their voyage.

Montevideo was the first sizable city they had been in since leaving Panama City way back on October 26th - over 3 months ago. Dan at first felt quite uncomfortable and rather out of place, but David found the city pleasantly European. While here, David came across a stray kitten which they cleaned up and adopted to replace Tiger.

David's vacation time was now about up so he flew back home from here leaving Dan to bring the boat the rest of the way back to New London. An old college friend Joe, flew into Montevideo to join Dan for the run up to Rio de Janeiro, which took a little over two weeks. This was the fellow's first experience on a sailboat and unfortunately he immediately got seasick. The fact that they quickly ran into heavy weather didn't help. The poor guy was sick for practically the entire time so when they reached Rio he was just as happy his sailboat trip was over. They spent several days resting and exploring the city before Joe flew out, leaving Dan to continue alone for close to 3,000 miles up to Antigua in the Antilles. While in Rio Dan acquired a monkey to take with him in addition to the cat.

Dan's next objective after leaving Rio was Fernando de Noronha Island east

Fig. SP-9 Route of the Sparrow
from "My Old Man and the Sea"– D. & D. Hayes

of the easternmost point on the bulge of Brazil. This was a slow uphill fight against wind and current. When he finally arrived there he was unable to land due to adverse winds and after making an unsuccessful attempt to get in, he gave up and headed on northwest for Antigua 2,100 miles away.

He now had the Trade Winds and the Equatorial Currents with him making for an easy and comfortable passage. At Antigua he was joined by his sister and her fiancé and the three then island hopped up the Antilles as far as St. Thomas. There Glenn, the fellow who had first started out of New London with him, joined Dan for the next run as far as Bermuda.

By then all that remained was the relatively short solo sail from Bermuda back to New London. The entire voyage, a distance of approximately 17,000 miles (Fig. SP-9) took 317 days from the time Dan left New London until he sailed back in. As he later laconically summed it up," We hung a right out of the Thames River, New London–went through the Panama Canal, then stayed left until we got back to New London."

CHAPTER 8

"Wild Goose" from White Sea to Black Sea

Part of the Song of Stenka Razin, a Cossack hero who sacrificed his bride to Russia's "Mother Volga"

Stenka Razin hears the murmur
Of his discontented band,
And his lovely Persian Princess,
He has circled with his hand

His dark brows are drawn together
As the waves of anger rise
And the blood comes rushing swiftly
To his piercing jet black eyes

Volga, Volga , Mother Volga,
Deep and wide above the land,
I will give you all you wanted,
Life and heart and head and hand

And that I might rule as ever
All my freeborn men and brave
Volga, Volga, Mother Volga,
Volga make this girl a grave

The Irish sailor and author, Captain Miles Clark, said after completing this voyage, that he had achieved his lifelong ambition. In 1992 he sailed a 60 year old, 34' long, British-built wooden sailboat, the *Wild Goose*, all the way through the heart of western Russia from **north** to **south**. He entered from the White Sea and came out in the Black Sea after sailing all the way through Russia's long, continuous, interconnected inland waterway system.

This may seem a curious project to be the lifelong ambition of an Irish sailor; however, he wanted to do it at a time when he was one of very few people outside of Russia, and for that matter probably very few inside as well, who knew that the inland waterway system of that country was connected in such a way as to make possible a complete north/south trip by water. His trip was notable for that reason and also because Clark, having determined that the voyage was possible, managed in 1992 to get permission from the Russian government to do it.

Prior to the time of Clark's voyage the Soviet government would never have permitted a foreigner to travel through so much of their heartland, since many places along the way were considered of strategic importance. Since the dissolution of the Soviet Union was in process when Clark asked to make his voyage, he was able to obtain the necessary permits. He started in the north at Archangel on the White Sea, then threaded his way south through Russia's huge, inland complex of rivers, lakes, and canals all the way down to the mouth of the Don. He then crossed the Sea of Azov to enter the Black Sea. Finally he went across to the north coast of Turkey where he turned his bow west to sail into Istanbul, and end his trip. The entire track of the voyage of *Wild Goose* through western Russia is shown for reference on the map Fig, WG-1.

After reading such great Russian writers as Pushkin, Turgenev, Tolstoy, and Dostoyevski, and seeing a great many WW II movies we in the west, tend to think of Russia as an almost endless stretch of *land*. Our picture of that country generally has become one of a boundless expanse of flat steppe country interspersed with forests extending in all directions as far as the eye can see. Then when we think of Russia under the Communists we may add a portrait gallery of huge, smoky, industrial complexes or vast areas of collective farms. As far as the Russian people themselves are concerned, most outsiders who have not been there haven't any very clear picture of them at all. Rest assured that whatever picture you have of them, particularly from movies, or perhaps from literature–it is wrong! Except for the language difference they are simply people like ourselves.

THE WATERWAYS OF INLAND RUSSIA

One actually has to see the multitude of sprawling rivers, lakes, and canals in European Russia to realize how very incomplete and inaccurate is our usual view of that country. Miles Clark knew long before he started his trip what Hitler and Napoleon had failed to consider before their ill fated attempts to conquer Russia. He was well aware that much of the countryside of Western Russia is crisscrossed by a complex network of inland waterways. This multitude of interconnected bodies of water have long constituted main arteries for the transportation of both goods and people throughout western Russia. The would-be conquerors also failed to note that the existence of these many waterways seri-

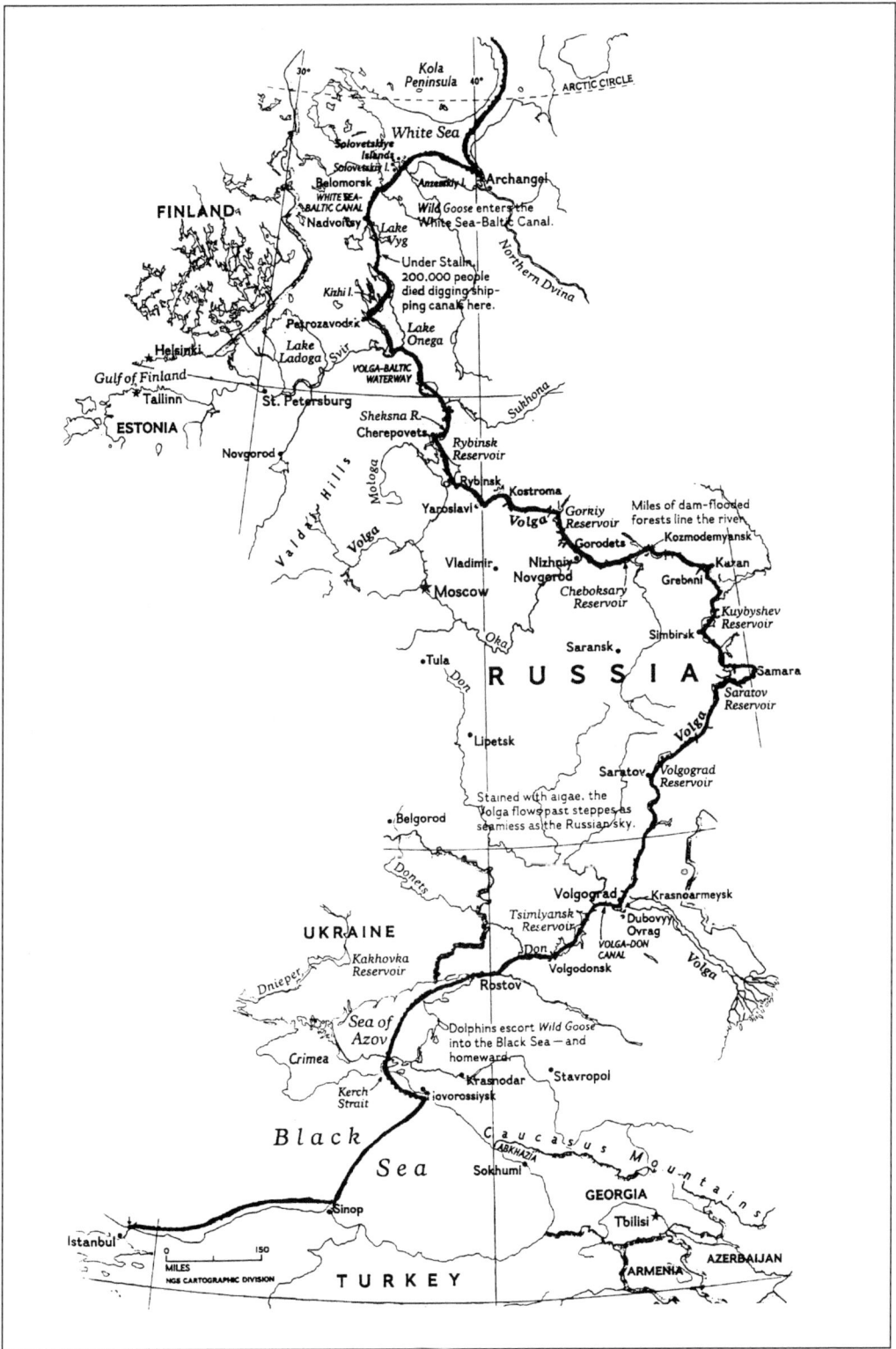

Fig. WG-1 Route of "Wild Goose" through Russia from the White Sea to the Black Sea
from "National Geographic"–Volume 185, Number 6

Fig. WG-2 Cargo handling at a port on the inland waterways
(Illustration : Author))

ously interferes with overland transportation over the vast distances required
due to the lack of well developed highways and rail lines.

As frequently happened elsewhere in Europe in the early history of this country, the rivers and lakes became major transportation arteries simply because they
were already there. Consequently, there was no great incentive to develop an
elaborate highway system Long distance surface transportation via trucks and
busses is hampered by a limited highway system. In addition, there are relatively few major rail lines as well. As a result, except for the period during the winter
when they are frozen in, a huge inland fleet of thousands of ocean-sized cargo
ships carry the majority of raw materials, as well as finished goods to and from
the major inland cities throughout western Russia (Fig. WG-2). These waterways
are also used by a fleet of high speed hydrofoil passenger boats that provide fast
and inexpensive transportation between many towns and villages which are difficult to reach overland (Fig. WG-3). They are also used by a large fleet of passenger cruise ships carrying touring vacationers.

Clark also knew beforehand that large cargo and passenger ships normally sail along the entire route he intended to follow. That being the case he knew that if he could manage to keep his little boat from being run down by these ships he would have no problem finding deep enough water to get his boat all the way through his desired route As it turned out, on one occasion he *did* have a very close call at a bend in the Volga with a pair of cargo ships.

NORTH FROM BRITAIN TO ARCHANGEL

Before he started Clark was well aware that due to the severe seasonal changes in weather conditions he would be limited by very tight time constraints. In order to sail his boat up to Archangel, the starting point of his intended trip at the northern end of the waterway system, he had first to get through the Barents Sea and across the White Sea. He knew he could not get through that area until about the middle of June. Until that time the heavy winter ice covering those northern seas would not melt enough to allow his boat to pass through. Once he arrived at Archangel he would only have until about the middle of September to complete his trip of about 3000 miles all the way to the mouth of the Don River, across the Sea of Azov, and on over the Black Sea to his final objective, Istanbul. This is because by late September, the oncoming fall would bring the first of the

Fig. WG-3 Typical Russian high-speed passenger hydrofoil
(Illustration : Author))

Fig. WG-4 "Wild Goose" passing a small Russian town
from "National Geographic"–Volume 185, Number 6

fall storms. These would produce, at best, uncomfortable, and at worst, danger-ous conditions for his final passage across the Black Sea.

This being the case Clark was going to need a bit of luck as well as skillful boat handling in order to get his 60 year old vessel (Fig. WG-4) all the way down Russia's vast waterway system and then across the Black Sea in time. If he encountered locks closed for repairs, if he ran aground damaging the hull, rudder or propeller, if contaminated fuel disabled his engine, or if his permission to pass was withdrawn or held up, any of these possible difficulties could stop him in his tracks or create delays causing him to arrive too late to get across the Black Sea ahead of the onset of the storm season.

The first step, obviously, was to get the boat up to the intended starting point at the north end of the waterway system as early in the year as possible. In late spring of 1992, with two British friends to help him he sailed from England up around Norway's North Cape into the Barents Sea, across it and then down through the White Sea to Archangel. Fortunately, they reached Archangel right on schedule by mid-June. Here, his two British crewmen got off to be replaced by Russians. One experienced Russian sailor named Vitaly Chankseliani came aboard here to remain with him for the entire voyage. Since Clark knew little or no Russian, 28 year old Vitaly, who came from Omsk, would also be his inter-preter when necessary.

A second Russian crewman, Nikolai Litau from Moscow, also a veteran mariner, was to come aboard at Belomorsk, the White Sea port at the north end of the inland waterway, and sail down as far as Nizhny Novgorod on the Volga There he was to be replaced by a third experienced Russian sailor, Arkady Gershuni also from Moscow, who would remain aboard all the rest of the way to the Black Sea.

Clark left Archangel with his first Russian crewman aboard to start across the White Sea on June 15. They began their unusual cruise from there to the Black Sea, in a driving rainstorm. Vitaly, while an experienced mariner had never before traveled on a small sailboat so he was not at all happy at the idea of starting out in such foul weather, but Cark felt it important to be under way as soon as possible.

On the following day the weather had calmed down by the time they reached the Solovetskiye Islands. These isolated islands have two claims to fame; one exemplary, and one sinister indeed. Their favorable fame was that back in the 1400s an isolated Orthodox monastery was started here that became widely renowned throughout the Russian Orthodox world for the piety and scholarship of its monks. The evil claim to fame was the unhappy fact that from 1923 to 1939 the Soviets set up an exceptionally brutal political prison colony, or gulag, here. The shocking total of something over 43,000 people were killed in this prison before it was finally closed and dismantled. When they went ashore here Miles and Vitaly met the small group of monks who had returned to carry on the tradition of the famous early monastery.

INTO THE NORTHERN CANALS AND LAKES

The next stop was Belomorsk at the White Sea end of the White Sea-Baltic Canal. This canal marks the start of the inland waterway system they will follow for nearly 3,000 miles until they emerge from the mouth of the Don River and enter the Sea of Azov. At this point, Clark and Vitaly picked up Nikolai Litau, the second Russian crewman. The three of them then entered the canal and motored through it to Lake Vyg. *Wild Goose* was the first foreign vessel ever allowed to enter that canal which had been built by forced labor between 1930 and 1933. It has since been revealed that the lives of approximately 200,000 people were sacrificed during its construction!!

After sailing across the 70 mile length of Lake Vyg they reentered the canal to emerge again at Lake Onaga. Toward the north end, and quite far out in Lake Onaga, they arrived at lonely Kizhi Island which has an unexpectedly interesting history. At very early times small groups of pious Orthodox monks, in order to avoid the temptations of the flesh, had already found their way to very distant and isolated corners of Russia such as this lonely island. Back in 900 AD a small group of Orthodox monks somehow found their way to this remote speck of land out in the lake, settled here, and built a unique church. (Fig. WG-5)

The "onion domes" for which Russian churches have become famous were already in use at that early date. Normally a Russian Orthodox church has five domes for a very specific traditional reason. The larger central one symbolized the Christ while the four smaller ones ranged around it symbolized the four major Apostles - Matthew, Mark, Luke, and John. For some now unknown reason the order of monks that had settled here at Kixhi Island was not satisfied with the usual five domes. From time to time as additions were made to the original church, additional domes were added as well. By the time they were finished the church had sprouted 22 onion domes which is the number it has today!

Certainly when they were built each of the 17 additional domes had a very specific significance to the builders, but when I was there in 1993, although that masterpiece of a church was still proudly standing, I was unable to find anyone

Fig. WG-5 1000 Year Old Wooden Church on Kizhi Island
(Illustration : Author)

surviving who knew anything about the meaning of the many additional domes. Everyone there was extremely proud of them, although no one knew why they were built. Captain Clark also indicates that he was never able to find anyone on the island who could explain their meaning either.

Another astonishing aspect of this 1000 year old church is that except for the foundation it is made *entirely* of wood. That means absolutely no metal fasteners whatsoever were used to hold any of its thousands of wood parts together. The framing, the sheathing, the roof shingles, the flooring, and all the interior furnishings are put together with a combination of pegs and interlocking wood joints.

Fig. WG-6 Sailboat with cargo ships off Petrozavodsk
(Illustration : Author)

There are absolutely no nails, screws, bolts, or other metal fasteners of any kind used anywhere in its construction. Think a moment - here is an all wood building 1,000 years old, standing in northern Russia where the winters are harsh indeed, and this entire original structure with no metal fasteners to hold it together, is still standing.

It is quite possible at that early time so far out there in the middle of the lake that the monks fastened everything with wood because they simply had no access to any source of metal. It is also likely that if the normal types of iron fasteners then available had been used they probably would have completely rusted away in the intervening 1000 years in which case the building would have long since completely collapsed. It may well be that those early monks knew *exactly* what they were doing and why.

After Kizhi Island the *Wild Goose* sailed on across Lake Onaga to the city of Petrozavodsk on its western shore. This city is the major port for handling heavy waterborn cargo on the lake. I took the photo in Fig. WG-6 in 1993, a year after the voyage of *Wild Goose*, but it gives you an idea of the type of cargo ships normally plying this lake and using this port. These ships are of seagoing size and the waterways provide them with access to the White Sea and North Atlantic

Fig. WG-7 Passenger Cruise Ship in a Typical Canal Lock
(Illustration : Author)

through Archangel, where *Wild Goose* entered, and to the Baltic and Atlantic again via connections from Lake Onaga to Lake Ladoga, and thence via the Svir River to St Petersberg and the Baltic (Fig. WG-1).

Dock space at Petrozavodsk apparently was at a premium at the time we were there because when we arrived many cargo ships were lying at anchor off-shore waiting to either load or unload. Incidentally, the sailboat shown here (Fig. WG-6) was the only one I actually saw under sail in the course of my own 1,100 miles of travel on Russia's inland waterways.

Clark makes no mention of what he did while here, but Petrozavodsk is a major city where he certainly could have picked up stores, fuel, and other sup-plies. Personally, I was particularly impressed at finding a Ben & Jerry's ice cream shop there in the middle of Russia. The Russians, it seems, are particularly partial to ice cream. I had an ice cream cone there for the ruble equivalent at that time of 25 cents! According to Ben & Jerry's agreement with the Russian government at that time, all purchases from them had to be paid for in rubles! Almost anywhere else in Russia in 1993, dollars were not only gladly accepted, they were preferred.

From Petrozavodsk, *Wild Goose* sailed to the northern entrance of the next major canal, the Volga-Baltic Canal. She motored south through that canal to

White Lake, crossed that lake and followed the canal the rest of the way southward to reach the huge Rybinsk Reservoir (Fig. WG-1), which is the most northerly one of the six great reservoirs along the Volga.

Passage through the Volga Baltic canal and the White Sea-Baltic Canal before it, required *Wild Goose* to pass through many locks. She would have to pass through a great many more locks by the time she got all the way down the Volga to the Volga-Don Canal, through that canal, and finally the rest of the way down the Don to its mouth at the Sea of Azov. These locks can raise or lower a vessel anywhere from 18′ to 53′ at a time, and throughout the entire waterway system they are standardized as to size in order to accommodate the large commercial passenger and cargo ships that ply these waterways The most commonly seen type of passenger cruise ship (Fig. WG-7) is 350′ long by 50′ wide. The standard lock can handle two of these ships at a time when placed end to end.

Cargo ships vary more in size than the passenger cruise ships which carry tourists, some carrying all foreigners while others carry only vacationing Russians. When I was there the cruise ships carrying foreigners were in far better condition than those the Russians assigned to themselves.

At all the locks in the entire Russian waterway system, vessels enter and leave under their own power. Embedded in the sides of each lock are sliding mooring bits (Fig. WG-8). These bits move up and down with the changes in the water level and the vessel maintains its position in the lock by tying off to these bits. When leaving they simply take their lines back aboard, and leave the same way they entered, under their own power. *Wild Goose* had to lock through with either passenger or cargo ships, and of course, had to carefully avoid being squashed in the process.

Fig. WG-8 *Floating Mooring Bit in a Typical Canal Lock*
(Illustration : Author)

No help from lockside "mules", such as we installed in the Panama Canal, is to be found in the Russian locks which makes their system simpler than the one in Panama. In addition, the floating mooring bits make it unnecessary while in the lock to adjust mooring lines to compensate for changes in the water level—a distinct improvement on the Panama system.

THE VOLGA

Emerging from the canal system *Wild Goose* now started down Russia's "Mother" Volga. This river drains an area of thousands and thousands of square miles—an area so large that it constitutes nearly 1/3 of European Russia. Altogether the river is about 2,300 miles long but *Wild Goose* only traveled down about 1,200 miles, or a bit over half of it, before turning off into the Volga-Don Canal at Volgograd.

Throughout Russian history, the water level of this river has been subject to extremely large seasonal changes in depth resulting from seasonal variations in rainfall. These changes often ranged up to as much as 50'. Along with these immense changes in water depth came tremendous variations in the velocity of flow in the river. Plainly, seasonal variations this great in the depth and flow of the water had, from earliest times, caused all manner of problems and interruptions in the use of the river for the transportation of both passengers and freight. For centuries, while the mighty Czars had absolute control over the lives and deaths of millions of their subjects, they had absolutely no control over the vagaries of the Volga. Taming the Volga had remained an impossible dream of all of the rulers of Russia until Josef Stalin arrived on the scene. He accomplished what Ivan the Terrible, Peter the Great, and all the other absolute rulers of Russia had found impossible. He tamed the Volga. The human cost was incalculable, but regardless, he was determined to succeed - and he did.

Dams and locks had long been in use in other countries to control rivers but not on the scale Stalin envisioned. Between 1937 and 1960, a series of major dams were built to harness the river and create a series of reservoirs varying in size from the comparatively small Uglich Reservoir covering about 150 square kilometers, up to the gigantic Kuibyshev Reservoir which covers 3,900 square kilometers. This series of dams and reservoirs is known in Russia as the "Volga Cascade". The Volga Cascade has substantially stabilized the seasonal changes in the river by storing and releasing the river water as required. At each dam there are locks allowing ships to move up and down the river. *Wild Goose* was dropped varying distances by the locks at each of the dams. The first one she reached was the one creating Rybinsk Reservoir, one of the largest. It is so large, in fact, that

Clark notes they were completely out of sight of land for much of the 14 hours it took to make the crossing from the south end end of the Volga -Baltic Canal to the Rybinsk Dam.

The next major city beyond Rybinsk is Kostroma which is particularly notable because it was the birthplace of the last line of Russian Czars, the unfortunate Romanovs. Their line tragically ended, as you will recall, when Czar Nicholas II, Czarina Alexandra and all their children, were shot by the Communist revolutionaries at Enkaterinberg in Siberia where, as been reliably determined by recent Russian excavations, the Princess Anastasia did *not* escape, in spite of various fascinating fantasies to the contrary. Finally in 1998, the remains of these unfortunate Romanovs were properly reburied.

The further down river they traveled the more congested it became, with both cargo and passenger shipping. A short distance below the dam that forms Gorky Reservoir at Gorodets, and in a narrow bend of the river, the Wild Goose narrowly escaped becoming the "ham in a sandwich" consisting of two 5,000 ton tankers passing each other in opposite directions. One of Clark's Russian crewman was at the helm. At that bend here was no space to allow him to get around them, so after several very tense minutes he found a wide enough slot between the two ships to allow *Wild Goose* to squeak through, much to the relief of Captain Clark who was not the least bit amused by the sudden danger of possibly losing his boat, ending his voyage, and having to swim out of there through very polluted water in the bargain.

At Nizhniy Novgorod (Fig. WG-1), the second Russian crewman, Nikolai, signed off and a third Russian named Arkady Gershuni came aboard and remained for the rest of the trip. This city was known as Gorky during the Communist period, and was then a completely closed area. It was a major military/industrial center, and also a place of exile for a number of important dissidents. The eminent Andrei Sakharov, for one, was exiled here for an extended period. By contrast this city is now very open and has become an extremely important commercial center. The crew of *Wild Goose* even came across an American fried chicken restaurant run by a chap from Texas who had moved here for this purpose, and who appeared to be doing a very lively business.

Clark and his crew had now begun to discover several disturbing facts about the condition of the river. Before the construction of the Volga Cascade, water entering the Volga at its source north of Moscow would reach the Caspian Sea in a period of about 50 days. With its water moving this rapidly the Volga was able to cleanse itself and keep healthy. Particularly in spring the seasonal freshets roared down the river turning it into a raging tumult and scouring out its entire length, Now, greatly slowed by passing through all of the many dams and reservoirs, water taking the same journey requires a leisurely 18 months! Instead of the river cleansing itself of pollutants what now occurs is a continual deposit of toxins and heavy metals on the bottoms of the huge reservoirs due to the combined effect of two factors: the sluggish movement of the water, along with the continually increasing discharge into the river of industrial wastes and pollutants from both industrial plants and farms along the way.

For much of its length Mother Volga looks cleaner than she is. However, as she flows south agricultural pollution feeding in from various tributaries and from her own banks as well, causes a strong algae bloom along great stretches of the river toward its southern end. As *Wild Goose* moved into the southern portion of the river beyond Saratov, her crew could clearly see in their wake the path she cut through this surface film of algae.

In early August while in the lower Volga, the *Wild Goose* crew heard on Radio Moscow that fighting had broken out between government troops and a local dissident group in a place called Sokhumi, which is a resort on the northeast coast of the Black Sea. Unfortunately, the wife and daughter of Vitaly, the Russian sailor who had been with Clark in *Wild Goose* all the way from Archangel, were on vacation there. Vitaly tried to reach his friend Nikolai, the crewman who had gone ashore in Nizhniy Novgorod, to find out about his family, but had no luck. During the following days news reports were not encouraging. There were reports of artillery bombardments and tank movements while attempts to broker a cease-fire were not successful.

Vitaly sadly realized there was nothing he could do. He knew full well that even if he could get to Sokhumi he wouldn't know where to start looking for his wife and child, nor did he have any idea what he would do if he found them. Since *Wild Goose* was heading toward the Black Sea anyway he decided to stay with the boat until he could get some reliable information.

The boat then sailed on down river to Volgograd, which, since WW II, is far better known to the world as Stalingrad. Fifty years after the city was besieged and destroyed by the Germans, whose Sixth Army was in turn destroyed by the Russians, the crew of *Wild Goose* found a new city built on the rubble of the old. It was then a major industrial center, and at that time its most powerful enemy was itself, in the form of massive industrial pollution. Stalingrad finally won the battle against the Germans, but Volgograd was fast losing the battle against its own chemical industry. The damage being done to both the river and the surrounding land was incalculable, and little if anything was being done to slow the damage or correct the situation.

FROM THE VOLGA TO THE DON TO THE SEA

The Volga empties into the Caspian Sea which is completely land locked with no connection to any of the world's oceans. However, at this point the mighty Don River flows quite close to the Volga. The Don connects to the Black Sea and through it, to the Mediterranean. The Volga-Don Canal was built to connect the cities on the lower Volga by water to the outside world, via the Don River.

Wild Goose then left the Volga through the Volga-Don Canal. She exited that canal into the huge Tsimlyansk Reservoir that for 130 miles tames the lower Don ,just as the reservoirs on the Volga Cascade tamed the Volga. They emerged at last from the locks by the dam at Volgodonsk into a river that still resembles the rural world of the legendary Don Cossacks, so beautifully described by Mikhail Sholokov in his books "Quiet flows the Don" and "The Don Flows Down to the Sea". Life in the old villages of this area is little changed since then. Heron and egrets fish in the shallows and there are even wild horses loose along the shore.

On August 31 at one o'clock AM, the *Wild Goose* reached the mouth of the Don and entered the waters of the Sea of Azov. She had now sailed for almost two and a half months, covering a distance of nearly 3,000 miles through the heart of European Russia to get here. Clark and his crew have had a remarkable view of the rivers, the lakes, the canals. the land, the inhabitants, and the accomplishments of the Russian people from 1,000 years ago until today.

On entering the Sea of Azov, Arkady, the sailor who had joined *Wild Goose* at Nizhniy Novgorod, remarked that after 20 years of sailing on the inland waterways he had finally reached the sea. Manning Russia's huge inland fleet of both freighters and passenger ships there are thousands of crewmen who, like Arkady, have spent years and years serving aboard seagoing-size ships but have never seen salt water.

To complete its cruise from the White Sea to the Black Sea, the *Wild Goose* now scudded south across the Sea of Azov driven by a northeasterly gale. Two days later she passed through the Kerch Strait between the Caucasus and the Crimea to enter the Black Sea. Vitaly still did not learn for a couple days more that his wife and daughter were able at last to get safely out of Sokhumi.

As far as is known, *Wild Goose* is the only sailboat ever to have made a north-south crossing through the heart of Mother Russia, a crossing that may or may not ever be repeated. *Wild Goose* completed her extraordinary voyage in September after Clark had sailed her across the Black Sea to northern Turkey, where he coasted westward to enter the busy narrow and twisting Straits of the Bosphorus, finally ending his long voyage in Istanbul.

CHAPTER 9

The 1700 Mile
Eastern Mediterranean Yacht Rally

This Turkish inspired event, the annual Eastern Mediterranean Yacht Rally (EMYR), is entirely unique in the sailing world. No sailing event elsewhere is even remotely comparable in terms of the number of nationalities represented among the participants, the distance sailed, and the number of different nations visited in the course of the event. This Rally regularly has a fleet of over 100 boats sailed by participants from about 20 different nations and sailing approximately 1700 miles for 49 days to visit 24 ports in 6 different countries.

WHAT IS A "YACHT RALLY"?

To the Turkish organizers of this event a "Yacht Rally" is *not* a race or series of races. It does not involve competition of any kind. On the contrary, it is rather a gathering of a large number of sailboats with their crews from many different nations, who then embark together on a carefully organized and extensive cruise. During this cruise they have many opportunities to meet, socialize, and share their experiences and backgrounds with other sailors, while at the same time meeting the people and exploring the histories and cultures of the different countries visited along the way. While in the many ports they visit they make numerous side trips to observe and learn about the many important historic sites in these countries.

All boats participating in the Rally must be privately owned. No commercially chartered boats are allowed to join, nor may any boat carry paying passengers. However, invited guests may contribute to the expenses of the host vessel. Crews consist predominantly of the owners of the participating boats, and their amateur sailing friends. Although chartered boats and paying passengers are forbidden, boat owners are permitted to carry paid crew, if they wish, which is done on some of the larger boats.

All boats entered in the Rally must be equipped with an operating diesel auxiliary engine. Diesels are specified because arrangements are made in advance for diesel fuel to be available at all ports upon the Rally arrival, because in some ports no gasoline refueling facilities exist.

Operating auxiliary engines are required because there are definite schedules to be kept. When the wind dies, or is adverse, it becomes necessary to motor in order to maintain these schedules. This happened a couple times during my sail with the 1999 EMYR Rally.

Another requirement is that each vessel must have a marine VHF transceiver since Rally communications and instructions are transmitted on various marine VHF channels. Further, if a vessel encounters a problem requiring assistance a call on VHF will quickly bring help from other Rally boats nearby. I also had an opportunity to observe how quickly competent assistance arrives in such cases.

All Rally boats are required to fly their flag of national origin, and fly the appropriate national courtesy flag on entering each foreign port. Also, while in port all Rally boats are to fly dress ship flags while docked. 100 boats all flying dress ship flags at once makes a truly festive appearance indeed!

The Rally has encouraged considerable development of marinas as well as support and service facilities for recreational vessels. In the years since the start of the Eastern Mediterranean Yacht Rally (the EMYR) in 1989 many of the facilities along its route have been vastly improved, several new marinas have been built, and others are under construction.

The Rally has, as a major objective, the encouragement of conditions that will allow the free and unrestricted movement of recreational vessels through the waters of the various nations of the Eastern Mediterranean Sea. This has not been easy, and they have not as yet been entirely successful, but conditions have already improved considerably. The various countries along the route have begun to notice that when these civilian yachts come in to port, a good deal of very welcome *money* comes in as well.

The EMYR now sails around western Turkey, out to Cyprus, back to eastern Turkey, then south to Syria, Lebanon, and Israel, to finally end its cruise in Egypt. While some of these nations are still extremely wary of each other, and most have unrest within their own borders as well, the fleet is warmly welcomed upon arrival everywhere it goes. Usually local dignitaries are on hand, and often a dockside party and/or entertainment are provided for the arriving sailors.

Lingering evidence of international distrust was still clearly perceptible at various points along the way. For example, when sailing south from Iskenderun in eastern Turkey to Lattakia in Syria we were required to stay at least 6 miles off the Syrian coast until Lattakia was directly abeam before turning in. Then, when we left Lattakia to go to Jouneih, just north of Beirut, Lebanon we had to stay 12 miles offshore. At that time, going directly from Lebanon to Israel was a "no, no", but if you first went to Magosa back on Cyprus and *then* sailed down to Israel, that was OK.

How much of this resulted from real fear or antagonism at the popular level in these countries, and how much was posturing by politicians, is impossible to determine when only quickly sailing by, as we did. Although there was occasional minor friction among the many disparate nationalities in the Rally fleet, generally they got along without difficulty on a one to one basis with each other. All of us, regardless of nationality, were most warmly welcomed by the local citizenry ashore in all the various ports we visited.

BACKGROUND OF THE EMYR

The original idea for this event came early in 1989 to a small multi-national group of sailors sitting in a bar at the Kemer Marina (Fig. EM-1) located in the small town of Kemer on the south coast of Turkey. This marina is a comparatively small one, but beautifully located with completely modern facilities.

These fellows were merely doing what sailors frequently do in a bar, having a few drinks and swapping tall tales. The group consisted of a Britisher named Bill Berry, Roland Boedt, a Belgian, Hilmar, a German, and Hasan Kacmaz, a young Turkish fellow who was also the manager of the Kemer Marina.

At that time the large port city of Antalya, about 15 miles east of Kemer, was

Fig. EM-1 Kemer Marina where it all began
(Illustration : Author)

as far east along the Turkish coast as pleasure vessels could go. In the ports further to the east there was limited dockage, fuel supplies, and repair facilities for fishing and small cargo ships, but nothing intended for recreational boats.

This group of four decided, perversely, they wanted to sail on their pleasure boats eastward beyond Antalya. Looking over possible destinations they settled on Girne-Kyrenia, the principal port on the north coast of Cyprus as their first destination. Hasan's wife was from Cyprus so she had relatives there. Since this harbor is in the Republic of Northern Cyprus they needed permission from those authorities for their vessels to enter. The family connections of Hasan's wife may have helped to expedite the permit process, but it still took a while. By the time the necessary permission was arranged word of the prospective trip had circulated in the local boating community, and several other venturesome sailors had joined them. When they finally sailed, their fleet consisted of 17 boats with a variety of crew drawn from eight different nationalities.

This first cruise was so successful they decided to make it an annual event. During the period from 1990 to 1994 the number of boats and the number of nationalities participating gradually increased and so did the number of ports and countries they visited, and the cruise took on the name of "The Eastern Mediterranean Yacht Rally". The route quickly extended well beyond Cyprus as more and more ports were gradually added, to include stops in Syria, Lebanon,

Fig. EM-2 Atakoy Marina–Istambul
(Illustration : Atakoy Marina)

Israel, and finally Egypt.

A major change in the Rally occurred in 1996. For a long time there had been another annual Turkish sailing cruise called the Inter-Continental Yacht Rally. That one began at the Atakoy Marina in Istanbul. This fleet sailed westward across the Sea of Marmora, through the Dardanelles, then southward stopping in various ports all along the Aegan coast of Turkey before turning eastward to follow its Mediterranean coast as far as Antalya. As previously mentioned, this had long been as far as pleasure boats could go.

In 1996 they joined with the EMYR to continue on from Antalya. Next, they went to Girne on Cyprus. Then from there sailed back to Mersin and Cevlik in southeastern Turkey before going on to Lattakia in Syria, Beirut in Lebanon, Haifa, Herzalia, and Ashkelon in Israel. From Israel they went on to Port Said and through the Suez Canal to end the cruise that year in Ismalia, Egypt. By this time close to 200 boats participated in the Rally.

In 1997 there were additional changes made in the Rally route. When they left Girne on Cyprus they split into two groups. One went around Cyprus to Magosa and then on to Israel. The other went first to Lattakia in Syria and then on to Beirut, Lebanon. Both groups then rejoined in Israel for the final run across to Egypt. About 120 yachts from 19 different countries were entered in the 1997 Rally.

Obviously, the route taken by the Rally has been vastly extended during the years since the modest 1989 excursion from Antalya to Cyprus. The combined Rally now starts in April every year at the Atakoy Marina in Istanbul. (Fig. EM-2) This is by far the largest, best equipped, and finest marina in Turkey, and can provide dockage for 700 boats with water, electricity, phone service, and TV connections at each slip. In addition, it offers its tenants a full service boatyard as well. Their travel-lift can handle vessels up to 70 tons.

MED MOOR

In the Mediterranean Sea the daily tide range is negligible–a matter of inches rather than feet - consequently floating docks are unnecessary. Boats can be comfortably docked by tying up to a stationary bulkhead. In order to maximize the number of boats using a given section of dock, instead of tying up alongside the bulkhead they tie up stern to with the bow held out on a bow anchor that is dropped as they back down to the dock. To facilitate docking in some marinas bow moorings have been permanently set in place. To further maximize the number of vessels tying up along a bulkhead there are no floating fingers between boats. They simply drop an anchor to hold the bow, and back down next to each other with their sterns to the dock. (Fig. EM-3) The stern is then tied

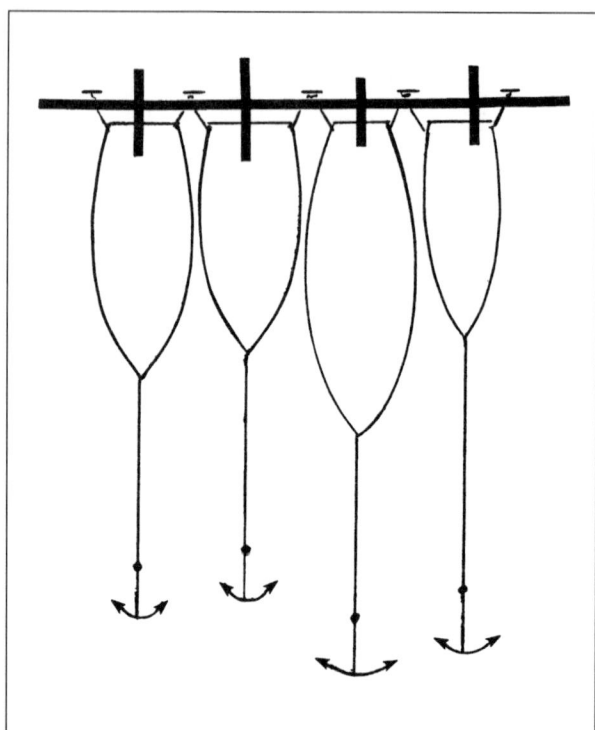

Fig. EM-3 Boats Med-moored
(Illustration : Author)

off to bits on the dock and a gangplank is swung across from the stern of the boat to provide access to the dock.

One night while Med moored in Girne we encountered beam winds of close to gale force. The major disadvantage of the Med moor was quickly obvious. In such conditions, if there is so much as one bow anchor not well set, chaos is likely. When one anchor drags allowing its boat to lose position, this strains both the anchor and dock lines of the boat alongside. The lateral movement of a single boat can quickly have an unfortunate domino effect.

Atakoy in Istanbul is the only marina in the area that provides most of its slips with dock fingers between boats, similar to what we are accustomed to in the U.S. Everywhere else I went, "Med moor" was the standard docking procedure.

THE RALLY ROUTE

The 10th Anniversary Rally was held in 1999 (EM-4) and went to 23 ports in 6 countries, sailing a total distance of 1760 nautical miles. This time there were 116 boats registered, flying the flags of 19 different nations.

From Istanbul the Rally now sails to 12 other ports along the Turkish west and south coasts before finally leaving Turkey for Cyprus. Most of the yacht marinas in Turkey that are visited by the Rally were originally built by the Turkish government in an effort to promote both yachting and tourism at the same time. In recent years, nearly all of these have been sold to private operators. A number of these marinas, such as Karada at Bodrum and Park Kemer at Kemer, offer full service boatyards as well as dockage, with electric, water, phone and TV connections.

Looking at the six countries to which the Rally goes: Turkey, Cyprus, Syria, Lebanon, Israel, and Egypt at the time this is being written in 1999, these nations are not known for having particularly cordial relationships with each other.

In addition, many are plagued with internal strife as well. There is serious friction between the Republic of Cyprus, which controls the predominantly Greek southern Cyprus, and the Republic of Northern Cyprus, which controls the predominantly Turkish northern Cyprus. Syria is not at all pleased by the agreements between its neighbors Turkey and Israel. The Turks have constantly had problems with the Kurds. The persistent internal friction between the Israelis and the Palestinians constantly makes newspaper headlines around the world. The Lebanese are not at all pleased at having their country occupied by

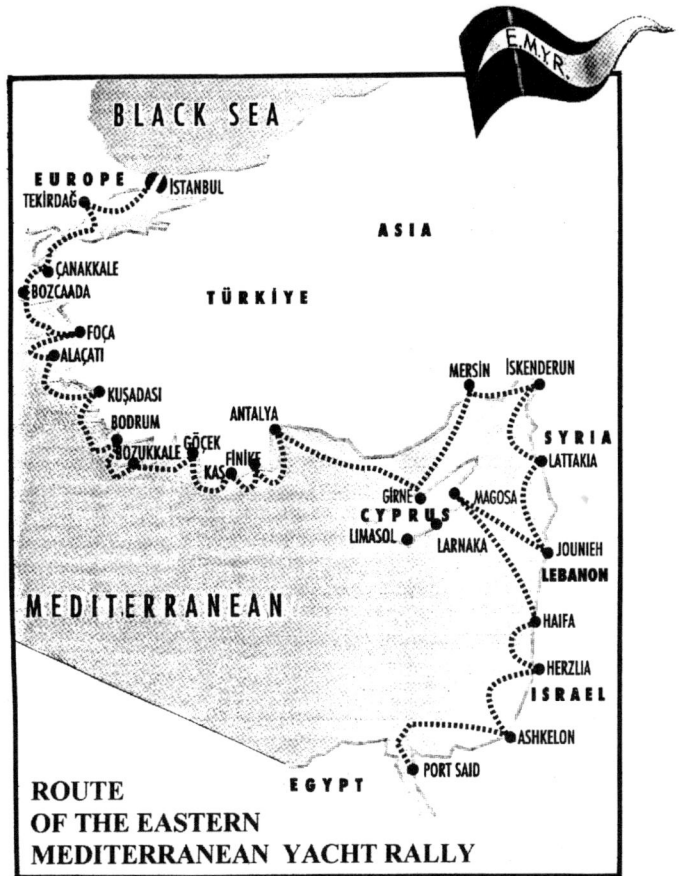

Fig. EM-4 Yacht Rally Route
Courtesy: Eastern Mediterranean Yacht Rally

Syrians, but they are not in a position to throw them out. At the same time, the Syrians would dearly love to take over Lebanon completely and incorporate it in a Greater Syria, but they are not quite strong enough to do that either. However, happily in spite of the various tensions plaguing the nations along the route at all the ports where Rally docks, the local population greets the them with the utmost cordiality. Wherever they go they are given ceremonial receptions by the local authorities and often, national dignitaries are present as well. The Rally has become firmly established in the area as an annual international good-will event.

THE RALLY ORGANIZATION

The running of the Rally is entirely in the hands of a group of volunteer organizers with no paid staff. Having been invited to sail a part of the 1999 cruise with them, I had an excellent opportunity to see how extremely well organized they were by that time. By then their long experience had prepared them for any emergencies that might arise, and consequently, the event proceeded effortlessly and smoothly.

Six participants from five different countries made up the Rally Committee in 1999. This committee enlisted sponsors, prepared the Rally brochure, registered the participants, and determined the route the Rally would follow. They also worked out the schedule for sailing the selected route, and enlisted local Rally Representatives at each port who arranged for docking, electrical connections, and water supply for the boats when they arrived. Since the start of the Rally, boats have *never* been charged for dockage, electricity, or water in any of the ports it has visited.

The Rally sponsors as of 1999 were a group of Turkish marina operators: Atakoy Marina in Istanbul, Karada Marina in Bodrum, Kemer Marina in Kemer, and the Setur Marina Group, with seven marinas along the Turkish coast at Istanbul, Ayvalik, Cesme, Kusadasi, Marmaris, Finike, and Antalya They provided the financing for the very impressive full color Rally brochure, as well as the Rally caps and shirts distributed to the participating sailors. At every harbor where the Rally stops, handsome memorial plaques are distributed to the port officials as a thanks for their assistance. Each yacht sailing in the Rally also receives a commemorative plaque as an enduring record of its participation.

The commercial sponsors of the Rally, along with the active cooperation of the Turkish Government make the Rally possible, but they have no control over the actual running of the Rally. That is entirely in the hands of the volunteer committee and its helpers. All entrants are required to contribute a mere 150DM (Deutchmarks) or the equivalent of about $80 U.S. to help pay for the many cocktails and dinners held at the various ports along the way. Many of the social events at ports along the route are totally paid for by organizations in the host cities.

THE RALLY UNDER WAY

The Rally sails under the command of a Rally Commodore who has full authority to decide exactly when the fleet will sail from each port. If, in his opinion, weather or sea conditions are unfavorable at any of the scheduled departure times, he may postpone that departure until he considers it safe to continue. He issues his instructions to the fleet by VHF radio in English, which is the official language used for voice communications. Therefor, on each boat there must be at least one person who clearly understands spoken English.

The other two most prevalent languages you'll hear around the Rally are Turkish and German. You'll also hear a good deal of French, Danish, and Dutch. At the time I sailed with the Rally there were also Italians, Swiss, Belgians, Bulgarians, and several Russians in the fleet, along with Israelis, Canadians, Maltese. and a very few sailors from the U.S.A. The existence of the Rally has not been well known among U.S. yachtsmen, in addition to the fact that it is held a very long distance away from here. The development of many excellent marinas along the Turkish coast has encouraged a number of the European participants to live on their boats for several months every year in the various Turkish marinas, and a few live there full time, returning to their home countries only on occasional visits.

Under way, the fleet is divided by size and speed into groups of 10 to 15 boats. When under way the boats in each group report by radio to their Group Leader, who was appointed by the Rally Committee, at such intervals as he or she requests. This system allows each Group Leader to keep track of the positions of the boats in his or her group, and to be made aware of any difficulties being experienced by any of them. Each Group Leader then reports on the progress of their group to the Commodore at such intervals as he orders. In this way, the progress of the entire fleet is constantly monitored and any vessels experiencing difficulties are quickly identified. In case of a disabling breakdown at sea one of the other boats in the fleet will go to the assistance of the affected boat and render whatever aid is required. A disabled vessel will be towed into port if necessary. In addition, the Turkish Coast Guard assigns two of its cutters to the rally. One sails ahead of the fleet, and the other follows, in case their assistance is needed.

NAVIGATION

Navigating along these coasts from late April to early June, when the Rally is in progress, is not difficult. The Rally has been timed so that the winter storms have passed and the intense summer heat has not yet set in. Normally mild weather conditions are likely at this time. Winds are generally moderate making for comfortable sailing. All Rally boats are equipped with GPS which is the standard positioning method used by all of them. I saw no one taking bearings and plotting positions from them, or using any of the various other navigational methods. Since the Rally sails close to the coasts, celestial navigation is not necessary unless some overachiever just wants to practice taking and reducing sights. I didn't happen to see anyone doing that either.

As noted above, the fleet sails in company and all boats report regularly to their group leaders, who in turn report regularly to the Commodore. Thus should anyone's GPS malfunction or his navigation prove to be inaccurate for some other reason, the regular reporting system will make his mistake apparent long before he is likely to get into any real difficulty.

The Rally Committee does not specify a set of charts to be used by the skippers of participating boats. Consequently, the charts I saw in use by participants came from a wide variety of sources. There were Turkish charts based on Turkish

Fig. EM-5 Folk dance group entertaining Rally sailors
(Illustration : Author)

Army surveys, and others based on British surveys; there were also British charts, U.S. charts, and even charts based on British surveys, but published in Italy. Unfortunately, I was unable to see what the Russsians and the Bulgarians were using.

In general, British surveys were the dominant source of charting information for the area. Distances on all charts are given in nautical miles, depths and heights are metric. The latest British survey date I saw was 1983, and there does not appear to be any designated authority, similar to our NOS, in the area that has charge of maintaining chart accuracy on any sort of regular basis. From the time of the British survey 1983 to 1999, when I sailed with the Rally, there had to have been a great many changes that were not yet on the charts they were using. If one were unfamiliar with the area, and sailing alone with charts so badly in need of current correction, it would seem imperative to consult sailors with local knowledge particularly when entering harbor or running close inshore. I noticed that the Rally generally stayed well off-shore until harbor entrances were about a beam.

The tide range here is in inches so tidal currents are non-existent. There is a large scale counter-clockwise current that circles the entire Mediterranean Sea, but it is by no means a strong current. There are also scattered localized minor currents, but none of these are very significant either. Thus, unknown currents are not likely to cause navigational errors.

Since the Mediterranean Sea is a relatively small, totally enclosed, and a rather shallow body of water, the large, long type swells typical of open ocean are not encountered here, although during a major migratory storm, conditions here can become extremely boisterous. When a strong breeze picks up what does develop rather quickly are short, steep, cycloidal type waves. Aboard the relatively small vessels making up the Rally, this produces conditions that, while not necessarily dangerous, can make sailing quite uncomfortable Also, because of the irregular coastlines and the various off-shore islands, swells are often refracted around obstructions that cause them to come in from directions very different from that of the wind.

The irregular Mediterranean coastline, coupled with varying local thermal effects over land and water, produces a complex variety of local wind conditions. Some of these local winds may reach gale force and are frequently subject to rapid onset and equally rapid cessation. The EMYR is scheduled from the end of April to the beginning of June when the severe traveling storms of winter have passed. As intended this leaves the weather along Rally route generally clear and comfortably warm. However, occasional severe localized weather disturbances are unavoidably experienced by the Rally.

SOCIAL AND CULTURAL ACTIVITIES

In each port the local Rally Representatives arrange various side trips from the ports to nearby sites of interest. Some are major historic archeological sites such as Ephesis, Palmyra, and Baalbeck. There are also many visits to local museums displaying objects from various historical periods. Activities ashore may range from local cultural events such as concerts, to visits to nearby amusement parks. Some of these activities are close by the port while others may be a considerable distance away, requiring a full day to get there and back. Some of these side trips go to places prominent in the histories of the earliest known civilizations in the area, such as the Hittites. Some to places prominent during the ascendancy of Greece, and later Rome. Still others are sites vital to one of three of the most prominent world religions: the Christians, the Muslims, and the Jews. The entire area is incalculably rich in such places. Rally participants are thus afforded an unusual opportunity to tour these historic places in company with highly experienced local guides carefully selected by the local Rally representatives.

The 1999 Rally lasted a total of 49 days of which 26, or just over half, were spent in the various ports, visiting nearby attractions and attending events arranged for them by these representatives. At many ports, the Rally is met upon docking by a local folk dance group (EM-5). At nearly every port the Rally Representative arranges for a formal Rally Dinner on the evening before the Rally is to depart this port–formal meaning, the male Rally participants are to wear jackets and ties, the ladies are to wear dresses. Everyday grubby sailing apparel is not acceptable at these dinners!

The Rally Dinners are always attended by local dignitaries, and often by representatives of the national governments as well. There, after appropriately complimentary speeches, the Rally officers present handsome memorial plaques to the local bigwigs who generally return the favor, after equally complimentary speeches, by presenting plaques to the Rally officers. The dinner is always a sumptuous Middle Eastern feast and invariably followed by a vigorous belly dance performance, and then general dancing to music by a local band.

Since the Rally sails 1700 miles and takes 49 days to do this many participants cannot, or do not wish, to sail the entire route. Consequently, at various ports all along the way, some boats drop out while others join the Rally. There is no requirement for any boat to sail the entire course. A participating boat may join wherever its Captain chooses and leave whenever he has gone as far as he wants to go. When a participating boat leaves the Rally at the Rally Dinner, its Captain is presented with a very handsome plaque as a memento showing where his boat entered and where it left the Rally.

BREAKDOWNS AND REPAIRS

On a trip this long there inevitably are boats that suffer a variety of breakdowns, ranging from minor rigging, electrical, or communications problems up to major engine or hull failures. The local representative's job also includes arranging to get necessary repairs completed promptly so that the affected vessel can continue with the Rally, if at all possible. Since the Rally makes a number of two day port stops a boat that is delayed and unable to sail from a particular port with the fleet, often can sail a day later and still catch up.

Here's an example of how efficiently the Rally organization handles a repair problem. As mentioned earlier, from time to time due to adverse winds or lack of wind it is necessary for the fleet to motor, in order to maintain its schedule. During the 1999 Rally, while motoring on the way from Girne, North Cyprus to Mersin, Turkey, the engine of one of the boats blew its head gasket and cracked the head. It was quickly taken in tow by another boat. By VHF, the Commodore was immediately informed of the problem and he in turn called the local Rally Representative in Mersin. A couple hours later when the boat docked, mechanics were waiting, and within an hour they had the head off, out of the boat, and I happened to see them wrestling it onto a pickup truck. By the time the Rally departed Mersin two days later the necessary parts had been obtained, and the engine reassembled and tested. The boat was then ready to depart with the Rally.

In another instance during the same Rally, at about 1900 hours about 5 miles off Lattakia, the boat I was on was motoring toward the harbor. Suddenly the engine simply stopped. Efforts to restart it failed. Within 15 minutes we were under tow behind another Rally boat. When in the harbor, the local authorities met us with a harbor tug to take us to our assigned berth. The cause of the shutdown turned out to be in the fuel supply. When the Captain of the boat was unable to clear it, the local Rally Representative quickly located an incredibly ancient and decrepit looking diesel mechanic who, contrary to appearances, proved himself an absolute wonder. In under half an hour he had the fuel blockage located, cleared, and the engine running. In this part of the world, mechanics are well acquainted with everything that can possibly go wrong with a diesel engine, and what is necessary to fix it.

SAILING DISTANCES

The distances between the various harbors on the Rally route vary considerably. On the 1999 course the shortest sail was only 15 miles from Kemer to Antalya. The longest single run was the one from Ashkelon in southern Israel 260 miles to Alexandria Egypt. However, most runs varied between 35 and 70 miles, making it possible to easily complete them in a single day. The 1999 schedule showed only three runs of over 100 miles requiring overnight sails.

The close spacing of most stops clearly shows that the Rally organizers are not out to make participants prove what tough, hardy old salts they are. Rather, the purpose is to make this cruise into a series of pleasant, comfortable sails on the beautiful, blue Mediterranean, interspersed with interesting social, intercultural, and educational events. For the host cities and countries, the Rally presents an excellent opportunity to present themselves in a favorable light, to a large group of well-to-do people, from a vide variety of countries, hoping this will promote tourism. For the participants, it is an unparalled opportunity to see a great number of historic places, and to meet and sail with a broadly international group of yachtsmen, such as they probably would never have an opportunity to know, otherwise.

BIBLIOGRAPHY

Boland, Charles Michael - They All Discovered America - Doubleday & Co. - 1961

Bloomster E.L. - Sailing and Small Craft Down the Ages - Naval Institute Press 1940

Bowditch, Nathaniel - The American Practical Navigator - DMAHC

Bradford, Ernle - Ulysses Found - Harcourt Brace - 1963

Clark, Miles - A Russian Voyage - National Geographic - Vol. 185 No. 6

Conway - The Earliest Ships - Naval Institute Press - 1996

Ellam & Mudie - Two Against the Western Ocean - Curtis Books 1953

Garland, Joseph E. - Lone Voyager - Little Brown & Co. - 1963

Gilmore & McElroy - Across Before Columbus - NEARA Publications, 1998

Greenhill & Morrison - The Archaeology of Boats & Ships - Naval Institute Press - 1995

Hays David & Daniel - My Old Man and the Sea - Algonquin Books - 1995

Hornstein, Howard - Favorite Sea Songs - The Ancient Mariners Chanteymen

Hugill, Stan - Shanties from the Seven Seas

Huschke, Ralph E. - Glossary of Meteororology - American Meteorological Soc. 1959

Maloney, Elbert S. - Dutton's Navigation & Piloting - Naval Institute Press

Markell, Jeff - The Sailor's Weather Guide - Sheridan House Inc. - 1995

Piver, Arthur - Trans-Atlantic Trimaran - Underwriter's Press - 1961

Piver, Arthur - Trans-Pacific Trimaran - Pi-Craft - 1963

Piver, Arthur - Trimaran Third Book - Pi-Craft - 1965

Rogers, W.L. - Greek and Roman Naval Warfare - U.S. Naval Institute - 1977

Severin, Tim - The Brendan Voyage - McGraw-Hill - 1978

The New Glenan's Sailing Manual - Sail Books, Inc. 1978